G000129001

How I Escaped My Certain Fate

by the same author

THE PERFECT FOOL

STEWART LEE

How I Escaped My Certain Fate

The Life and Deaths of a Stand-Up Comedian

faber and faber

To Ted Chippington

First published in 2010
by Faber and Faber Ltd
Bloomsbury House
74–77 Great Russell Street
London WC1B 3DA

Typeset by Ian Bahrami
Printed in England by CPI Mackays, Chatham

A CIP record for this book
is available from the British Library

ISBN 978–0–571–25480–4

2 4 6 8 10 9 7 5 3 1

Contents

Introduction: Alternative Comedian

I never wanted to be a comedian. When I was very young I wanted to be a writer, first of all a writer of philosophically inclined thrillers like Robert E. Howard, Ray Bradbury or Stan Lee, and then later a writer of thrillingly inclined philosophy, like Albert Camus, Franz Kafka or Samuel Beckett. But then, at the age of sixteen, I saw a comedian called Ted Chippington open for The Fall in Birmingham in October 1984 and literature's loss became stand-up comedy's loss also. However, unlike generations of would-be comedians before me or after me, I never really wanted to be a 'comedian'. I wanted to be an Alternative Comedian, because all other types of comedian were sell-out scum and whores of the system.*

* The editor of this book worries there might be people perusing this introduction who were born in the eighties, or even the nineties, and who will therefore need help understanding the archaic term 'Alternative Comedy'. I don't think my editor really knows much about the reading habits of young people, and like everyone in publishing, a dying industry with no future, he has his head in the sand. Do they still read at all, the young? I understand from the newspapers that teenagers spend an average of nine hours a week watching internet pornography. Are they supposed to find time to read as well now? Perhaps they are all experts at multitasking. As I understand it is known.

Nonetheless, my editor feels that for many potential readers

1

I started out as a stand-up in the eighties, just as the Alternative Comedy scene that shaped me was coalescing into a commercial entity; by the end of the nineties, I had co-starred in four television series for the BBC and performed over 2,000 stand-up gigs. But by the turn of a new century, all my broadcasting work was cancelled, and I'd been circling the stand-up comedy circuit apparently aimlessly for over a decade. So sometime around the back end of 2000 or the start of 2001, I gradually, incrementally and without any fanfare – or even much thought – gave up being a stand-up comedian. By the time I quit, 'Alternative Comedy', and the machinery around it, was hardly recognisable from its beginnings in the late seventies anyway. 'Alternative comedy?' said the *Bullseye* host and old-school comic Jim Bowen every day from 1979 until his tragic end choking to death on a slice of bully beef. 'It's the alternative *to* comedy.' And it had been, thank God.

I was born in 1968. For my generation of London-circuit stand-up comedians there was a Year Zero attitude to 1979. Holy texts found in a skip out the back of the offices of the London listings magazine *Time Out* tell us how, with a few incendiary post-punk punchlines, Alexei Sayle, Arnold Brown, Dawn French and Andy de la Tour destroyed the British comedy hegemony of Upper-Class Oxbridge Satirical Songs and Working-Class Bow Tie-Sporting Racism. Then, with the fragments of these smashed idols and their own bare hands, they built the pioneering stand-up

---

today's full-spectrum dominance of stand-up comedy across all media, in the form of panel shows, top-selling DVDs, live stadium gigs and cash-in books, might be something they take for granted. It was not ever thus, and apparently some context is necessary else these pages appear as nothing more than 'the demented ramblings of an inexplicably bitter man'.

clubs The Comedy Store and The Comic Strip. In so doing they founded the egalitarian Polytechnic of Laughs that is today's comedy establishment. Every religion needs a Genesis myth, and this is contemporary British stand-up comedy's very own creation story.*

However, this simplified fable ignores the rather more complex nature of British comedy in the seventies. It's a romantic exaggeration to claim that The Comedy Store had an ideological position. It did, for about a week in 1980, but it didn't when it started and obviously its policy today is defined by commercial imperatives alone. It is true there was an enormous bulk of increasingly dated and dubious working-men's-club comics laughing at Pakistanis, poofs and their wives' mothers. Their hot piss regularly cascaded into my childhood home via the conduit of ITV's *The Comedians*, where enthusiastically dissipated tap-room whimsy and economically compressed racial hatred (the latter dishonestly edited out of the series' cosily nostalgic DVD releases) were interspersed with trad jazz tunes from Kenny Ball or Shep's Banjo Boys. Like an iceberg barely visible above the waterline of light entertainment, these twats nevertheless made up the majority of live stand-up in Britain at the time.†

Meanwhile, the slowly dissipating after-fart of the fifties

* In his autobiography *I Stole Freddie Mercury's Birthday Cake*, the late, great Malcolm Hardee says it was he who first coined the term 'Alternative' in relation to comedy or cabaret, for a night he hosted in a pub called The Ferry Inn in Salcombe in 1978, in order to differentiate it from the more mainstream fare offered by the local yacht club. This is probably the only true 'fact' in Malcolm's book.
† Bernard Manning remained the liberal press's chief old-school whipping boy until his death in 2007, largely because he was the only one of these fools anyone could even remember the name of. Personally, I always preferred George 'Welly' Roper.

and sixties Oxbridge satire boom meant that posh kids still helmed the high-profile left-field TV and radio shows, such as *Not the Nine O'Clock News* or *Radio Active*, as they do again today, and got to tour a Cambridge Footlights show to mid-range theatre venues in the south of England every year, still dressed in matching outfits and singing funny songs about the news at the piano.

Of course, there were dozens of superb seventies acts that didn't fit this bipolar model and who were guilty of few, if any, of the ideological crimes now retrospectively ascribed to all British stand-up before 1979. It is difficult to pigeon-hole the rarely bettered bone-dry stealth bombs of Dave Allen, the variety-circuit shtick of Les Dawson, the snug-bar surrealism of Chic Murray, the art-house proto-Alternative Comedy of John Dowie, the punk poetry of John Cooper Clarke and the storytelling folk-singer comedians Billy Connolly, Max Boyce, Jasper Carrott and Mike Harding. So, for the sake of simplicity, I will ignore them. (There is probably something on the internet you can read instead.)

Another conveniently ignored factor in the development of the Alternative Comedy scene is economics. For example, when I started on the circuit in London in 1989, Roland and Claire Muldoon's CAST organisation was a relatively high-profile promoter of New Variety nights, usually with a textbook balance of performers of all racial and sexual persuasions on the bill. But in the seventies, CAST had been a touring radical theatre group, expressly formed to bring about the collapse of capitalism and to encourage mass drug-taking and compulsory homosexuality, its funding continually questioned in the Commons by the perpetually outraged Tory MP Teddy Taylor. After the Conservative landslide of 1979, the ever-adaptable Muldoons smelt change in the air and scaled down their theatre shows into Alternative Cabaret

4

evenings that espoused the same ideals but didn't rely on funding that was clearly going to disappear. As the comedy historian Oliver Double noted in his study of the early circuit, 'Alternative Comedy: From Radicalism to Commercialism', refugees from left-wing theatre groups also found themselves key players in early Comedy Store line-ups or shows by Tony Allen's Alternative Cabaret collective. There are few forms of entertainment cheaper to stage than stand-up. In some ways the Alternative Comedy scene was initiated on an economic model that was incongruously Thatcherite.

But the comedy community I joined in the late eighties still retained traces of its birth in opposition to both the political and the entertainment establishments of its day. As well as being an ethical, admirable and even brave thing to do at the time, working within these politically correct parameters forced the Alternatives to find new subjects and new styles. And if these new comics' jokes *were* ever sexist or racist, then they were at least aimed at totemic female figures, like Margaret Thatcher, or at races that had previously not been overtly stereotyped. 'I'm an Albanian, I'm an Albanian!' shouted Alexei Sayle on Chris Tarrant's bandwagon-jumping zoo TV show *O.T.T.* whilst leaping up and down and hitting himself on the head with a tea tray. I stayed up late and watched, thrilled. If you told me that nearly thirty years later I would be fat and appearing on TV doing comedy in a too-tight suit just like Alexei Sayle's, I would have swallowed my own fist.

And how long ago the eighties seem now. Suddenly the decade has the dusty, foggy flavour of the forties or the fifties. When did we grow old, we who guffawed at Monty Python and Spike Milligan on BBC2 as children, and learned *Young Ones* scripts off by heart in our teens? It was a different world. This was the era when you could still scrape

5

by on dole money, full student grants, like mine, or Enterprise Allowance Schemes and call yourself an artist without needing to earn a crust from art itself; when regional arts centres and the long-lost Arts Labs still hummed with a sense of community and common purpose, rather than just being used as tour stops by covers bands and hypnotists; when stand-up comedy and rock music were still not deemed worthy of reviews in broadsheet newspapers, except under special circumstances; and when alternative and underground culture was bush-telegraphed direct to your brain by inky fanzines and word of mouth.

In those dogmatic days, sexual relations with women, who could often be found wearing earrings depicting men being castrated, were a complex ideological negotiation. How many student-union anti-sexist men's groups were staffed by young boys who wanted only to be kissed? How many heroic lesbians first headed south only as a result of political expediency? Frequently, the most a man could aspire to was to be described as 'a sound bloke', an epithet which mixed left-of-centre political inclinations with a suggestion of unpretentious solidity. Yet in many ways things were simpler. The teenage girls we tried to date did not wear T-shirts saying 'Whore', 'Slut' or 'No Gag Reflex', nor queue up to get talent-spotted by lads' mags in the Student Union Super-Pub, formerly known as The Mandela Bar. Oh, Winnie, how fortunate that you did not live to see your memory sullied so.

Back then, under the shadow of an unattainable ideal of ideological purity, nobody, not bands or stand-up comedians or comic-book creators, wanted to be seen to 'sell out to the Man' by doing an advert or appearing on *Top of the Pops* or achieving any level of commercial sustainability. Gigs were performed on pallet stages in smoky pubs and scary squats, and were advertised on photocopied sepia-toned flyers pinned to walls. This was before computer graphics programs meant that even jumble-sale adverts have the production values of Hollywood movie posters, and before the internet could rally a crowd to see minor cult figures at the click of a mouse.

And today's young consumers would not tolerate our lack of sophistication. The first cappuccino I ever tasted was in the Queen's Lane Coffee House in December 1985, when I went up to Oxford for university interviews, and it came with a tuna mayonnaise roll, served in a seeded bun with salad. At that time, the mid-eighties, these two items comprised the most exotic meal I had ever seen, and I remember the shock of the taste to this day. Back then, exciting food was still a novelty. Even pizza was regarded with suspicion. Pubs stopped serving at 10.30 p.m. and closed all afternoon. There were only four delicatessens in the whole of the country and all they sold was Belgian biscuits.

And it was cold back then! It snowed all the time and we wore fingerless gloves and black woollen beanies and dead men's Crombies and Dr Marten boots every day, not out of punkish affectation, but out of sheer necessity. There was no shame in a duffle coat in those dark days. Michael Foot, the last socialist leader of the Labour Party, a man who had actually put his life on the line voluntarily, fighting Fascists in the Spanish civil war, wore one. (He always said he didn't, but he did.) And so did Alan Davies, who, along with Jack Dee, was the first Alternative Comedian of any profile to break ranks and do a big advertising campaign, flogging Abbey National policies sometime in the early nineties.*

* Alan Davies later became infamous for biting the ear of a homeless man who shouted at him one night as he left Soho's exclusive media hangout the Groucho Club. I am sure there are mitigating

Writing this now, God, how I miss the cultural side of the eighties – the rhetoric, the raggedy clothes, the politics, gigs you were frightened to go into, Radio 1 when it had weird bits, Channel 4 when it was radical, the *NME* when it had writers, and the thrill of discovering underground music and new comedy for yourself. Or maybe I just miss being eighteen, and like all those columnists who turned forty sometime in the late nineties and wrote simultaneous think-pieces on why Punk was the best thing ever, I'm just confusing the thrill of being young with the notion that the era in which I was young was in any way especially creative or remarkable.

Nevertheless, because various brands of bespoke comedy are now ubiquitous on television, in clubs and on the internet, I don't think anyone today will have the same experience we had, of stumbling across a slice of that new Alternative Comedy when it was fresh and unformed. And to find it you had to dig. There were a paltry two editions of Paul Jackson's well-intentioned BBC2 circuit sampler *Boom Boom Out Go the Lights*. There might be specially recorded sessions on the John Peel show, from John Hegley or Eric Bogosian. And occasionally, in some provincial town that didn't have London's burgeoning comedy scene, you'd catch one of the Alternatives opening for your favourite band. To me, growing up in a conservative suburb south-east of Birmingham, these voices seemed like transmissions from Mars. I saw Peter Richardson from

---

circumstances in this story – perhaps the tramp had an especially delicious ear – but it is too good an event not to use as a mile-high metaphor for the way the Alternative Comedian's role has drifted somewhat since the early days of the circuit. Once we stood shoulder to shoulder with society's outsiders. Now we view them as a late-night snack.

The Comic Strip opening for Dexys Midnight Runners as a Mexican bandit, and a young Phill Jupitus doing performance poetry at a Billy Bragg gig under the name of Porky the Poet. And in October 1984, I saw Ted Chippington, the man who made me a stand-up, supporting The Fall, and everything changed.

Ted Chippington took the stage at The Powerhaus, Hurst Street, Birmingham, in Teddy Boy regalia, to a crowd that wasn't expecting him. For the next half an hour, he stood rooted to the spot, scowling and supping beer, and in a flat Midlands monotone delivered variations on the same joke, involving a torturous misunderstanding of a place name, or a make of car, or an abstract concept, and all of which began with the phrase 'I was walking down this road the other day'. These he interspersed with listless interpretations of pop hits. People were paralysed with laughter or furious with irritation. At the point tuned-in comedy consumers were beginning to process the new stand-up styles of Ben Elton and Alexei Sayle, Ted was already dismantling the form itself. With every frill removed, and with the very notion of what a joke was boiled down to the barest of bones, Ted was stand-up in its purest form, belonging neither to the politically charged world of the new stand-ups nor the reactionary hinterlands of working men's clubs. I was utterly transfixed and my heart was racing as I realised that stand-up could be anything you wanted it to be. You didn't even have to look as if you were enjoying it. And I thought, 'That's what I want to do.'*

* 'Eventually, Ted became a minor cult, though he never played any conventional comedy clubs, preferring to perform where he was not necessarily wanted. In 1986, a collaboration with Birmingham bands The Nightingales and We've Got A Fuzzbox And We're Gonna Use It nudged Rocking With Rita to the bottom of

Not long after seeing Ted, in the spring of 1985, I applied to St Edmund Hall at Oxford University to read English Literature. I did so for two reasons. Firstly, I loved English Literature, and the Anglo-Saxon poetry course really appealed to me (although sadly I turned out to be particularly poor at this subject, lacking the requisite

—————

the charts, and the DJ Steve Wright's fascination with Ted's oddly moving take on The Beatles' She Loves You led to brief major label interest and three TV appearances. Years later Vic Reeves arrived by another route at a similar, but more sophisticated, form of bent light entertainment. At the dawn of the nineties, Ted's audiences were in on the joke, so he split to seek fame and fortune in Los Angeles, eventually ending up driving trucks to Mexico and working as a cook. And then the trail went cold.

'In the late 1980s, at university and the Edinburgh fringe, I met other teenage, would-be comics who knew Ted's lone album, Man In A Suitcase, off by heart. Ted's releases documented him struggling with hostile crowds, though his indifference seems now almost sublime. Ted taught us that a bad audience reaction didn't necessarily mean that what you were doing was worthless, and we co-opted his low-energy insolence and fed off it. At the risk of seeming delusional, I now think you can hear second and third hand echoes of Ted in the routines of comics who probably never even heard him. The relentlessness of Ricky Gervais' Aesop's Fables bit is Ted with a tailwind, and in 2005, when I had the superbly baffling young Edinburgh fringe award-winner Josie Long open for me on tour, a disgruntled Leeds punter remarked, "This is the worst thing I've seen since Ted Chippington, twenty years ago." I couldn't have been happier.

'It's difficult to say who the first alternative comedian was. Ben Elton? Alexei Sayle? Victoria Wood? John Dowie, if you really know your stuff? But one thing is for certain. Ted Chippington was the first post-alternative comedian, and without him, everything would be different. Not necessarily worse. But different.' (From a piece written for the *Guardian* upon the release of the Ted Chippington box set *Walking Down the Road* (Big Print records), in February 2007.)

grammar-school Greek and Latin). And secondly, a doctor for whom I did a Saturday morning filing job had told me about going to the Edinburgh Fringe in the seventies with an Oxford University student comedy group that had included some of *Not the Nine O'Clock News*, and it sounded superb. I passed the exams and got a place. I still can't believe I was really allowed to study there, with all those clever people, reading books all day in the midst of the Cotswold-stone cathedrals of culture. However, the wind of change was already blowing across the comedy continent.

Everything I ever read, and every documentary I ever saw, about the fifties satire boom and its inheritors seemed to suggest that going to Oxbridge was a passport into a BBC Light Entertainment career, irrespective of your actual ability. But the Alternative Comedy scene that was swiftly becoming the dominant trope was expressly and understandably against this privileged old guard. In my early days on the circuit, I kept the exact location of my education a secret, as it would have been held against me; on the rare occasions it leaked out, I felt I had to be twice as good to prove myself.*

---

* I remember the anarchist comedian and 'godfather of Alternative Comedy' Tony Allen being extremely keen to book me for a night he ran in a squat in Hackney after he found out I'd got a 2:1 in English from St Edmund Hall. I'd like to think that the days of fast-tracking are long gone, but a disproportionate amount of television comedians who rose to prominence in the last decade do seem, just like in the pre-Alternative days, to be from Oxbridge. Mitchell and Webb, Katy Brand, Lucy Montgomery, Simon Bird, John Oliver, Johnny Vegas and Frank Skinner, for example, all are former presidents of the Cambridge Footlights. What is undeniable is that going to Oxford gave me a degree of confidence, and some organisational skills when it came to writing. But then, I would deny any outright

I moved to London to be a comic in September 1989. There was a comedy micro-economy in the city where a few thirty-quid gigs a week, in the tiniest of pub back rooms, almost added up to a living wage. I got a flat in Acton with Richard Herring, with whom I had written some student comedy shows, and two other friends from university. From nine to five, I worked in temp jobs orange-juice packing, data inputting and finally the luxury of fact-checking for a horticultural encyclopedia. Every day I'd hassle the forty or so comedy clubs in *Time Out* for the live auditions they called Open Spots, laboriously dialling dozens of numbers on the revolving disc of the telephone, round and round, day after day. I don't think the young people of the twenty-first century, with their mobile telephones, can possibly imagine what it was like actually having to dial phone numbers. Kids today! They don't know they're born.

Maybe I'd be slotted into an unpaid five minutes, anywhere from the thirty-seater Guilty Pea above The Wheatsheaf on Rathbone Place, where various thirties bohemians drank themselves to death, to the sprawling 180 seats of the old Comedy Store in Leicester Square. The stand-up guru John Gordillo, then in a double act called The Crisis Twins, saw my act and liked it, and gave me his private-promoter

---

privilege, wouldn't I? I'm a special case. My excuse is that I'm from a single-parent family, got a full grant, and went to an independent boys' school on a part-scholarship and a charity bung, so I ain't the same as all them Oxford toffs. Nobody likes to think their own success is anything but hard won and deserved. I expect even David Cameron and George Osborne maintain, privately, that they're 'not like those other Oxbridge-educated Eton fuckers', and think they have somehow achieved their positions as puce-faced masters of the known universe on merit alone.

phone-number list, which seemed like an astonishing act of trust and kindness. Click, whirr; click, whirr. After a few weeks of pestering, most places called back.* Every evening, I travelled home across London on night buses, back when you could smoke and drink on the top deck – epicurean allowances which made the most inconvenient journey a hedonistic pleasure – and I'd feel like I was living the mythical life of some *fin de siècle* artist, despite the looming threat of another early start at the data-input desk.

In February 1990, after six months in London, I got through the heats of the Hackney Empire and *City Limits* magazine New Act of the Year competition, and won the final, beating Simon Munnery's Security Guard character, which was much funnier than my act. ('I went to work today. Nothing happened. That's what I get paid for.')†

Even the host of the event, the hypnotically lugubrious Jewish veteran Ivor Dembina, knew I'd been lucky. 'You were the best on the night, fair play,' he said, in a tone

---

* It took nine months of two calls a day for Jongleurs to give me an open spot at their Battersea club, the only one they had in those days. The gig that night was compèred by Jack Dee, who was about to become famous off the back of some beer adverts. I died and was never allowed back.
† I had seen Simon in a remarkable double act in Edinburgh the previous summer, the iconoclastically named God and Jesus, and first spoke to the skinny genius (and that's a noun I use sparingly) that same week. I found myself trying to shield his tiny body from an attack by Jeremy Hardy's wife, the comedienne Kit Hollerbach, who had flown at Simon like a harpy from the darkness of the Pleasance Cabaret bar to accuse him of being a neo-Nazi, as one did in those days, and seemed to be saying that I must be a neo-Nazi too if I was speaking to him. But I wasn't and nor was he. Not then, anyway, but we all get more right-wing as we get older.

typically laden with world-weary wisdom and an indefinable regret. 'Well done,' said John Connor, the head judge, who was also the comedy critic of *City Limits* and the producer of The Comedy Store's Cutting Edge night, 'we'll show these Oxbridge wankers like Rob Newman and David Baddiel what real comedy is.' 'Oh,' I answered, not thinking, as we walked into the backstage darkness, 'I went to Oxford.' 'Did you?' said Connor. 'But you're not like those wankers, are you?' he added with all the desperation of a disappointed sex tourist who has just discovered his beautiful Thai prostitute has a penis, and is wondering whether just to try and make the best of it. 'I like David Baddiel. I think he's good,' I said. I'd seen Baddiel in Edinburgh the previous summer. He was the first stand-up who seemed to speak in an idiom that was recognisably aimed at our generation. His distinctive tone of voice was soon to be imitated across all media for the next decade.

My prize for winning the Hackney Empire and *City Limits* magazine's New Act of the Year competition was £500, a booking at the Hackney Empire, a booking at The Comedy Store and a slot on a TV show I can't remember the name of. I received the money on the night, but the Hackney Empire slot took a decade to materialise, The Comedy Store hasn't booked me to this day, and the TV show never called. And the winner's certificate was made out to 'Steward' Lee.

Ivor Dembina told me that because of the sort of act I was, stiff and still, I should always have the microphone-stand boom set in a vertical position. 'Who is this guy?' I thought. Well, he was Ivor Dembina, the Obi-Wan Kenobi of comedy, and he was right. Learning that I needed a vertical boom stand, which I now call Dembina's Upright Position, was the best thing I got out of being The Hackney

Empire New Act of the Year. That, and an upsurge in circuit bookings, which meant I soon gave up my temping jobs. Since November 1990, I can honestly say, with some degree of pride, I have never done a decent day's work in my life.

In 1990, I was taken on by a newly moulded stand-up comedy management agency for Alternative Comedians, run by a failed impresario, the thwarting of whose theatrical ambitions had forced him to apply his enormous brain and Cheshire Cat charm to the blossoming stand-up scene. There were only two other similar outfits: Off the Kerb, which specialised in the sort of gay, transsexual, animal-based, drag and novelty acts beloved by its flamboyant founder Addison Cresswell; and Stage Left, which managed and booked more overtly hard-line performers such as Jeremy Hardy and a young Mark Thomas. My new agency's roster made them seem like the future and they did the deal on a handshake, in the days before binding contracts, promising that they were about to set up a national network of money-spinning student gigs. 'I'll just pass you to our live department,' the big manager would say, cupping his hand over the phone and passing it along the sofa he shared with the little manager, then the company's only other employee and a vocal fan of the hardcore anarcho-punk band Conflict. 'You cannot win a nuclear war!' ran the spoken-word sample at the beginning of *The Ungovernable Force*, played full blast as he drove me to my undeserved Jerry Sadowitz support slots in a Ford Fiesta.

The new agency's client list was already impressive: the aforementioned Sadowitz, a comic I remain quietly in awe of, who was then involved in a complex, controversial and hilarious reaction against the politically correct orthodoxies of the day; Simon Munnery, who was now pushing his

Alan Parker Urban Warrior character, a satirical love-letter to the punk revolutionaries he'd worshipped as a teenager; and David Baddiel and Rob Newman, whose sassy pop-literate acts and shoe-gazers' haircuts were about to create a whole new audience for Alternative Comedy – girls. Today, I and all those other acts are long gone from the agency. Only David Baddiel remains, a once proud raven, his head now bowed, pecking the dry earth and tethered to the ground by the heavy chains of history, for fear that he too should fly away.

When I went back to the Edinburgh Fringe for my fourth visit in 1990, no longer a student comedian, my management company introduced bold new ideas to the stand-up comedy scene, such as advertising and two-colour posters. (The innovative idea of insurmountable performers' debts, paid off piecemeal by working for the management company's other departments, was yet to come.) The photocopied bits of paper everyone else pinned up in Edinburgh newsagents' windows suddenly seemed so drab. The eighties were over. The bright new dawn of nineties comedy was rising, and we drove around Edinburgh under cover of darkness in a panel van, flyposting illegally with pots of paste and brushes, like the A-Team with jokes. The romance of it! Me, Simon Munnery, the comedy musician Jim Tavare, our brave two-man management team and a German crusty they had press-ganged into joining them, all of us pasting over Jeremy Hardy's face again and again and again and again, like pathetic and ungrateful school-boys vandalising a photo of the headmaster. Nobody on the Fringe had ever seen anything like it. Advertising! It was outrageous, and flew in the face of all eighties ideals. But in retrospect, the Stage Left acts, smoking rollies in their Red Wedge T-shirts and supping pints of Special Brew in the

Pleasance courtyard, were right to be annoyed. It was the beginning of the end, and I was an accessory.

With regard to earning a living week to week, there weren't the nationwide opportunities for comics to play all over the country at arts centres and provincial theatres and local comedy clubs that there are today. But my new management were as good as their word and established an almost viable network of student comedy gigs at polytechnics and universities nationwide. No one had really thought to do this before. It seemed like Simon Munnery and I were always the advance party, sent out to colonise uncharted educational territories. We would find ourselves required to perform in the corner of a bar, with no stage, no lighting, no microphone, no seating and no posters advertising the show or its start time, booked by a forgetful Entertainments Officer who seemed disgruntled that our presence might mean he would have to turn off MTV, the jukebox, the fruit machines and the Space Invaders. In the end, to try and explain to the students how to set up a comedy gig, we sent out a drawing of a stick man holding a microphone with lights pointed at him.

Comics would head off in twos and threes and split £300 or so a show, after commission and before tax. We slept in dodgy DSS bed and breakfasts for as little as six pounds a night, or else saved the money and crashed on strangers' sofas. Although I did tours of these universities and polytechnics, in various combinations of different acts, on and off for the next decade, they were often a struggle.*

* At Bangor student union, forcing the comedians to leave the stage by whatever means necessary had become a point of pride for both the audience and the Entertainments Officer, who would then dock your money in proportion to your shortfall in stage time, despite essentially orchestrating your early exit. Playing this

17

But these shows paid the bills. And we were young, and I loved riding the motorway network in second-hand cars, especially with Simon, hopped up on fags and lager, listening to tapes of The Fall and pissing in hedges, all the way from Peckham Rye to Jerusalem.

During the same period, 1990 to 1995, I'd been chipping away at writing for radio with Richard Herring, who had gone as far as buying an Amstrad word processor the size of a Mini Clubman, while I still clung to my electric typewriter, with its futuristic correction-ribbon facility. Richard had given up on stand-up after a string of frustrating try-out spots, though lots of the material people baulked at in 1990 has proved a perfect fit for twenty-first-century audiences who love the fine line he now walks between hilarious obscenity and criminally prosecutable obscenity. Instead, Rich approached the puzzle of trying to write for radio with a tenacity, enthusiasm and originality that dragged me along in its wake.

In those days, BBC Radio discovered new comedy writers by simply inviting anyone who wanted to write for Radio 4's long-running weekly shit satire show, *Weekending*, to just come into the building, without even the most basic identity check, and meet with the producer of that week's show. He or she would tell the assembled mass of stinking eccentrics what sort of sketches the show was still short of.

---

venue in 1994 with Richard Herring, and already wise to the trick, I told Rich that we had to stay on for our full time come what may. When the Ents Officer invited the rugby team in to heckle us off, I copped an old line of Simon's and said we'd only leave the stage if they threw glass. Bottles duly flew. The security staff tried to get us offstage but, as glass smashed around us, I forced them to establish that our removal was their decision, not ours, thus ensuring receipt of our full fee of £140 each.

These wannabe writers, smelly and covered in food, shaggy of beard and baggy of trouser, sockless often, sometimes howling drunk and without a clean shirt between them, then sat in an airless room for the next twenty-four hours, tapping away at typewriters, as no one had laptops back then, before finally submitting some formulaic sketch in which John Major was Robin Hood or Darth Vader or a cat or something.

Some of the non-coms, as 'non-commissioned' writers were known, would sleep under desks overnight, curled up in their beards. The nightwatchman would always turn a blind eye when his torch flickered across their dreaming faces, for he could see the non-coms for what they were: spirits come to earth, voodoo children, faerie folk adrift in the world, gnomes and leprechauns in human form, harmless as flies, but with less hope of careers in radio. But if you could get stuff used regularly by *Weekending*, you might get a contracted commission for a minute of material every week worth £25.*

Even though I was often away doing gigs, and my main interest remained stand-up, Richard's enthusiasm for writing for radio pushed us through the process fairly quickly, and after getting a commission to write for *Weekending* we then wrote for *On the Hour*, the Steve Coogan and Chris

* Non-commissioned writers who finally found fame include Al Murray, Harry Hill, the screenwriter Georgia Pritchett and the merchant seaman and Pot Noodle Goth Peter Baynham, who eventually wrote the Borat movie and then moved to Hollywood to grow his hair. Most of the regular non-commissioned writers faded from view, but what a superb system. 'How do we discover new writers?' ask the BBC think tanks. Just invite them in, whoever they are, irrespective of the security risk they might pose, like *Weekending* used to before you cancelled it. Then you will find them.

Morris vehicle that became TV's *The Day Today*, though it transferred without us due to a petty argument and our delusional and insolent sense of entitlement. Throughout the mid-nineties we did various shows as Lee and Herring for Radio 4 and even Radio 1, which back then had many spoken-word and specialist shows, and developed the rudimentary chemistry of a viable double act. I was thinner than Richard at the time, and as some kind of contrast between the two players is all that is required in a double act really, we were soon able to elaborate our minimal weight differential into a fully formed comic relationship and take the act to BBC2 with the series of *Fist of Fun*.

In 1993, Newman and Baddiel played Wembley Arena, where Rob Newman flew high up into the air on a wire whilst talking about how he liked Crass as a child. Janet Street-Porter saw a picture of this in *The Face* and declared 'comedy is the new rock and roll'. But when Rob Newman flew up in the air at Wembley it changed comedy in Britain for ever, probably for the worse. Suddenly stand-up looked like a career option for ambitious young people, and a cash cow for unscrupulous promoters. Could ye olde eighties Alternative Comedy still be 'alternative' when there were T-shirts of its latest stars on sale in skinny-fit sizes at stadiums? Rich and I had the same management as Newman and Baddiel, and perhaps they had hoped for the same stadium-filling results when we did TV, but we just didn't have that kind of fan base. Knickers were rarely thrown at us, and if they had been, we would have worn them as hats, or just as knickers, our own having been cast away, filthy, in the lane.

Despite this obvious lack of exploitable teen fans, throughout the second part of the decade Richard and I were put on the road, rock-and-roll style, in a tour van, for heavily and expensively advertised tours. We usually

played to largely empty rooms in unloved council-run theatres, where disillusioned programmers booked whatever
was pushed at them, regardless. The overheads prevented
us from seeing a significant share of any profits. Comedy
was the new rock and roll, perhaps, and as in the early days
of rock and roll the cash rarely trickled down to the acts.
Our second series, *This Morning with Richard not Judy*, was
ignominiously cancelled by the then BBC2 controller Jane
Root in 1999; our final tour as Lee and Herring, in 1998,
actually appeared to have lost money. Most of what we'd
earned from the first television series was eaten up by debts
from Edinburgh, as we insisted on going back every year
with more and more new shows, sometimes doing three or
four performances of different things every day, trying to
remain loyal to the egalitarian ethics of the Fringe that had
formed us as teenagers, and thus losing more money and
sinking deeper into debt.

We ceased trading as Lee and Herring in 1999. People
still ask me why we split up the double act, but we never
really did. I remember when I was a teenager I loved The
Moodists, a gang of beatnik Australian blues punks based
in London which dissolved in 1987. The following year, I
saw their guitarist, Steve Miller, loading gear into a venue
for The Triffids, another expat Australian band. 'Why did
you split up The Moodists?' I asked. 'We didn't split up,'
he said, wearily, presumably remembering a decade of
struggling to make ends meet in the face of indifference
and mismanagement. 'We just stopped.' At the time I was
confused. The Moodists were brilliant. Literally dozens of
people loved them. How could they just stop? But Lee and
Herring didn't split up either. We just stopped.

Even while we were touring the double act and writing television, I'd always had other projects on the go.

21

Regrettably, Cluub Zarathustra, a Dadaist live show initiated by Simon Munnery and featuring a brilliant revolving-door cast including the likes of Kevin Eldon, Sally Phillips, Richard Thomas, the future Mighty Boosh mover Julian Barratt and Roger Mann,* came to nothing. Perhaps ending the rather short pilot we submitted to Channel 4 in 1997 with the words 'Insert More Money' flashing across the screen didn't help.

In between commitments to the double act I did hundreds of stand-up gigs a year on the circuit, which was always my principal creative outlet, and usually knocked

---

* Roger Mann was a superbly strange comic whom I first saw at Marco's Leisure Centre in Edinburgh in 1989, when he was known as Paul Ramone. His ability to make a sudden mid-stream switch from genial rambling into a kind of highfalutin Regency fop register, complete with the appropriately constipated face and pursed lips, was certainly an influence on his friend Frank Skinner's subsequent use of the same tic. Roger, who resembled Herman Munster's rakish younger brother, combined off-the-wall surrealism and coquettish whimsy with a kind of threatening suppressed rage, and we all loved him. His timeless party piece, the role of the decadent storyteller Edgar Allan Poo, began with the superbly portentous sentence, 'I had been called upon to invent a new kind of pig.' Roger and Kevin Eldon's 1992 Channel 4 sitcom Packing Them In, while roundly panned at the time, would probably stand up rather better than most recent offerings, and included the line, 'Look. It appears that, all along, Alan was a mechanical eagle.' Roger retired early, destitute and disillusioned, to veg out somewhere in the Pyrenees foothills on a bottle of red a day and a baguette a week. Nevertheless, the Swindon Advertiser recently voted him Swindon's twenty-ninth most famous person, beating XTC's Dave Gregory at number 34. Roger gave me loads of gigs early on in tiny clubs he ran in south London, and I am eternally in his debt. Not financially though, if I could just make that clear, as I understand his paltry savings largely disappeared in the 2009 crash.

out a new solo show for Edinburgh and in theory beyond, although the low-level, solo comedy show touring network of today didn't exist. But there were other problems too. By the late nineties, my management company had grown from a two-man operation into a massive conglomerate, with dozens of subdivisions staffed by hopeful serfs. It was hard to feel the same sense of all being in it together. The days of acts and management out in the van behind enemy lines on flyposting missions were long gone. And now, the live department was run like a tele-sales desk, with hungry young operatives trying to place acts around the country for maximum fees, to ensure a healthy turnover, often irrespective of the suitability of the venue. This meant we tended to be sent to council-funded places anxious to tick boxes by showing they'd had some comedy, unaware that the event wasn't going to fly. And because I gave each subsequent solo show a new title, rather than just being billed as 'Stewart Lee', and a theme, and a poster that tried to reflect that, all the information would get jumbled up by my bookers and I'd arrive at some regional arts centre somewhere with a show totally different to the one advertised, a two-year-old poster and press pack having been sent out. And all the while, audiences dwindled away.

In the early part of 2000, the big manager booked me a one-off gig at Dundee Rep. I paid the 15 per cent commission. I paid the support act. I paid for travel. I paid for accommodation. And then there was almost nothing left of the fee. The audience barely reached double figures. I arrived and left in darkness, with little to show for my trouble either financially or creatively. It seemed like a metaphor for my career. Creatively, I was in Dundee. By now, I'd hoped at least to be in St Andrews. I'd been on television to two million viewers less than a year ago, but now it seemed there was no one out there interested in what I did. I sold out a new stand-up show called *Stewart Lee's Badly Mapped World* for a month in a 150-seater in Edinburgh in August 2000, but lost money as usual. The show received dreary middling reviews, saying I was boring or monotonous or drunk. I performed it a few times subsequently, but the momentum soon petered out.

In the spring of 2001, I was supposed to be doing a mini-tour of Scotland and the friendlier parts of the North, supported by the clown-haired satirist Andy Zaltzman, but the venues showed me contracts that proved his presence on the bill had never been confirmed, and because they'd already booked their own opening acts, they refused to pay him or allow him to go on. Thus, Andy accompanied me on a strange holiday, a bizarre and unwanted chaperone figure visiting random and largely empty rooms in faraway towns where his contribution was not required, watching me lose my way emotionally, creatively, geographically, while I paid all his hotel bills and made him tramp across Scottish moors in search of uncharted stone circles during the long dead days off.

At some stage during this downward spiral of a tour, I found myself onstage at the Rawhide club in Liverpool, going mechanically through the motions of material I knew inside out, hoping that something would happen to wake me from my torpor and invest these stale riffs with some spontaneity. And it did. A drunken young man in a suit in the front row kept shouting that he didn't want to hear about anything I had to say – admittedly voicing the feelings of most of the room – and that I should talk about illegal immigrants. 'Talk about illegal immigrants,' he grunted, 'talk about fucking illegal immigrants.' I decided to take a bold course of action and get him onstage and hand him the mic, probably having just read a biography of the erratically inspired American comic Andy Kaufman or some other dangerous piece of literature, to see what he came up with on the subject of illegal immigrants, while I watched from his now vacant seat. I knew it would be incoherent and awful, which it was, as he slurred and stammered about asylum-seekers and how they should be sent back, but my plan was to let the room boil in irritation and fade away, before flipping the mood with a perfectly chosen bon mot. But as the crowd turned, security came and got the man offstage and told me, in no uncertain terms, that I had to go back on, utterly undermining any status I had left. There I was in a cellar in Liverpool, standing in front of a drunk racist, but somehow in the wrong. And what was a man like that even doing in one of *our* comedy clubs, being all racist, in his suit and tie? Did Tony Allen, the Godfather of Alternative Comedy, die onstage, repeatedly, night after night, for this?

Suddenly everything was clear. It was the twenty-first century and I was a mumbling relic from an earlier age. The crowds had changed. The rules were different. The management weren't out flyposting with the acts, and Alternative Comedy was dead. I was spent. I was trapped. I listened to the material as I was saying it. I watched it float out of my mouth over the bored faces of the Rawhide regulars like a brown tongue of acrid smoke, stinking the place out. Arch, cynical, tired, fake, conceited, formulaic and flat. I was no longer the person that wrote it, and the audience that it was written for weren't to be found at any of the places I was playing. I didn't believe in it any more; even people that liked me had seen through it. And for the racists at the Rawhide, everything I was saying was irrelevant anyway. So, quietly and without any fuss, I decided, then and there, to stop. Not that anyone noticed.

I spent a long time wondering how best to explain to you, dear readers, what I was doing in the period I disappeared from view. Then I was sent the text of a blog by The Spirit, the silver-haired member of the multi-billionaire Brixton country hip-hop group Alabama Three, who had spoken to me when I was signing DVDs after a recent live show. The Spirit, who is in fact a fully corporeal human, summed up my career post-Lee and Herring at the beginning of a piece called, unpleasantly, 'I Bum Stewart Lee'.

> Stewart Lee. He was the edgy, handsome half of the duo that did 'Fist of Fun' in the nineties. For four years he was very hot. Then he wasn't. He spent a decade getting fat and doing increasingly bitter and surreal sets to uncomfortable social workers in provincial arts centres, before suddenly bouncing back into the public eye by accidentally co-writing 'Jerry Springer – The Opera'.

The timescale is a little out of whack, but I don't feel I can really better The Spirit's brutal and unsentimental assessment of my career from 2000 to 2004. Nonetheless, here goes.

In the spring of 2001, Richard Thomas, a composer and former member of the musical comedy double act Miles and Millner, asked me to contribute some storylines to, and effectively direct, a new idea he was working on. I had directed Richard's opera shorts for Simon Munnery's BBC2 series *Attention Scum*, and he'd been happy with them. Now Richard had begun a project called *How to Write an Opera about Jerry Springer*, which featured him alone at a piano, playing snatches of tunes and talking about how you could write an opera about the American talk-show host Jerry Springer. His initial explanation of the genesis of the idea remains perfect: 'One night I was watching *The Jerry Springer Show*, drunk, and there were all these fat people shouting at one another and you couldn't understand what they were saying, and I thought, "That's an opera."'

But Richard's keen ear for a musical motif, and his keen eye for human suffering, found tragedy and comedy in *Springer Show* dialogue, which had previously just sounded profane, and his experiment played to a packed forty-seater room at Battersea Arts Centre. BAC's genius move of the noughties was the introduction of Scratch Nights. You could use their facilities for free to develop new pieces, as long as you showed the work in progress to the public and appeared to entertain their inane suggestions in the bar afterwards. In the light of the now punitive costs of road-testing new ideas at the Edinburgh Fringe through my management, it was a real lifeline, and I doubt I would ever have written or performed anything new ever again without BAC's encouragement.

There was no money in the opera at this stage, and no obvious future. I didn't give up stand-up to work on Richard's opera, which I wasn't being paid anything for in any case. I just gave up stand-up anyway, because I was sick of it and no one came to see me outside London and the Fringe. Instead, I was scraping by through writing weekly record reviews for my default arts patron at the *Sunday Times* Culture section, Rupert Murdoch. The mortgage on my flat was £500 a month, I wasn't on drugs and got lots of free records. I managed on very little.

On paper, the story of the opera's success looks like a showbiz dream. Every few months we'd add another scene to the piece, expand the cast of enthusiastic operatic volunteers, and restage it during another little run of Battersea Scratch Nights, under the auspices of their dramaturge Tom Morris, who quietly changed our lives, and will doubtless do so again. And the audience, and the buzz, would grow.

In August 2001, I declined to go to the Edinburgh Fringe for the first time since 1987. Instead, we staged a lengthy run of all the Jerry Springer material we had in the big, 200-seater room at Battersea. The great and the good all pitched up. Nick Hytner, the future director of the National Theatre, sniffed around like a funny little cat. We were written about in American newspapers by critics whose names excited people. We headed off a writ from the *Springer Show*'s production company. And our manager, now the producer of Richard's opera as well, began to try and find investors who would take the show forward commercially.

By the following summer, we'd sold out the 600-seater room at the Assembly Rooms for the month of the Edinburgh Fringe, and Nick Hytner wanted to open his tenure at the National Theatre with *Jerry Springer: The Opera* the next year. Amazing. Our manager's hustling had worked. Maybe we'd even get paid. That same summer, I wrote and performed a little theatre piece I'd also 'scratched' at BAC, *Pea Green Boat*, at the Traverse in Edinburgh, dealing directly with the theatre via the promoter Hils Jago. I made £600. It was the first money I'd earned in Edinburgh in twelve years, since the £450 I got as one of the four acts in Comedy Zone in 1991. Things were looking up.

But three years later, after all the awards, and after steering a cast of now nearly fifty through the ever-expanding show and moving it from the cocoon of the National Theatre to the bloody commercial reality of its West End run, there were things I realised about the production, and by implication the wider world, that thrust me back towards stand-up.

First of all, it was clear to me, even with the costly fire-power of our management's marketing department and all the goodwill of the critics behind it, that *Jerry Springer: The Opera* was a piece of art. It was essentially confusing and opaque, whereas commercial musical theatre hits, and commercial hits generally, tend to be about comforting certainties (see Appendix I). No matter what production values and lush orchestration and full-colour posters you threw at it, it was at base a genuine piece of work, created by artists, initially without a commercial end product in sight. Once you stuck it in the West End at £50 a ticket, you'd already priced a significant proportion of discerning arts consumers out of the market, and located it somewhere they didn't particularly want to go.

Secondly, having spent my twilight years as a stand-up complaining about the limitations of the art form and the low expectations of its audiences, it now seemed wonderfully adaptable. Richard Thomas hadn't let the fact that all people who like musical theatre are divs frighten him away from trying to expand the limits of the genre. And the simplicity of stand-up, the fact that you can think of an idea in the afternoon, after a long lie in, and implement it in the evening, suddenly seemed very attractive to me, now that I was a commercial theatre director whose attempts to make even the slightest change to the work required separate sets of instructions to literally dozens of people. Nor did you need an elaborate and literal stage set, though Julian Crouch's tasteful and minimal design for *Jerry* had grappled subversively with commercial theatre's institutionalised insistence on extravagance. But onstage, alone, as a stand-up, you could suggest anything with a few well-chosen words.

And thirdly, from an economic perspective, stand-up suddenly didn't seem such a bad bet. With *Jerry*, I was in the midst of a palpable hit, but I still didn't have anything much to show for it. Our manager, who was also the producer of the show, had narrowly missed out on a lucrative deal for the publishing rights to the opera's critically acclaimed songs, but as he explained to his loyal client Frank Skinner, who recalled a conversation with him in a *Guardian* interview, 'When you give someone the job of manager, you are basically giving them the right to play poker on your behalf.'*

We worked on the show from spring 2000 to the autumn of 2001 for nothing, before getting a salary at the National, but we ended up waiving our royalties towards the end of the West End run to cover a legal battle with the *Daily Mail*. I used up all my savings to work on the show. From an economic perspective, I'd have been better spending the *Opera* years doing stand-up in rooms above pubs every night than swanning around the West End, drunk, brandishing a financially worthless Olivier award.†

* Discussions with Sony about an album of songs from the show initially approved Lee Perry, Scott Walker and John Zorn as contributors, but eventually the head of Sony, Rob Stringer, started floating Ronan Keating from Boyzone, so I stopped attending the meetings or going to the studio. An awful house mix of one of the songs slunk unnoticed into the gay clubs as a white label, with the classical section in the middle that redeemed it snipped out. I was hugely relieved when the whole deal finally died.
† But I wouldn't have traded the experience of collaborating with Richard, Rob Thirtle and Julian Crouch from Improbable Theatre, David Soul, who played our final London Jerry, and the rest of the cast and creative team for a lifetime's worth of tickets to *We Will Rock You*.

But in a sense *Jerry Springer: The Opera* made me. Looking at what I'd observed of the strengths and weaknesses of the show as a business proposition, I realised that if I could aim my stand-up act at a small but loyal audience that would get it, in small and tasteful venues where it would work, raise my game with the raw material and the form of stand-up in the same way as Richard Thomas had done with musical theatre's, and somehow find a way of not spending more on promoting shows than I could possibly earn, it ought to be possible to be a commercially and creatively viable – and maybe alternative – stand-up comedian once again.

Around that time, my teenage comedy hero John Hegley told me you only need a few thousand fans. And if they all give you ten pounds a year, you're away. And I thought about all the musicians I like – the folk singers and free jazzers and alternative country cowpokes and persistent punk veterans who all hang in there, on small labels, selling self-released CDs for cash out of suitcases after gigs and operating within viable margins, tour, rest, tour, rest and sell some CDs. They survive.*

In early 2010, I arranged to meet one of the stars of *Jerry Springer: The Opera*, Wills Morgan, in a West End pub. Wills had made the role of Jesus his own, and Richard essentially wrote it for him, but he had been through a rough patch and had recently become a minor human-interest news story. The idea of a homeless opera singer was too good for journalists to resist. Wills was back on his feet again, and housed, and had enough of a sense of perspective to find the humour in his recent woes. He also had a headless Olivier award in his rucksack, Sir Larry cleanly decapitated at his replica bronze neck. I declined to ask Wills how this accident had befallen the great knight of the theatre, but thought the image the final coda to my relationship with *Jerry Springer: The Opera*.
* As an F-list celebrity and amateur arts journalist I have been able

However, as well as these three reasonably rational reasons why I wanted to start stand-up again, I had another, less rational, more disconcerting motive. I had been on nodding terms with Ricky Gervais since he was the Entertainments Officer at the University of London student union in the early nineties, where he was an enthusiastic promoter of stand-up nights and smitten fan of comedy. The compliments he would pay us were so extravagant that it often made interaction with him awkward and embarrassing, a natural characteristic he was subsequently able to siphon, to great effect, into the brilliantly realised role of David Brent.

At first I hadn't made the connection between the former comedy promoter and the man who, in 1999, took on the persona of an ignorant right-wing irritant on Channel 4's *The 11 O'Clock Show*. At the time, Ricky was around the circuit occasionally, doing the character of a man with learning difficulties. However, nothing in Ricky's work to date suggested the consummate and genre-redefining bombshell he was soon to drop, alongside Stephen Merchant, in the form of *The Office*, one of the all-time great television shows.

On the back of the success of *The Office*, Ricky was suddenly able to do his first full-length solo stand-up shows, to large and enthusiastic audiences. It was drawn to my

---

to meet many of my favourite musicians, and the way Howe Gelb of Giant Sand, Dave Graney, the former frontman of The Moodists, and the free improviser Derek Bailey all ran their affairs, direct-marketing their work to sustainably farmed fan bases, was something of an inspiration, economically as well as artistically. And the comic-book writer Alan Moore's refusal to engage with big money's misappropriation of his work clearly left him free to concentrate on the job in hand.

attention that he always praised me and Sean Lock in interviews, and cited us as his main inspirations. Ricky was preparing his second live tour, 2004's *Politics*, when I drifted back onto the circuit. I hadn't seen any of his stand-up.

The first time I was informed that I had copied Ricky Gervais was at The Amused Moose in Soho, sometime in late 2003 or early 2004. A mother and her daughter, who had enjoyed my set but never seen me before, said that I was 'clearly very influenced by Ricky Gervais', with the implication that they had rumbled me and I really ought to find my own shtick. Then it happened again two or three times. And then I started to wonder why Ricky was always praising me to the skies in interviews, and so I took up an offer of tickets to his new show at the Bloomsbury Theatre.

I sat there, dumbfounded. It wasn't that Ricky was the same as me. He wasn't. And I'm not saying he had copied me. There wasn't a single line that exactly duplicated anything I'd ever done. But Ricky had the calmness, and the way of offering up contentious ideas as if they meant nothing and were merely idle thoughts, that I felt was a hallmark of my work, and which had always made it such a difficult fit for mainstream audiences at populist clubs. And there was enough coincidental overlap, in terms of tone and subjects I might cover – Aesop's fables, a long routine on 'The Boy Who Cried Wolf' – to mean that now Ricky was a big name, I could understand why the casual viewer would mistake *me* for an imitator of *his* approach. I hadn't realised how much my stand-up mattered to me until I considered the possibility of never being able to do it again. I became aware that the two people I had come with, sitting either side of me, were looking at me, concerned, and one of them took my hand in a supportive gesture. My face was frozen in numb shock. All around us people were laughing and clapping. I felt like I had died, or had never been born. Had my friends guessed what I was going through?

At some point during the show I experienced an emotion I rarely feel. It was jealousy. I had honestly never been jealous of another comedian, and after working with musical theatre performers my admiration for stand-ups had reached a point where I loved them all indiscriminately. And there were lots of friends and acquaintances of mine I'd started out with who had been much more successful than me – Al Murray, Steve Coogan, Harry Hill – but I didn't ever feel like I was in competition with them because they are so different to me, and the choices they have made are theirs and not mine. And there were also people whose talents far outstripped mine, who produced work I thought I'd never be capable of in my life – Daniel Kitson, Simon Munnery, Jerry Sadowitz, Richard Thomas, Johnny Vegas, Kevin McAleer – but I didn't want to be them, because I could never be them. But watching Ricky I felt myself thinking, 'This is the kind of thing I used to do. And all these people in this massive room are loving it. Whereas in the dying days of my stand-up career, I was reviewed as if I didn't know what I was doing, and found myself playing to fifteen people in Dundee.' I hadn't minded not being popular when I'd thought that what I did could never be popular, but seeing something not dissimilar to what I might do being enjoyed by 500 people, already sold on the strangest bits by virtue of Ricky's celebrity, was bewildering.

Ricky had invited us backstage, but I felt too shaken up to go. The upshot of that evening at the Bloomsbury was that I realised, somewhere within my dead and defeated hulk, I had an ego. For better or worse, I did not want to be Ted Chippington, a fondly remembered and influential cult back to doing a day job. And I did not want to be a footnote in stand-up either, cited as the comedian that the famous Ricky Gervais always said he liked. I wanted to get what I did as a stand-up back in the public eye, even if only on a low level, before whatever had been unique about me became subsumed into the general mass of comedy.

I also knew that if I did start again and took it seriously, I would have to move what I had done onwards a stage or two, in case the mother and daughter from The Amused Moose were in the room. A few months later, I rang Ricky up and asked him if I could use one of his flattering interview quotes about me – 'the funniest, most cliché-free comedian on the circuit' – on a poster. He agreed, glad to help, and I think this single-handedly sold out the show *Stand-Up Comedian* on tour and in London and Edinburgh. But I often wonder what happened to Ricky Gervais. He never crops up on London circuit gigs now. I assume that, like all those long-forgotten names of my open-spot days – Two Gorgeous Hunks or The Singing Fireman or The Amazing Mr Smith – Ricky must have just given up.

As I tentatively crept back into the clubs to assemble my new hour, now brazenly endorsed by Ricky Gervais, in short spots on regular comedy nights, I found the flavour of the London circuit had changed subtly. Sure, there were still lots of packed rooms of lads laughing at jokes about football, and I went to silence before some City types somewhere out east, and died so badly in a room in Hammersmith that a member of the audience took me to task afterwards, refusing to believe that I had ever made a living out of comedy. But the appliquéd surrealist Josie Long was running evenings with an almost arts-and-crafts flavour during which young weirdos read half-formed ideas off crumpled bits of paper, Robin Ince had started his unashamedly pretentious Book Club nights, and pre-TV

Miranda Hart was fronting a vibrant women's comedy night downstairs at The Albany Arms, where I was allowed to be the monthly guest man.

There was now an obvious split in the circuit. You could make a living doing your regular twenty minutes at Jongleurs and The Store, with some lucrative Christmas corporate gigs thrown in during the festive season, and never bother to go north to the Fringe. Or you could shuffle about in what seemed to be this new underground scene, and take your show to Edinburgh at a massive loss, and get written about in a broadsheet, and try and get some arts centre gigs, and let nerds all over the land know about your work via these newfangled social networking sites that I, like a nut-hungry ape staring at a nutcracker, was just beginning to see the possibilities of. If the phrase hadn't lost its meaning once already, you could almost say we were witnessing the birth of a new Alternative Comedy, in opposition to the crowd-pleasing composite that the Alternative Comedy of old had become.

The same trend was evident beyond the M25. Most major cities now had a branch of one of the big chains of comedy clubs, a Comedy Store or a Jongleurs, showcasing simple man-and-a-mic stand-up to audiences of stag and hen nights. But the ubiquity of these big chains meant that in every city that had a Franchised Laff Retail Outlet™, at least one alternative venue seemed to be thriving in opposition to it, such as XS Mallarkey in Manchester, or The Glee Club in Birmingham, or The Comedy Box in Bristol, none of which had much crossover with the franchises in terms of acts or audiences. It was the same sort of schism that, thirty years ago, pitched the non-sexist and non-racist Comic Strip against Bernard Manning's old-school Embassy Club.

These counter-Jongleurs were the places where I needed to be playing. Instead of going on for guaranteed fees in empty council venues and failing to build an audience, or boring the shit out of Friday night punters who just wanted to have some fun between work and the disco, I needed to be in the dedicated comedy clubs that had flourished in my absence from the circuit, playing for smaller fees to smaller crowds composed of people that would get it and would come back next time with a friend. Could I have a second chance at building the following I had failed to find in the previous decade?

My management had a new live booker, Charlie Briggs, a young woman whose favourite act was the sentimental misanthropist Daniel Kitson, as everyone's should be, and who had thought, in the light of watching how this fiercely independent comic conducts his business affairs, that there may be a live model that suited me better than my management's usual telesales approach to booking dates. Charlie knew all these small and sussed venues, and she travelled the country to check them out on her own time, without any encouragement from her employers, even though these places weren't all going to pay the kind of big fees that the telesales-style bookers needed to bump up their turnovers. With Charlie happy to eschew the larger fees I might have made by selling me on underwritten guarantees to big empty spaces, and booking me instead at this sustainable lower level, I thought I could get on the road after an Edinburgh Fringe run and maybe, before it was too late, claw myself out the beginnings of an audience that might stay with me for life. That was, if the August shows went well.

So in early 2004, I began to scrape together a show from the few bits of my vast back catalogue that I could still stand to repeat and some ideas I'd had during my time off. I called it *Stewart Lee – Stand-Up Comedian* as a blunt statement of intent and a method of sidestepping the fact that I had no idea what it would be about as the Fringe listings deadline approached. My management winkled out an offer from a relatively new venue on the Edinburgh Fringe, the hip subterranean firetrap called The Underbelly, which was keen to have what it viewed as a big name, and the deal was weighted favourably enough to mean I wouldn't actually lose money on an Edinburgh show they promoted for the first time in fifteen years.

Stand-Up Comedian hit the ground running, in the corrugated silo of The Underbelly's White Belly room. I was thrilled to be away from negotiating the needs of the massive cast of the opera and to be back on my own. Now that I had been ladled with theatrical accolades, previously puzzled critics had to assume that my apparent inability to write and perform stand-up properly was in fact the result of positive artistic choices, rather than an indication of a basic lack of ability, and they adjusted their star ratings accordingly. Plus in my absence I had been fêted by their new favourite, the mid-noughties sensation Ricky Gervais.

I took every small-hours Fringe festival club set going, revelling in my freedom, choked ecstatically on a million fags, long after midnight, in steamy attics and dripping cellars, turning comedy fat back into tentative muscle. And I saw dozens of superb new acts I'd never seen before, like the disarmingly honest Chippenham skinhead Will Hodgson and the brilliantly realised character comedy of Will Adamsdale in *Jackson's Way*, which I attended half a dozen times at least, and which was to alter the whole way I thought about performance. Watching Will, an uncategorisable Etonian performance-art eccentric who never blinked in the face of audience disbelief, maintaining the most improbable and engaging of conceits in the face of mass irritation and total audience boredom proved to me that one man on a stage in a room could be anything at all, go anywhere, say anything, suggest anything, do anything. This was what I needed to see.

Comedians' memoirs, about how they got back on the road after a lay-off, or their fully approved fly-on-the-wall documentaries on the same subject, tend towards the sentimental journeys of thoroughly made millionaires, peeping out from their Chelsea penthouses and Hollywood Hills adobe ranches to try and recapture their youth. Understand this: it was not nostalgia that drew me back to stand-up. I was pushing forty. Nothing had worked out, not even the theatrical hit of the decade. For the middle part of my thirties I'd been barely earning a living. I was like a punch-drunk prizefighter with no other viable skills who thought maybe there still might be a battle to be won. And I realised that stand-up was just one man on a stage in a room. And so stand-up was infinite. And I had been a fool to doubt it. I might never be a proper comedian, like friends and acquaintances who had achieved fame and wealth and mass acclaim, but perhaps I could still be an Alternative Comedian, which, I gradually remembered, was what I had wanted to be in the first place.

Stand-Up Comedian

A transcript of the show recorded on 10 March 2005
at The Stand, Glasgow

PRE-SHOW MUSIC: 'THE BREATH OF COLDNESS'*

* 'The Breath of Coldness' is a ten-minute saxophone solo, using the circular breathing technique, from the album *America 2003* by the British free-jazz saxophonist Evan Parker, with whom I share a birthday. During the missing years of being an award-winning opera director who once shook hands with Michael Portillo at a buffet at the National Theatre, I'd moved to Stoke Newington in Hackney. Stoke Newington is the spiritual home and elephants' graveyard of British free improvised music. In Stoke Newington, the streets are littered with puzzled musical mavericks still trying to figure out how to improvise non-idiomatically within a now established idiom.

I was first exposed to this kind of music by my flatmate, the guitarist Michael Cosgrave, in 1992, when he was briefly press-ganged into the musique concrète noodlers Morphogenesis, who described themselves, with hopefully knowing humour, as 'Britain's most theoretically rigorous group', an epithet I subsequently cannibalised into my own late-nineties poster strapline 'Britain's most theoretically rigorous comedian'. I'd attended the Red Rose Club's out-there Momposo evenings when I lived in Finsbury Park in the mid- to late nineties, and I'd seen the ever open-minded Sonic Youth jam with representatives from the scene at various events in the nineties, and made curious trips to London Musicians' Collective events at the ICA and the South Bank. But in Stoke Newington, gigs at The Vortex and improvised music club nights at The Red Lion and Ryan's Bar meant I was now regularly immersed in splurge and skronk. Evan Parker was a monthly fixture at The Vortex, a listed building a few hundred yards from my new flat that was eventually demolished under mysterious circumstances to make way for a Nando's, and I saw him dozens of times in the first few years I lived there. And this stuff got under my skin.

I do appreciate it's always dangerous, and potentially shaming, for comedians to claim inspiration from great musicians, or indeed any other legitimate artists. When TV's Russell Howard cites, in an interview, Bob Dylan's mantra 'every great artist needs to be in a permanent state of becoming' as an influence, one wonders what relationship this profound phrase has with appearing on *Mock the Week* and making fun of Susan Boyle for having a hairy face?

But I feel that the sheer bloody-mindedness of the free-jazzers was something of an example, as was their take-it-or-leave-it attitude to critical and public approval. One felt, romantically I am sure, this music had to be made, and would somehow issue forth whatever, out of sheer necessity, irrespective of people's response. Listeners had to come to it on its own terms, suspend their expectations and forget what they had learned. I'll never be one of those comics who genuinely jam a whole set off the top of their heads, like the mighty Phil Kaye or the fiery and fluid Ross Noble, but I admired the musicians' fearlessness in the face of apparently perilous artistic precipices.

Thus it was a very deliberate and self-conscious decision to use the Evan Parker solo, on a loop, as the pre-show music for *Stand-Up Comedian*. The normal pre-show procedure for stand-up is to play something upbeat and jaunty, slightly too loud, through the PA. (The Amused Moose Club's endless repeat plays of that Supergrass song about something pumping on the stereo to introduce every act is a case in point, and I am always inwardly amused, whenever I do gigs there, to slouch on as non-triumphally as I am able.) But in the small and stifling space of The Underbelly's soggy dungeon, The White Belly, in August 2004, the Evan Parker solo was a warning, before the show began, that this was not intended to be like other stand-up shows.

Playing the Parker solo was also a good way of identifying troublemakers, of spotting punters that had probably come to the wrong gig. I'd stand at the back of the room watching the audience

STEW APPEARS. MUSIC CHANGES TO 'MR. LEE' BY THE
5.6.7.8's.*

STEW INVITES FOUR PEOPLE ONSTAGE. HE GIVES THEM
PARTY POPPERS AND TELLS THEM TO EXPLODE THEM ON
HIS SIGNAL. THEY DO SO AND RETURN TO THEIR SEATS,
LEAVING STEW ALONE AT THE MIC, A FEW STRANDS OF
PARTY STREAMER DRAPED OVER HIS HEAD.†

---

file in. Anyone who got up and remonstrated with the sound guy, insisting that the music was turned off, as some would, was probably not going to go for the show. In New Zealand, some English fans of Peter Kay and the sport of rugby accidentally arrived at my show as a result of a wrongly assumed national kinship. It was their furious reaction to the Evan Parker solo that immediately alerted me to problems ahead, which eventually and inevitably ruined the show (see Appendix II).

Since 2004, I've always thought very carefully about pre-show music. It's all part of set and setting. A show begins the moment the audience walk into a venue. When *Jerry Springer: The Opera* was at the National Theatre, the grandiose vibe of the building and the dignity of its discreet and helpful staff were already heading the audience into a beautiful crossfire of high cultural surroundings and low cultural content. But when the show transferred to the West End and punters trooped in past loads of people shouting at them and trying to flog them Maltesers and souvenir hats, this was lost, and the initial impact of the show suffered as a result.

In essence, I don't want the pre-show music to seem like I am eager to please. I want to start wrong-footing the audience before they've even sat down.

* I chose this Japanese garage-punk song because it is fast and exciting and the ladies' foreign accents are funny. Is this lacist? I am velly solly.

† The more fun I could have with the punters here, getting them to join in the party atmosphere, the funnier and more disconcerting it would be to hold the silence after the celebrations were over and then shift the mood by beginning to talk about the tragedy of

43

So, on September the 11th, 2001 . . . I was actually on holiday, right. That seems distasteful now. But I wasn't to know
at the time. You know, I didn't plan it. The holiday, I mean,
not the attacks.* And I was actually in the city of Granada

---

the World Trade Center whilst still draped in party-popper streamers. Reading this now it probably seems in poor taste, and perhaps
it was when it was written, but three years after 9/11, when I first
began performing this show, the event was still inescapable on a
daily basis, percolating even apparently unrelated media. It had
changed everything, as the cliché goes, but often in the strangest
places. There was a bizarre Marvel comic where Spider-Man and
The Avengers deferred to the true heroes, the firemen and the
police, as they contributed to the clean-up operation. I'm a huge
Marvel Comics fan, but had I lost someone on the day, even I might
have felt this was an inappropriate tribute (though it's always good
to know that a fictional character who has been given the ability
to climb walls by the bite of a radioactive spider shares your pain).
Closer to home, I remember talks about scrapping a projection of
Bosch-like figures falling down to hell in *Jerry Springer: The Opera*
because suddenly they echoed the tumbling bodies of 11 September.
But reminders of the attack were everywhere, intentional and unin-
tentional, to the point where it was beginning to lose its meaning.
Could the mere mention of it still kill a room stone dead if the person mentioning it had streamers in their hair?
* It's an ongoing source of annoyance to me that initially self-
contained jokes and comments are suddenly, and often wilfully,
made to seem contentious or offensive by media commentators
who reposition them in the orbit of events or shifts in attitudes,
subsequent to their telling, which no one could reasonably have
foreseen. Again, in *Jerry Springer: The Opera*, we were required by
the producers and stars to rewrite and re-rehearse an existing scene
involving a severed head after a hostage was decapitated in Iraq, the
suggestion being that audiences watching this vast, massively choreographed, two-and-a-half-hour spectacle might assume the severed head scene had been rapidly included that week specifically in
the interests of appearing topical and tasteless. Soon after the death

in southern Spain, right. It's an interesting place. Granada was kind of the last point of Muslim occupation in medieval Europe. It's still a very mixed city – lots of mosques, lots of churches, lots of Arab Spaniards and white European Spaniards, all getting on fine.*

And I was walking around there on nine-one-one – the 9th of November, reclaim the calendar, we invented those dates† – I was walking around there on the 9th of

---

of Boyzone's Stephen Gately I saw an episode of *Most Haunted*, Living TV's ethically dubious ghost provocation show in which the restless souls of the dead are taunted into activity by entirely unqualified amateur parapsychologists and occasional F-list celebrities. In this particular edition, the tormented wraiths suffered the attentions of Gately's false Irish group and their lucky shit-at-the-wall svengali Louis Walsh, who were taken into some haunted cellars in Edinburgh to search for the spirits of furious Scottish troglodytes. Rather than thinking that it was intended either as a calculated insult or some kind of misplaced tribute to the now deceased teen idol, who had fled the scene three times in terror during the show, I simply assumed that the timing of the broadcast was nothing more than an oversight on the part of the schedulers, and went about my business.

* The quietly seminal Irish comedian Ian Macpherson, a formative influence on my stand-up, used to have a joke: 'Everyone can remember where they were when they heard that JFK had been shot. I was leaning out of the second-floor window of a book depository in Dallas, Texas,' or something like that. Similarly, we can all remember where we were when we found out that planes had flown into the World Trade Center. I was on holiday in Granada, Spain. And pretty much everything in this routine is true.

† Watching American responses to the attack on the news in the bar, and later in the hotel room, it was clear that semantic difficulties – the unintentionally jingoistic use of the word 'crusade', for example – were instantly amplifying existing tensions. Even the numerical naming of the event itself showed how we are divided by a common language.

November, nine-one-one, and I went into, er, a little Spanish bar. And on television there was all this film of buildings on fire, and things falling down, and people running and screaming. And I said to the barman, 'Where's that?' – in Spanish, '¿Dónde está?' And he said, 'Nuevo Yorica.' And I thought, 'Oh, it's in Colombia or somewhere, it doesn't matter.' And then I watched for a bit longer, Glasgow, and I realised that it was New York, where English-speaking people live, and therefore a terrible newsworthy tragedy.

And I don't know if you remember, do you remember the planes, flying into the, yeah, the World Trade . . .? 'Cause we got that on the news in London, I don't know if you had it here. And . . . I don't want to make any assumptions, you know . . . Um . . .*

* This transcript, remember, comes from a show in Glasgow. Scottish audiences, or Scotch audiences as I prefer to call them, like to manufacture unnecessary grievances by wilfully imagining that visiting English comics know nothing about their culture, and that we have assumed everything in Scotland is the same as in England. This is a misconception I am happy to play on by doing everything I can to make it appear true. I was always scared of Scottish audiences, especially the legendarily feral ones of Glasgow, until I decided to go out to cultivate an air of deliberate cultural insensitivity, which eventually induced their grudging respect.

Likewise, deep in the days of the Troubles, any English stand-up in Northern Ireland was always, understandably, walking on eggshells, many of them deliberately placed in their path by the regular host of Belfast's Empire comedy club, the TV personality Patrick Kielty. Fearless as ever, the legendary Simon Munnery went onstage in Derry in his anarcho-punk Alan Parker Urban Warrior persona and began his set by apologising for English complicity in the potato famine and emptying a compensatory sack of spuds onto the stage. The Irish republicans loved it! Audiences can actually enjoy being insulted. If they are abused with enough originality, confidence and verve, the time and trouble

So I was watching that in this, this Spanish bar. And then George Bush came on the television news, and he said, 'We are gonna get them folks what done this.' And that annoyed me for two reasons. One, because it was grammatically inaccurate. And secondly, 'cause you could already see the terrible kind of cultural fallout of what this was going to mean. There was suddenly a horrible tension between the Arab Spaniards and the white European Spaniards in this previously happy bar. And after a while, I, I couldn't stand the tension any more, so I went into the Gents to do a wee, and, er . . . A couple of people over there sniggered at the word 'wee'. That's fine, I know this is a tense subject to open with and I'm, I'm happy that the word 'wee' has helped defuse the atmosphere a bit. So . . . So I was standing there in this Spanish bar on the 9th of November doing a wee . . . out of my cock . . . and . . . and it was yellow . . . and smelt of wee.*

And while I was doing it, this thing happened that happens when you get a bit older, where, when you kind of release the pressure on the front sphincter, the, the, the back sphincter kind of loosens off of its own accord, you know. While I was there, this Arab guy came, and he, and he, and he stood next to me but I didn't make eye contact with him, 'cause I was embarrassed, er, about the wee. And world news events.† But, you know, while I was there, 'cause

---

an act has taken to disrespect their core values actually appears flattering.

* I suppose what I was doing here was trying to exploit the tension of discussing something puerile in the midst of something terribly serious, and I would go into greater or lesser detail about the act of weeing depending on the feel of the room. Also, wee is funny, especially if the wee is being weed out of a cock. Into a toilet. On 9/11.

† This is absolutely true. I did feel like I couldn't make eye contact

I was a bit older the, the, the front sphincter slackened off, the back sphincter went of its own accord. And suddenly, a little fart came out, right.* But it was only a really tiny fart,

───────

with the man because of both weeing and the World Trade Center falling down. Similarly, I remember as a thirteen-year-old boy being taken by my mum to see Richard Attenborough's *Gandhi* at a cinema in Birmingham, back in the days when they still had intervals in films. After Edward Fox had presided over a massacre of innocent Indian demonstrators at Amritsar, we went and queued in the foyer for an ice cream, the only white people amongst dozens of Brummie Indians, to whom I remember feeling very strongly that I should apologise in some way, firstly for the Amritsar massacre, and secondly for Ben Kingsley blacking up and doing a Dick Emery voice.

* I did not do a fart at this point during the tragic events of 9/11. But I did have a kind of momentary Tourette syndrome panic that I might do, even though I couldn't feel any gas pressure in my bowel, and I was terrified at how this might seem utterly inappropriate to the man standing next to me, given the seriousness of the events unfolding on the television in the bar. Once, when I was a teenager, I bumped into a friend in the street who was distraught, having just seen an acquaintance run down and killed, and I remember having an out-of-body experience where I realised that the worst thing I could possibly do would be to laugh, as I became paralysed by the fear that I would do so. Similarly, a few days after a terrible child murder in a grim northern city in the mid-nineties, I found myself floating above myself, looking down on myself while onstage doing stand-up in the said city, and watching as I made idiotic and insensitive comments about the incident, and then, as my personalities merged once more, I was greatly relieved to find that I had not said anything of the sort. But my mouth was dry, my tongue large and lifeless, and I was bathed in a cold sweat.

Richard Herring is to be both praised and condemned for having exactly these kinds of mad impulses to say the worst possible thing in any situation, and for somehow lacking the self-censorship facility that prevents most of us from acting on them. His mid-nineties

like the kind of fart a vole might do. Or Anna Friel. It was a fart that smelt mainly of hair and was comprised principally of ideas. But it was a fart nonetheless.* And the Arab

---

flatmate, the Pot Noodle advert actor and disgrace to Wales Peter Baynham, returned home one afternoon, Rich having been forewarned that Pete's dad had passed away earlier that day. Rich's first words were 'Pete, can I just say how delighted I am to hear of the death of your father,' a bold gamble, but one that was accepted in the spirit it was meant. Since then, Richard has progressed beyond the shock-hack's default setting of 'saying the unsayable' to 'saying the unthinkable' and to articulating ideas so sexually and morally twisted that it wouldn't even occur to the average punter to imagine them, let alone say them.

There was a school of comedy in the nineties where the audience would warm to a comedian who seemed to be expressing opinions and feelings they themselves had had but never expressed. There's an incredible and admirable skill in doing this, and Michael McIntyre perhaps represents its apogee, his rapid-fire observations about everyday life being so accurate and instantly recognisable that he is absolved even of the obligation to develop them into actual jokes. But I've always liked the kind of comedy that makes you go, 'My God, I would never have thought that!'

* In long-running shows that I have to perform many times, where there are long sections that need to stay more or less the same to convey dramatically necessary parts of the narrative, I look forward immensely to tiny details that I can change every night to keep myself amused. Each night the mammal and the celebrity in this section would change, as would the exact composition of the fart they had supposedly issued in the subsequent sentence, though it was always necessary for there to be some kind of believable relationship between the mammal, the celebrity and the texture of the fart. For me, the 'vole/Anna Friel/hair and ideas' combo, the version recorded for posterity here, wasn't at all as strong as, say, something like 'shrew/Paul Morley/Vimto and affectation', whereas 'stoat/Victoria Beckham/custard and regret' is somehow not quite right at all. Or maybe it is? Cynics think free-associating surreal stuff is easy,

guy, he, he heard the fart. And he looked across at me. And I looked back at him. And he laughed. And then I laughed. And I realised everything was going to be OK.*

And then I went back into the bar. By now the situation was even worse, even more tense. The room had kind of split along racial, religious lines. There was a horrible tension in the room.† And then suddenly Co-lin – *Colin* – Powell went on the television – we invented those names, his name's not . . . he's not Co-lin the Barbarian, his name's Colin, he should be running a photocopier repair workshop – Colin Powell went on television on the 9th of November, Spanish bar, and he said, 'We are gonna launch a crusade against them folks what done this.'‡ And being

---

but it's much harder than simply putting the word 'fish' into normal sentences at random points, as advertising creatives and whoever wrote the piss-weak parody of *The Mighty Boosh* in Mitchell and Webb's cash-in book might want to note.

* On sticky nights, when the audience were uncomfortable and uneasy and silent, this was usually the point at which things finally swung my way, and the laugh would come like a great wave of relief as people in the room realised I was working towards some kind of point, rather than being gratuitously offensive. Not in Aspen, though.

† Sometimes, if the atmosphere at the gig was bad enough by this point, I was able to play a game in the performance of this section whereby I would gesture around the emotional topography of the uncomfortable room I was in to stand in for the emotional topography of the uncomfortable room I was describing.

‡ Co-lin Powell did not say this on 9/11. He never really said it, but he did use the word 'crusade' a couple of days later. I lied for comic effect. But who is the real criminal? Is it the humble stand-up comedian, slightly changing what someone said a bit for comic effect? Or is it the American politician, laughing and touching himself inappropriately while he rains death and destruction on the heads of millions of innocents? (Answer: it is the American politician. He is the real criminal.)

in a largely Muslim town, full of murals of crusaders cutting the heads off Muslims, you realise what an inappropriate word 'crusade' was to use on the 9th of November. It went down really badly. And as a, a world statesman, Colin Powell should be aware of how words change their meaning, culturally. Saying 'crusade' on the 9th of November, it's a bit like if I were to get a job as a maths teacher, teaching maths in a German town somewhere near Belsen. And I was to say to the kids, 'I'm going to set you a maths problem. I want you to work through it, and on the last page, fill in your final solution.'* You know, it would be received badly. And as a world leader, Colin Powell should be aware of these kinds of cultural shifts in language. But he said 'crusade' and it went down really badly with everyone in the room, so there was an even worse atmosphere than before.

And then the Arab guy that I'd had my kind of moment of epiphany, of kind of human trust with in the toilets, he was standing just in front of me. And he looked across at me with these eyes full of hope, as if to go, 'What are we going to do?' And I didn't know what to do. I mean, I couldn't just do another fart at will. You know, I'm not a nineteenth-century French music-hall entertainer. I'm the

---

* When I performed this show in Solihull, where I grew up, a bloke I was at school with, who was now an Alpha Course born-again Christian, tried to engage me in a conversation about the rights and wrongs of the supposedly blasphemous *Jerry Springer: The Opera* that I had worked on. He suggested that this line, for example, was anti-Semitic and that Jews would be offended by it, though he wasn't personally. It's so obviously not the point of the line at all, to me, but I mention this only as an example of the fact that you can't always worry too much about what people think, as some people are just beyond help.

opposite of that. In four main ways . . . there isn't time to go into now. But . . . But someone went, 'Aw,' disappointed there. If you seek me out afterwards, I'll clarify the exact position.*

But I knew I had to do something, so . . . It was my moment. So what I did was, I just kind of lifted my leg up like that. And I sort of acted it out. I went, 'Ugh, fuck, smell, ugh, horrible!' And he laughed. And the guys he was with laughed. Gradually the laughter spread all around the room. There was a critic from the *Independent* at the back not laughing. But he didn't really get what I was doing, you know. It was a kind of mixture of the sacred and the profane, it just went over his head.†

But eventually everyone in the room was laughing. And I realised that with that one inane, puerile, scatological gesture I had achieved more for world peace than any politician had all day. 'Cause farts are funny, Glasgow, right? That is the international baseline of all humour, farts, right. And you can be as sophisticated as you like, Glasgow, but at the end of the day you have to admit farts are funny.

---

* I never did decide what the four main ways I differed from Le Pétomane were, and this is another example of me making spaces in the material to amuse myself. Perhaps I hoped I would be called upon to explain this unsatisfactory sentence at some point. Or maybe, in my eternal love–hate relationship with the very idea of being a stand-up, I did feel that all I was at the time was a turn, a turn farting gags out towards bemused onlookers, who craved the sweeter smells of roses and lavender.

† I am thinking specifically of Julian Hall of the *Independent* here, who always gives me three stars but comes back to my shows every year out of the goodness of his heart to try and encourage me further in my sadly misguided endeavours, like a dog returning to a pile of old shit and sniffing it again to see if it has suddenly turned into ice cream.

And you go, 'No, we don't actually agree with you, Stew. I saw a hilarious, satirical cartoon in the *New Statesman* at the weekend, satirising EU farming policies, it was hilarious.' Was it? Was it as funny as a fart? No, it wasn't.

'But I saw Ian Hislop on television at the weekend, Stew, satirising the government, with his voice going up at the start of the sentence and going down at the end. It was hilarious.' Was it? Was it as funny as some gas that smells of shit coming out of an arse? No, it wasn't. And nothing Ian Hislop ever says or does or secretly imagines will be as funny as that.*

And I ran this show in the Edinburgh Fringe Festival, right, in August and, um, every year in Edinburgh they have a prize for comedy, right, organised by Perrier – the Perrier Awards. Perrier of course owned by Nestlé, Nestlé top of the World Health Organisation list of unethical companies. It suggested that their milk-marketing policies contribute to the death of 1.5 million children every year. So every time you laugh at a Perrier-nominated act, a little baby dies. Bear that in mind.†

* I chose Ian Hislop here because he seems like an utterly blameless figure with whom no sensible person could take issue, which seemed to make the attack on him funnier, painting me as a 'demented, inexplicably bitter man', which I am, as you will see. It's probably worth pointing out that during my short-lived and misguided attempt to appear on TV comedy panel shows, in late 2006, Hislop was easily the most helpful and supportive person I encountered.

† When this show was due to be issued on DVD in 2005, the legal department of the production wing of my old management, who filmed it, initially said it would not be possible to describe Nestlé in these terms. I told them to look into it. And, after the briefest bit of research, they decided it would be fine. Make of this what you will. By the following year, Perrier was no longer the sponsor

And every year in Edinburgh, they always give that award to comedy to a human being speaking about some stuff. But if they had any integrity, they would give the Perrier Award to the genuinely funniest thing that's going to happen in Edinburgh all August, which is just going to be an old Scottish tramp doing a fart in a wood. But, Glasgow, if a tramp farts in a forest and no one hears it, is it still funny? Yes, it is. 'Cause it's some shit that smells of shit coming out of an arse. And if the Perrier had any integrity, which it doesn't, it would sign up that fart for its own twelve-part Channel 4 comedy series deal.

Some laughs, some doubt in the room. People going, 'We're kind of with you theoretically. We understand this is some kind of satire of something. But how would that actually work, Stew? An invisible cloud of shit-smelling gas with its own Channel 4 series?' I don't know, Glasgow,

———

of Nica Burns's Edinburgh comedy award. It is entirely plausible that Perrier no longer felt the increasingly coarse and volatile world of once 'alternative' comedy sat well with the sophisticated nature of their brand, but romantics like to imagine the sustained anti-Perrier campaign by Baby Milk Action and the Tapwater Awards team may have helped sway their bloody hand, as every story on the Perrier Comedy Awards ceremony was always accompanied by information about the protests. Delightfully, Jason Trachtenberg, of the lo-fi, outsider art, comedy singing trio The Trachtenberg Family Slideshow Players, was booked as the entertainment at the 2005 Perrier Awards party and, having learned of their parent company's disgraceful and unethical record, used his platform to improvise lyrics about Nestlé's well-known and proven complicity in the deaths of millions of children. Typically, the TV-industry weekenders present were too pissed to notice, and continued looking for the future of comedy in the bottom of their champagne glasses, I expect. I don't know. They don't invite me. And if they did, I wouldn't go. So there!

I don't know. But what I say to you is, could an invisible cloud of shit-smelling gas with its own Channel 4 series be any less funny than *The Friday Night Project*?*

So the day after the 9th of November – which is the 9th of December, nine-one-two.† Do the math . . . s . . . I flew back from Spain to Heathrow Airport. I got a mini-cab from Heathrow Airport to Stoke Newington, Hackney, north-east London, where I live.‡ And on the way, I had to go past the Finsbury Park mosque, which you'll know if you read the news is the kind of hotbed of Muslim radicalism in Britain, run by Abu Hamza until recently. That's the guy who has an eye patch and hooks for hands. An eye patch and hooks for hands. That's not a good look for a religious leader. It's a good look maybe if you're considering auditioning for extra work in the sequel to *Pirates of the*

---

* Writing these notes six years on, it seems bizarre to single out *The Friday Night Project* for abuse, as the bar for bad comedy has been lowered so far by the broadcasting on BBC3 of *Horne and Corden* that *The Friday Night Project* now seems like a product of a long-gone Age of Enlightenment by comparison. What a different world we live in, here in the 2010s! I flew up in the air to throw my copy of *Lesbian Vampire Killers* into a skip wearing my own personal jet pack!
† By this point, I had entirely lost the audience at the Aspen Comedy Festival, culturally, politically and, most crucially, mathematically.
‡ Stoke Newington is a great place to live for a comedian, if for no other reason than it's a funny-sounding address. I love saying it onstage, I like setting stories there and I love the resonances that go with the name, from Alexei Sayle's classic 'What's on in Stoke Newington?' routine that all comics of my generation remember fondly from their childhoods, to the air of shabby would-be bohemianism that hangs around the area today. I was unfavourably described by a reviewer in 2009 as 'Britain's most middle-class comic', but I'm not. That is Michael McIntyre. I am the most Stoke Newington comic there is, with all that that suggests.

Caribbean. But it's not a good look for a religious leader. The Archbishop of Canterbury does not have an eye patch and hooks for his hands. He has a big festive Christmas beard in which robins might nest. And that helps us to take his pronouncements on the ethics of the family and modern society more sympathetically than we would if he had hooks for his hands. We'd be suspicious.*

AUDIENCE MEMBER: Only one hook!

No, a woman there saying it's only one hook. I think that it's hooks for hands, I think he's got two. But of course luckily the element of doubt's been introduced here. Umm . . . I'm able to go away and check that. Er, if it's factually inaccurate, I can remove it from this video . . . [*male audience member heckles unintelligibly*] . . . as I can everything you've said.

---

* I would try and improvise the Abu Hamza stuff differently every night, aware subconsciously, I suppose, that I was sort of taking on the persona of a proper normal stand-up comedian, riffing around the kind of news personality whose unusual physical appearance always makes him a regular occurrence in panel-show comics' bits, irrespective of his actual newsworthiness. I even went on to satirise this kind of Hamza riff in 2007's *41st Best Stand-Up Ever* show. I don't remember doing stuff about the Archbishop of Canterbury and his beard other than in this performance, but maybe the perceptible shift into a genuine conversational, improvisational idiom is what prompts the heckler to feel they can contribute, both helpfully and amusingly, leading to an off-the-cuff splurge about the deceitful opportunities of the editing suite that seems really neat on the finished DVD recorded at this performance.

Live comedy DVDs rarely address the fact that the viewer at home's experience is clearly different to that of the audience on the night. I always try to crank something in, and made it a central plank in my approach to considering the shots and the directorial approach to my 2009 TV series, *Stewart Lee's Comedy Vehicle*.

So it'll just look like a sixty-minute stream of uninter-rupted success. Although, ironically, I may consider leaving this part in to give the illusion of it being a genuine event. What do you think of that, viewers at home? This is simul-taneously dishonest, and yet also satisfying.

But Abu Hamza of course, he's in Belmarsh at the moment. He's in the process of being deported to America, where he is guaranteed a fair trial. Irony there. One of the many comic tools we'll be using tonight.*

So. So I was driving past the Finsbury Park mosque on the, er, 9th of December, the day after the 9th of Novem-ber, and it was all kicking off outside. There's Muslim dem-onstrators on one side of the street complaining about the reprisals they've suffered, police in the middle trying to keep order. And on the other side of the Seven Sisters Road, British National Party members standing near the Arsenal shop, their spiritual home. And they're shout-ing out, 'SEND THEM BACK! SEND THE MUSLIMS BACK TO WHERE THEY CAME FROM! BRADFORD, WOOD GREEN, LEEDS, LIVERPOOL, MANCHES-TER, BIRMINGHAM AND OTHER BRITISH INDUS-TRIAL CITIES WHICH REQUIRED CHEAP LABOUR IN THE NINETEEN-SIXTIES AND SEVENTIES.'

And it looked, Glasgow, like there was going to be a full-scale religious race riot. And so I said to the minicab driver, 'Stop. Let me out. I can help here.'†

---

* Again, this never worked in America, where the average person's perception of the situation is entirely different.
† Looking at this years later, I suspect this routine has its genesis in two things: (1) Seeing this demonstration outside the Fins-bury Park mosque, which is about a ten-minute walk from me; and (2) a Simon Munnery routine where, in the character of the naive anarcho-punk Alan Parker Urban Warrior, he tries to quell

57

And I got out the minicab. I pushed through the British National Party blokes. I pushed through the police line. I pushed through the Muslim demonstrators. I ran into the mosque, some guy tried to get me to take my shoes off, I don't know what that was about, there wasn't time, I carried on through. It was a nice, hospitable gesture, but it was ill-timed. And I ran up the prayer tower to the minaret, where the call to prayer is broadcast out to the faithful of North London, and I snatched the little microphone out of the stand there, and I pulled down my underpants and I shoved it up my anus. And with a concerted effort of mental and physical willpower, I farted into it. But on that occasion, it didn't really help.

In fact, some eyewitnesses to the ensuing carnage were subsequently to suggest that it may have made the situation worse. And my heartfelt message of peace and goodwill to all men was misunderstood. Although I take some comfort in the fact that a similar thing often happened to Jesus. I'm not saying I am Jesus. That's for you to think about at home. But if I was Him, this is the kind of place I would come, isn't it? A simple, humble place. Not the Glasgow Empire, I'd come here. But I'm not saying I

---

a sectarian squabble in Glasgow by tying together the scarves of Rangers and Celtic supporters against their will, which ends with them all beating him up, as he explains triumphantly, 'together'. I've never consciously stolen any of Simon's material, but his shadow hangs heavily over everything I do. I bought two lines off him for my 2009 TV show, and I consider him one of the all-time greats, the Peter Cook of our generation, without whose influence the entire comedy landscape would be entirely different, even if he is far from a household name. Indeed, even in his own household his name is barely known, as Simon's wife and his three beautiful little girls are in the habit of referring to him simply as 'Mr Poo Poo Head'.

am Jesus. Not in the current climate. Erm . . .*

But I think there's a kind of European smugness where we look at America's hysterical overreaction to the events of the 9th of November and we go, 'Thanks for that, America, thanks. You've set us off on a course of the destruction of world civilisation as we know it. Thanks for that. Thanks.' But you mustn't hate the Americans, right? America is currently the most hated country in the world. Americans don't know that. They don't read, or watch news. If they did, they would be unhappy. Osama bin Laden flew planes into the World Trade Center, it was a waste of time. If he'd really wanted to hit America hard, where it hurts, he should have carpet-bombed the country with a weapon that Americans would never be able to understand – world geography examination papers. Shops which don't have the word 'barn' in their name. And the metaphysical concept of shame.†

But you mustn't hate the Americans. Don't hate them,

* The Irish comedian Ian Macpherson, mentioned earlier, has written a book, *The Autobiography of a Genius*. I have not read it, but I am told it begins with the line 'It is not for me to draw parallels between my own life and that of Christ,' a set-up similar to one both Richard Herring and I imagined independently of each other, which we may have used in the double act at some point.
† I probably wouldn't write or perform something like this now. It seems glib, stereotypical, cheap and simplistic. It was funny at the time, though. Also, our failure to act entirely honourably in Iraq and Afghanistan alongside the USA means that, to the rest of the world, we're both the bad guys. You'd have to address that now. Today, this approach to the topic would be dishonest, ignoring the elephant in the room. How different the world is in the futuristic days of the 2010s! I'm going to fly alongside the funeral cortège of British servicemen's bodies passing through the Wiltshire town of Wootton Bassett on my own personal hover-saucer!

Glasgow. Americans live in a kind of state of ignorant, prelapsarian bliss. They don't know what's going on.* And because of that, it can be very relaxing to go to America and watch them. If you go to America and look at Americans in their natural habitat – er, the theme park, the shopping mall, the race riot, the high-school massacre – and you watch them walking around, looking at colours and shapes . . . and lights . . . and words . . . sometimes imagining what the words might mean . . . It's very relaxing, Glasgow. It's like watching carp in a pond in a stately home, er, their mouths opening and closing. It's charming.†

But you mustn't hate the Americans. They're not a naturally curious people. Most Americans do not own

---

* As a rule I try to avoid using long and complicated words that not everyone understands, as it seems like something Russell Brand would do to try and make *Sun* readers think he was an intellectual. But 'prelapsarian' is the perfect word to use here.

† There are echoes here of how I would describe Richard Herring's home town of Cheddar in the routines we co-wrote for our Lee and Herring double act in the mid-nineties about him being a bumpkin peasant, so some credit must go to him here, as it must for much of what I have done since meeting him in 1986. When we first arrived in London, we shared a flat in Acton, and I was complaining bitterly about some aspect of modern life which irked me. Rich, finding my position untenable and unintentionally amusing, said I should try expressing this point of view onstage, thus helping me to realise clearly, I think for the first time, who my 'clown' was: an outsider, inexplicably annoyed about things that don't really bother most people.

On the whole, the double act necessarily involved more compromises than my solo work, but you can't help but carry parts of a partnership like that with you, and sometimes, I have noticed, in the absence of a second voice to argue with live onstage I am given to fabricating a second one of my own – 'Oh, Stew!' etc. – which sounds uncannily like Richard Herring.

60

passports. They're not a naturally curious people. If you were to lock an American for sixty years in an empty underground bunker which contained nothing but a woolly tea cosy, the American would not even be curious enough to be tempted to see if the tea cosy would make a serviceable hat.* They're far more likely to arrest the tea cosy, intern it illegally in Guantanamo Bay, and then repeatedly anally rape it until such time that it admits that it was actually a member of an al-Qaeda training cell. Even though at the time of the alleged offence the tea cosy was actually working as a shop assistant in a branch of Currys in Wolverhampton.†

* This line about the Americans' lack of curiosity was adapted from an old routine from the mid-nineties about babies and their lack of curiosity, which in turn was based on something my friend Giles Clarke said at school, describing a mutual acquaintance as 'the sort of person who, if they were locked in a room with a tea cosy, wouldn't even be tempted to try it on'. Years later, I rejigged, or stole, Giles's witticism for my set, though even at the time I remember it seeming an uncommonly well-rounded bon mot in the mouth of a thirteen-year-old fantasy war games fan.
† One of the British inmates at Guantanamo Bay had been working in a branch of Currys in Tipton at the time he was supposed to have been training with al-Qaeda. Which doesn't mean he wasn't a sympathiser, but I thought it was a funny juxtaposition. Obviously this bit died in Aspen, as it often did in the UK. I was quite happy for it to die, as it opened up enormous possibilities for improvising around its failure, as happens in the subsequent section. I really enjoy this aspect of stand-up – how failure presents opportunities to create subsequent victories – and increasingly I build pseudo-failure into the shows to give myself and the audience the thrill of a struggle. In the nineties, I was often criticised for losing the room and then fighting for ages to win it back, when in fact that was what I had been trying to do all along. It seemed that what I imagined were my strengths were perceived as weaknesses, that my successes

Some laughs there, other people are a bit confused. 'What's he talking about?' Right? OK, well, again, that's a kind of bit of satire of the fact that some of the British citizens held in Guantanamo Bay were tortured into saying that they'd been in al-Qaeda camps, even though at the time they were supposed to be there, they were actually working as shop assistants in a branch of Currys in Wolverhampton. Other people I sense are going, 'Yeah, we know about that. That's not what's confusing us. What's confusing us here in Glasgow is the idea of a tea cosy working as a shop assistant in a branch of Currys. How could that possibly work?' And again, Glasgow, I say to you, I don't know, I don't know how that would work. But what I say to you is, could a tea cosy working as a shop assistant in a branch of Currys actually be any less effective than some of the people currently employed there?*

'Hello. I don't know if you can help me. I'm interested in buying one of those iPods.'

'I'm sorry, sir. I won't be able to help you, on account of the fact that I am fashioned entirely from colourful wool.†

---

were viewed as failures, and that my positive choices were viewed as accidental errors. At least these days most critics realise I am doing this deliberately.

* Again, I probably wouldn't make a joke about stupid shop assistants today. Not because it's not necessarily true, but because it's the kind of joke you see on all those production-company landfill TV comedy sketch shows on BBC2, BBC3, Channel 4 and ITV3, in which privileged middle-class actor-comedians do impressions of what they imagine the working classes are like.

† 'Wool' is a brilliant, all-purpose funny word. Few things are not made funnier if one imagines them being made out of, or coated in, wool. I believe it was the feckless Australian comedian Greg Fleet who drip-fed the idea that the word 'wool' is funny into the international comic subconsciousness from his smegma-smeared

Perhaps you'd like to ask one of my colleagues – the cardigan, the mitten, the balaclava helmet.'

And again, you'll notice there a list of three things. Really they ought, comedically, to build. But the balaclava helmet was a disappointment. It didn't get the laugh one would be hoping for there. Umm . . . And I knew that was going to happen, right, 'cause like I say, I ran this show in Edinburgh for a month last August. And I thought – I'll be honest with you, Glasgow – I thought the balaclava helmet was going to get a big laugh. Ironically, I've been touring this. The only place the balaclava helmet did get a big laugh was in Aldershot, which is a military town, so they probably have a different relationship with it.* But on the whole,

---

seaside lair in St Kilda, at some point in the mid-nineties. Greg is responsible for much of the whole tone of contemporary stand-up in Australia, but is unable or unwilling to take any real advantage of his statesman status. If he were given a Lifetime Achievement Award, he'd only take it to Cash Converters anyway. The rurally named musical comedian Boothby Graffoe has a tattoo of Greg's name on his leg, as a tribute to the beaver-toothed funnyman. Greg is more than loved; he is universally tolerated, like a beloved family dog. That stinks. Two or three particular moments of watching Greg onstage in the nineties have undeniably shaped what I do in stand-up for ever, notably his heroin addiction/kidnapping show *Thai-Die*, which I saw in Edinburgh in 1995 and which was the first ever narrative-driven stand-up show I'd seen, and his shark-attack routine, as performed to uninterested lunchtime drinkers at Adelaide University in 1997. In the event of his death, I would certainly make the effort to travel to Australia to attend his memorial service alongside his family, friends and creditors. Greg Fleet – that wool guy!

The Canadian stand-up Glenn Wool, meanwhile, even has the word 'wool' in his name. How cool is that? Imagine if Wool was, like, your actual name! Awesome! Sweet as!

* This is true.

people don't find it funny. Now I was confused, because for me, the balaclava helmet is one of those inherently absurd items. I thought it would be a good topper there, but it never works.

So the first kind of week of the run, the month run, I kept swapping the order around, I was going, 'Perhaps you'd like to talk to one of my colleagues, the balaclava helmet, mitten, cardigan. Cardigan, balaclava helmet, mitten,' whatever. And after weeks, still nothing . . . It never got any laughs. Then, after about ten days, um, one of my friends in the audience, the Actor Kevin Eldon, who you may remember from Channel 4's *Packing Them In* in the early nineties – the best, the best work he did.* And erm . . . I said to him, 'Why do you think that isn't working?' And he said, 'Well, the problem is, all the items in your list are made of wool. And the tea cosy has already said to the customer that it won't be able to help him on account of the fact that it is made of wool. So for the tea cosy to suggest to the customer that he seeks assistance from other exclusively woollen items, you know it simply adds insult to injury, it makes the situation worse.'†

* I met the Actor Kevin Eldon, as Richard Herring and I always insist on calling him, when he and I started out on the stand-up circuit at around the same time in 1989, I think at a club called Oranje Boom Boom above the De Hems pub in Soho. You can look for it, it is still there. He was thirty at the time, which seemed impossibly old to me, and I wondered what he had been doing with his life. The Actor Kevin Eldon is always a great comedy problem solver, a good person to ask why something is or isn't working, but he is a Buddhist, and conceitedly believes that he has lived a good life and so will be reincarnated as a rich king or a pop star or something.
† Critics often talk about me 'deconstructing' comedy. I don't think it's as complicated as that. I just think it's funny to take a joke and show the working out in the margins. If you remove the surprise of

So I said, 'Yeah, I'd never thought of that, you know. What shall I do?' And he said, 'Well, just think of three things that aren't made of wool and you'll be all right.' And I thought, 'Yeah, I will, right, but I won't write them down. I'll come out every night and I'll just make them up. I'll exist in the moment. I'll trust it to chance. I'll improvise like Eddie Izzard . . . pretends to do.' And . . . no! And, when you've tried to do it, you realise why he doesn't. It's hard. It's hard to do. It's much easier to just go 'er' in every sentence and give the illusion of spontaneity.*

And so . . . So I came out . . . let it go, let it go! . . . so I came out the first night, I went, 'Yeah, perhaps you'd like to talk to one of my colleagues.' And I said, you know, 'The stick, the wood.' And then I said, 'The toaster.' And again, there was no laughs. I thought, 'Why's that?' And I went home, and I thought, 'Yeah, the problem is the toaster is an electrical item and people are thinking, "Is that working in Currys or is it for sale there?"'

Yeah, but I was chasing the problem down. Basically, I realised I needed three things that were neither electrical nor woollen. Right. But it's quite hard to think of that.

Sir, think of a thing.

---

the punchline by telegraphing it, deliberately, then instead of waiting to laugh at the pay-off the punters have to enjoy the texture of the extended set-up. In theory.

* It puzzled me that Eddie Izzard was always reviewed positively in the nineties for his supposed improvisational abilities, when in fact his real skill was to make his prepared ideas look as if they were utterly spontaneous, thereby involving everyone in the room, even in massive stadiums, in a succession of beautiful moments of apparent conception that all seemed to be unrepeatable. I can't fake things. I have no acting skills. I have to build actual improvisations in to achieve the effect, and over the course of a long run I can feel the scripted sections of a show ossify and stiffen.

AUDIENCE MEMBER #1: Weather vane.

Weather vane.

AUDIENCE MEMBER #2: The act of cunnilingus.

Weather vane. The act of cunnilingus. And . . .

AUDIENCE MEMBER #3: A banana.

What?

AUDIENCE MEMBER #3: A banana.

A banana. Weather vane, the act of cunnilingus and a b– . . . Well, admittedly, those are, those are quite good. They're not electrical nor wool. And weather vane, banana – good. The act of cunnilingus is particularly good 'cause that takes us into an area where actual concepts, not just things and objects, are working in a shop. It's certainly . . .*

I was in Aspen, Colorado, two weeks ago, in America. You beat them hands down. Their first two suggestions were a scarf and a kettle.† Woollen and electrical, straight

---

* Whatever happened here, it didn't really matter. If the audience's suggestions were funny, that worked, and if they weren't, it was also fine. Something would come up. I suppose it was interesting in trying to get them to think as comedians might, to try and give them a sense of how some apparently random objects seem utterly apposite and some don't, and to show them how this is almost alchemical, beyond reason.

† These are the real suggestions of the Aspen Comedy Festival audience, many of them TV professionals. Having seen this show in Edinburgh, the Aspen Comedy Festival booked it for a short run in a room in an oxygen-free skiing hotel high above the snowline, and some short warm-ups in New York clubs the weekend before. The New York clubs were all awful, full of dreadful hack comics trying to hone seven-minute sets about nothing into tight three-minute sets about even less for Letterman and such like, standing in front of paintings of brick walls while bored people ignored them on a two-drink minimum. Needless to say, I went down to utter silence. I can't do anything in seven minutes any more. I don't have the

. . . Although, to be fair, this wasn't the part of the set they liked least, you know? After the nine-one-one opening, a lot of the American audience had been shaken off in, in Aspen. If anything, arguably the New York warm-ups were worse. But . . .

It's weird, 'cause, 'cause about two weeks into Edinburgh, some kid emailed me and he went, 'You know that bit you do about people being so bored they wear tea cosies as hats?' I went, 'Yeah.' He goes, 'Um, there's a Spike Milligan or a Billy Connolly joke like that,' he said, 'from 1972.' So, basically, I must have kind of remembered that and copied it.*

So that bit, the first half of it is plagiarised and the second half doesn't really work.†

But I was making a number of crass generalisations about Americans there. I don't really believe any of them and I did it for comic effect. And I don't understand how anyone can have a kind of generalised view about another nation or race. I certainly don't, and I think it's because I'm, I'm different to a lot of you. I'm not necessarily better,

---

skills. I wouldn't have had time to do the 9/11 stuff there, even if I had wanted to, but I wonder if I'd ever run the show in New York, whether I'd have had the guts to do it. Would the risk of offence be worth the possibly cathartic outcome?

* As the run progressed a number of people claimed this was either a Billy Connolly or a Spike Milligan line. See? It turns out Giles Clarke didn't think up that phrase.

† For me it's funny to go on this long, quasi-improvised, meta-textural riff about the tea-cosy joke, and then to just piss the thing away into nothing at the end. In fairness, though, I can also understand why people might feel their time had been wasted. Having sat in on the edits of three live DVDs and a TV series, I have nothing but sympathy, generally, for people who find my work intolerable.

but I am . . . I'm different. And I'm better, let's face it.*

But . . . But . . . And I think it's because I feel a little bit kind of removed from your human society, 'cause I'm actually, I'm adopted, I'm an adopted man† . . . so I'm suspicious of notions of identity or nationhood. For example, I grew up thinking that I was English, right, but about two years ago I found out – and this is true – I found out that

* I often read on the internet and in newspapers that I am arrogant. I am arrogant, I admit, but when I say things like this onstage I have chosen to be arrogant for comic effect, and hope in part that the comments reflect badly on me, creating a distancing effect between me and the audience. I hope they admire the comedy, but I'd rather they didn't enjoy the show just because they think they liked me as a person. It seems cheap.

† Interestingly, about 50 per cent of the time the phrase 'adopted man', as opposed to the less specific 'adopted', would get a tentative laugh, allowing me to go off on improvisations about the specific age ranges of adoptees that seem the funniest. I think the phrase 'adopted man' was funny because it suggested the image of a fully grown man being delivered to a hopeful couple's door, perhaps with his record collection and personal artefacts in tow. I think it also contains an unconscious echo of one of Harry Hill's first jokes, back in the early nineties, when we were on bills together and he was called Harry Hall. I forget what the set-up was, but the punchline was 'I am a diabetic man and have missed my lunch.' To me, this always seemed much funnier than it would have done if the pay-off had been 'I am a diabetic and have missed my lunch.' The word 'man' is so utterly unnecessary here that I find it amusing.

Here in the age of Twitter I am continually reading the wise words of Twittering comedy writers who speak of the incredible skill and satisfaction of honing their witty jokes down to the bare minimum of information, so as to maximise the value of the few characters the medium allows. Presumably, free-floating and yet inexplicably powerful words like 'man', as it occurs in Harry's joke above, will be the first casualties of this charmless, technology-led approach to what's funny, Graham Linehan.

my real father is Scottish, right, which of course means that I'm Scottish, 'cause, as you'll know, Scottishness is passed on through the male genes.* Like a disability. And, er . . . it . . . it overwhelms all female chromosomes. And that's why there are no Scottish women, are there? There's no Scottish women. There are men in kilts, but that's just nature trying to find its own level.

And if a Scottish man wants to breed, of course, you have to travel south of the border. Normally, you get as far as a major English railway station, get off the train, lie down in a gutter, drunk, and hope some pollen lands on you. And . . . and I can say that, remember, because I . . . technically, I am Scotch. Yeah, Scotch, yeah.† Genetically, if not culturally.

---

* I was adopted and am under the impression that my real father was Scottish. Some comics, and some whole schools of comedy, and most American stand-ups, base their routines on a specific regional, racial or national identity, and the accepted behavioural connotations that come with it. Many of the most successful American comedians elaborate upon this idea by pretending that, or describing how, each of their parents is from a different racial or cultural background, and they are often able to derive whole seven-minute sets from the collision of these two presumed sets of different exaggerated social values or genetic traits, often involving the consumption of specific food items or the practice of particular sexual acts, presumed to be unique to the culture or race chosen. I am happy to be without portfolio. I have chosen to become what I am, a stereotype of the kind of middle-class arts graduate that would live in a beatnik enclave of north-east London, and I have chosen the character I portray to the public. You will notice there is precious little personal information in this book. This very paragraph, going into extremely dull and lengthy detail about a not especially interesting comedy trope, is in itself a diversionary tactic. I am no one. No one.
† I can remember the rough point at which I learned that the Scots do not like to be called Scotch, and have found it a funny word ever since. It was sometime during the period I lived with my

But I think that, even though I grew up thinking I was English, I think I always knew that I was one of you, you know. 'Cause I'd go into school, Monday mornings, and people'd go, 'Did you see the sport at the weekend, Stew? The brilliant sport that all men must like, with England winning in it? It was good, wasn't it?' And I'd go, 'No, in fact it filled me feelings of revulsion and disgust.'* Then

---

grandparents as a child, 1971–5, and we were watching an episode of the Edwardian drama series *Upstairs, Downstairs* in the back room, which was yet to be knocked through into one big rectangular space, the front room still being a parlour, where tea was served on Sundays, with radishes and tomatoes from grandpa's garden, and antimacassars hugged the backs of the armchairs in case of a visit from some heavily Brylcreemed freemason. In this edition of *Upstairs, Downstairs*, the family had gone to stay in Scotland, and the servant played by Pauline Collins said to the Gordon Jackson butler bloke, while he was polishing a glass, something like, 'You must be delighted to be in Scotland, Mr Hudson, what with you being Scotch and all,' to which he stonily replied, 'It's Scots.' I have no other memories of *Upstairs, Downstairs* whatsoever. Who'd have thought, that thirty-five years later, the late Gordon Jackson's words would come back to taunt his countrymen from out of my sneering English mouth?

* I am always pleased whenever the opportunity arises to say onstage that I don't like sport and have no interest in it. In the early nineties, style magazines, nascent lads' mags and Sunday supplements were thrilled when the 'alternative' comedians like David Baddiel, Rob Newman and Frank Skinner began talking about football in their comedy routines in Alternative Comedy clubs, at the Edinburgh Fringe and on Radio 4 and BBC2, where previously football would have been considered of no interest or relevance. Soon there was *Fantasy Football*, a low-fidelity television comedy series that applied the sort of irreverent, witty and intelligent humour usually reserved during the period for the subjects of politics, pop, sex and drugs to football, raising the bar considerably in an area in which Jimmy Hill had previously been thought of as a great wit.

70

But the floodgates were open, and try as he might, with his considered BBC2 series and public love of Samuel Johnson, Frank Skinner could never get the djinni back in the bottle. Football fans and so-called 'new lads' began to feel welcome at once 'alternative' comedy venues, in their Ben Sherman shirts, and within five years the comedy counter-culture which our illustrious eighties stand-up comedy forebears shed blood to build, in the post-punk shadows of fat working men's club comics and elitist Oxbridge satirists, was destroyed. Suddenly, sport-loving scumbags began to comprise a significant percentage of any comedy audience. I think it was *Fantasy Football* and the introduction of football as a subject into Alternative Comedy that ultimately destroyed the values and the unrealised artistic potential of the Alternative Comedy community which I so desperately wanted to contribute to as a teenager. Indeed, all responsibility for the collapse of the entire sixties, seventies and eighties counter-culture in Britain can probably be extrapolated from *Fantasy Football* and laid at the door of Baddiel and Skinner, who shared a flat, and presumably a door, at the time.

Rob Newman subsequently recognised the monster he had helped to create, and tried to make amends for his crimes. By the end of the decade Newman had changed his name by deed poll to Robert Newman and retreated from the front line to became a humble aesthete, quietly trying to save the world with his thoughtful and moving live shows, and with a carbon footprint the size of an ant's. But in contrast, today David Baddiel and Frank Skinner have massive luxury homes on the moon and their own private spacecraft made of gold and seal fur. The rest of us, who wanted Alternative Comedy to offer us merely the chance to subsist in an endless utopia of CND benefits and Women Only Cabaret Nights, have only shattered memories and shat-upon dreams.

When I was fourteen, I had a massive poster on my wall of a giant pop-art mouth advertising a Swiss exhibition of abstract art. My friends and family mocked my pretention, but I loved that poster and the hope it offered of an exciting world of thought beyond the boundaries of stifling Solihull. But one day the poster fell off the wall and the dog pissed all over it, ruining it for ever, while my mother laughed. That poster is what the Alternative Comedy

they'd go to me, 'What about the rich tapestry, the tableau of English culture and history? Do you take no pleasure in that?' And I'd go, 'No. In fact, the whole notion of English culture just makes me feel kind of mentally, physically and spiritually bereft.' And they'd go, 'What about the English language, the tongue of Shakespeare, Shelley, Blake? Churchill? Does that not stir some residual national pride in you?' And I'd go, 'No. In fact, whenever I hear an English accent, I have to be physically sick.' And I would hear my own voice answering their question and I would start vomiting as I spoke.

So I hated, as a child, I hated being English. And yet conversely, I always harboured secret cravings for shortbread, offal and heroin.* (You seem to like that.) You know, deep-fried heroin if I could get it. With sauce ['soss']. Heroin supper, £2.95.

But . . . So . . . I think I always knew, Glasgow . . . I can hardly believe this is happening . . . I think I always knew that I was a Scotch man. And so I always knew, and . . . But . . .

AUDIENCE: Scottish!†

Yeah, Scottish. Thank you for correcting me, sorry. Er . . . you know . . . it was an error I made on purpose for comic effect. And I'm glad that there's so little trust in me

---

dream meant to me – the possibility of a better world. And now it is covered in dog's piss.

* Again, there is an echo of the always apposite Simon Munnery here, who I think planted the word 'offal' in my mind with his joke 'Why do the Scots like haggis? The truth is they don't. Haggis is just a means of selling offal to tourists.'

† During the Glasgow gig from which this text is transcribed, a foolish Scotchman has misunderstood my deliberate misuse of the word 'Scotch', leading to a hilarious improvisation.

in the room that people are going, 'He's a fucking idiot! He doesn't know . . . He's insane! What's he talking about? He hasn't done the most basic research.' But . . . No . . . Even despite that, I always knew that I was Scottish . . . In my heart, in my brave heart, I always knew that I was.*

OK, shout out if you've seen the film *Braveheart*. You've all seen it, shout out.

AUDIENCE: Yes!

OK, now you'll know more than any other audience I've played in the last three weeks that *Braveheart* is the shittest film ever made, right? It was. It was directed by the reactionary Catholic bigot Mel Gibson, and it's full of basic, fundamental historical errors which insult your race, and mine by association. Right? Here's . . . Here's just three off the top of my head.†

---

* I found here that if I intonated the word 'braveheart' as if I thought it should get a laugh, it would only get a groan, but if I threw it away as if it were just an accidental collision of words to which I had given no actual conscious thought, and which only coincidentally echoed the folk name of the Scotch national hero William Wallace, then it would get a big laugh. Audiences, in my experience, are like cats. They don't respect you if you seem too desperate for their affection, but disguise your desperate need for their love as a kind of bored indifference, and soon they will be eating out of your hand.

† I remember some reviews at the time criticising me for doing material about the film *Braveheart*, which had been released almost a decade earlier. But *Braveheart* had such a totemic role in the rise of the SNP and the drive towards a Scottish parliament, and is also famous for its typically Hollywood approach to the troublesome niggle of historical accuracy, that I think it's a great subject in which to package a discussion about Scottish national identity, and by association, all the myths, lies and macho nostalgia that go towards forging any national identity. I don't really believe that there's such a thing as dated subject material, or clichéd subject material. There

Firstly, William Wallace, Braveheart, your national hero, he wasn't some, you know, noble savage living in a mud hut, we all know that. He was a privileged, educated noble-man, right?

Secondly, it's not mentioned by Mel Gibson in the film, but there's some evidence to suggest that he actually fought as a mercenary for the English as a teenager. That's conveniently missed out.

Thirdly, you know that French princess he's supposed to have sex with? This French princess, in the film, you remember? And the implication is that he gets her pregnant and she marries Edward II of England, so it's his kid. Now – she was a real historical figure, that French princess. But at the time of the death of William Wallace, Braveheart, your national hero, she was only four years old.

Now, Glasgow, I'm not saying that William Wallace, Braveheart, your national hero, didn't have sex with her . . . You know . . . He probably did. But if he did – and he did, he definitely did, right – it would have been a far less romantic scene than the one enacted by Mel Gibson in the film *Braveheart*. It may have happened in a tent, but it would still have been not a romantic scene. Because that would have made William Wallace, Braveheart, your national hero, a paedophile. A Scottish paedophile. The worst kind of paedophile that there is. Coming at you . . . through a bothy* . . . with shortbread on its face . . . mut-

---

are only dated and clichéd approaches, and even some of them are still funny.

* One way of avoiding the ire of the people you are mocking is to refuse them the easy option of assuming that you are ignorant by including within the abuse some detail or turn of phrase that shows you are in fact fully acquainted with their culture, nation, faith or city, and so presumably have made a positive choice to denigrate it

74

tering unintelligible sexual threats in a frankly incomprehensible dialect.

Another weird thing about that film is, you know in it, like, um . . . Fine, leave at this point. Er . . . It gets, it gets worse. A man leaving there to go away and think about the idea of a paedophile Braveheart in the privacy of a toilet cubicle.*

---

from a position of strength, rather than by dint of just not knowing anything about it in the first place. I remember a BBC Radio 4 religious bigwig describing an early-nineties radio sketch Richard Herring and I wrote about the primitive Christian mystic and pole-dweller Simeon Stylites as 'ignorant', but to be honest, if you're even considering writing a sketch about Simeon Stylites, you're already some degrees away from a simple position of 'ignorance'. 'Bothy', in turn, is a Gaelic word for a small cottage. Unique to the Highlands, these structures are now mainly used as mountain shelters for walkers and climbers. Only someone who really knew their way around the Scotch culture in all its manifest variety would be able, with such casual confidence, to introduce a word like 'bothy' into a comedy routine with such obvious nonchalance, and the unruly Glaswegian audience see this and realise that they must submit to the comedian's iron will.

* This may seem clever to you, but it is a standard move by me, at the point of an unexpected exit by a member of the crowd, to imply that they are leaving to masturbate over the thought of whatever I have just been talking about, though this is funnier, I always feel, if the subject is not actually sexual in any way, suggesting that the escapee has some very specific sexual fetish. In recent years, my standard move at the point of an unexpected punter exit is to pretend to assume they have been offended by whatever I am talking about and are leaving in disgust. I usually say something along the lines of, 'I didn't pay to hear a man talk disparagingly about . . . [insert whatever here].' Since the mid-noughties, this approach has the added advantage of usually seeming like a clever, topical ad-lib, as there is usually some absurd story bubbling along in at least one tabloid concerning an outcry about some largely

Another weird thing about that film is that in it, if you remember, like, er, Mel Gibson makes a big deal about the fact Edward II, the English prince, was gay, right, as if not only did he oppress the Scots, but he did it in a kind of gay way, which makes it worse. But . . . the irony is, again, it's not mentioned in the film that William Wallace, Braveheart, your national hero himself, was actually gay.* And . . . No, he was, sir . . . And we know this from some information that's come to light in the last couple of years. Firstly, about two years ago, they found a cache of love letters hidden in a

---

innocuous comedy routine by someone about something.

* Here it was absolutely necessary to use vocal inflections that suggest that Wallace's homosexuality was entirely acceptable, and not a matter of controversy in any respect. Thus, any audience objections about this apparent abuse of a Scottish folk figure would hopefully freeze in the mouth of the heckler, for fear of them appearing homophobic. It was not difficult for me, personally, to say these sentences without appearing that I had any issues with homosexuality, as I absolutely don't. At least two of my best friends are gay, and the composer Richard Thomas, with whom I worked for five years continuously, is a minimum of 80 per cent gay. I even enjoy the work of many gay writers and some of the world's gayest musicians. That said, even though I have lived in heavily multicultural areas for two and a half decades now, I still do not have a huge amount of black or Asian friends, apart from Andrew Mallet, whom I see every Christmas and who is Malaysian or Hawaiian or something. I appreciate that this looks bad and am already working to correct it. I have always got on reasonably well with the Labour MP for Hackney, Diane Abbott, when I have met her on TV politics shows, and may try to cultivate a friendship with her, because as well as being an individual black woman she also represents the black community as a whole, which would help me enormously in meeting my friends diversity quota with the minimum of effort. That said, I said hello to her in the street the other day and I don't think she recognised me.

76

nook at, er . . . at, er . . . Glamis Castle or somewhere.* And the letters were exchanged between William Wallace and Robert the Bruce. And they were full of declarations – they were – they were full of declarations of love and details of their, of their sexual encounters, the very vigorous sexual encounters that they had. That's one thing. Then, about a year ago, they found some, um, graffiti on, er, a wall . . . on an old Scottish wall, on the wall . . . on the wall of a broch, actually, which is . . . the Broch of Gurness, which is a real place in, er . . . the Orkneys.† They found it there. And it said, um . . . The graffiti, which is real, it existed, it said, er . . . 'I am a gay, signed William Wallace, "Braveheart"'. And the 'Braveheart' bit was in inverted commas, so they knew that meant it was real. 'Cause it was like a fun nickname, you know, it was, like, real.

So . . . Now . . . So, er . . . Wow, Braveheart, our national hero, was gay. And when – you know – when I was

---

* Again, here I would stave off the psychotic boredom of doing this show for months on end by always changing the love-letter location, but the trick was to find somewhere suitably obscure that would delight an audience by its apparent oddness, but at the same time ring enough bells to get laughs. I suppose that's a trick many of us employ throughout our stand-up – trying to employ a reference or a structural device that's just close enough to the edge of comprehensibility to make the audience feel flattered, whilst at the same time not doing something so arcane that it deliberately freezes out the majority of the room.

† Again, who could object, here in Glasgow, to a man familiar with specific technical terms for specific Scottish Iron Age archaeological structures in the Hebrides? The exact purpose of these ring-shaped stone structures is not clear, but the Broch of Gurness, in Orkney, is particularly beautiful, and Clickimin Broch in Lerwick is one of the few real attractions of Shetland, where my wife Bridget and I erroneously spent our honeymoon in December 2006.

talking about this in Edinburgh in the summer, people were going, 'Well, why didn't we know about that, you know? Why . . .?' And the reason is 'cause the graffiti and the letters were written in Gaelic, so it wasn't translated. And people are going, 'Well, why wasn't it translated? That's just the ancient language of our nation, of the Scots. Why wasn't it translated?' Well, it wasn't. What Gaelic actually was, was a very kind of highly evolved form of medieval Scottish homosexual patois. And the clue's in the name if you look at it, right. Gae-lich. That means 'gae' – homosexual, gay – and then 'lich' is language or tongue. So Gaelic is literally the language of gays.

And . . . you know . . . I was booed off at the Assembly Rooms for saying this in Edinburgh. But it's true. And I don't think it's . . . I think it's really great that, that our national hero, er, William Wallace, was gay. Because Scotland's always been a much more progressive, liberally minded kind of a nation that's not afraid to show its feminine side.* And I think that, um, compared to England, which is a very backward kind of bigoted place. And I think that it's really good that as we enter the twenty-first century, one of your national folk heroes can embody a kind of progressive notion of sexual identity. I think that's a really brilliant thing. And I wish that some of the English, er, folk heroes, like, er, King Alfred or, or Robin Hood or

* Again, this would get derisory laughter from the Scots, and yet at the same time, they were confused as to their correct response. Shouldn't they be pleased that I am saying their land is liberally minded and progressive? I love the confusion of a room that doesn't know how it's supposed to respond. I'd rather the punters scattered like startled birds, flying off into all different directions, than all in one direction, waving their Union Jacks and cheering.

King Arthur had, had been gay. But . . . but they weren't. And . . . it's only William Wallace, Braveheart, the Scottish one, that definitely was gay.*

And of course another . . .

AUDIENCE MEMBER: Robin Hood, surely.

Sorry?

AUDIENCE MEMBER: Robin Hood, surely.

Someone, er, said that Robin Hood was, surely . . .

AUDIENCE MEMBER: Men in tights.

And someone there saying 'Men in tights'. But of course the 'men in tights' addition to the Robin Hood legend was made in the nineteen-eighties by Mel Brooks. The, er, facility to make those kind of tights didn't exist in medieval England. If it had have done, maybe they would have worn them. I'm sure that a thin denier tight is, er, an ideal garment for medieval combat, offering as it does no

---

* I don't think it's funny in and of itself to suggest that Braveheart was gay. My point here is that Mel Gibson, and to be honest many small-minded nationalists, are usually engaged in quite macho mythologising of notions of nationhood, of which Gibson's ugly and homophobic movie is just one example. So therefore it's funny to turn this on its head, and also to complicate things by appearing to praise the Scottish folk hero for his assumed homosexuality, taking the gamble that while my audience might feel a little insulted by this, their usually impeccable liberal mindsets won't let them attack the routine in terms that could be misconstrued as politically incorrect. When I played this routine to Scottish audiences that hadn't specifically come to see me, such as on a mixed bill at the Edinburgh Assembly Rooms late show in August 2005, they were not slow to boo me off and threaten me for saying that their national hero was gay. You see, this is the problem with David Baddiel and Frank Skinner having opened up the exclusive club of Alternative Comedy to football fans – suddenly you can't assume that the audience is just weedy liberals.

protection whatsoever to the human leg.*

But . . . of course the other major inaccuracy of that film was that in the Middle Ages there was no such country as Scotland. Scotland was actually invented, as you all know, in 1911, by the McGowan sweet company as a way of marketing Highland toffee. Because of course, traditionally, we think toffee's better if it's manufactured at a high altitude.†

But again, I was making a number of kind of crass generalisations about, about the Scots, about my country there. And I don't, I don't believe any of them. Again, I did it for comic effect.

But you do meet people who have very fixed notions about other groups of people. I'll give you an example of what I mean. I got in, er, a cab in, in London in December, and about five minutes into the journey, a propos of nothing, early on a Sunday morning, the cab driver turned round to me and he said, 'I think all homosexuals should be killed.'‡

* This was off the top of my head, in response to the heckle, but one of the advantages of having stolen, as a younger man, the slow and ponderous delivery of Ted Chippington, Arnold Brown and Norman Lovett is that, compared to the average comic, I get extra thinking time between each word, and so really ought to be able to come out with something at least half-coherent.
† I didn't bother improvising around the theme of Highland toffee if I was south of the border. In Scotland there might be five minutes in it, but a man has to know his limitations. Readers of these footnotes may find this surprising, but I do not think that everything that occurs to me is worth saying.
‡ This actually happened to me, in the summer of 1999, as I pulled off the Westway towards BBC TV centre in a car that had been booked by the BBC. If you're driving someone to the liberal bastion of the BBC, it's reasonable to assume they won't think all homosexuals should be killed, and of course there's always the high

Now, whatever you think of that, Glasgow, as a statement, you have to admit it's a bold opening conversational gambit. You know, with a stranger. And I was a bit taken aback. I went, 'Oh, why do you think that?' And then there was a pause, 'cause he'd obviously never had to go to the next level of the argument, fraternising mainly with cab drivers, so . . . where that was just accepted as a point. No . . .*

And he said, 'Well . . .' after a moment, he said, 'Well, because homosexuality is immoral.'

And I said – this is honestly true – I said, 'Um, I'm not sure how much weight you can afford to place on the notion of morality in this argument, because morality's not a fixed thing. It changes its parameters, culturally, historically, over time.' I said, 'For example, look at ancient Greece. To this day, we still take most of our most fundamental principles about ethics, aesthetics, er, philosophy, medicine, science, whatever from ancient Greece. And yet', I said, 'in ancient Greece, love between two men, far from

---

statistical chance that your passenger will themselves be gay. Where did the comment spring from? Was there something on the radio that I didn't hear, or a billboard I didn't see, that provoked it? Also, why say it at all? Even from a business point of view it can't make sense for a service-provider to risk causing such massive offence. Why are cab drivers not concerned about appearing to fulfil, completely, their stand-up comedy stereotype? It's almost as if they enjoy it.

* Yes, I am aware that, paradoxically, I am arguing for more humane attitudes towards the gays while at the same time stereotyping all white, working-class cab drivers as being ignorant bigots. All I can say is that there are times in the act when I deliberately move into a kind of persona of a bigoted, middle-class, über-liberal for comic effect, but even I am not sure exactly where this character begins and I end, especially when I find myself behaving like this in my actual life.

being immoral, was actually considered the highest, most ethical, most profound, if you will, most moral form of love that there could be. So all I'm saying', I said to him, 'is I'm not sure how useful morality is, given its flexible nature, as a cornerstone of your argument on this subject.'*

And then he said to me – this is honestly true – he said to me, 'Well, you can prove anything with facts, can't you?'†

For a minute, I went, 'Yeah.' And then I thought, 'Hang on! That's the most fantastic way of winning an argument I've ever heard! "You can . . . I'm not interested in facts. I find they tend to cloud my judgement. I prefer to rely on instinct and blind prejudice."'

And I came of age, for want of a better phrase, in the, in the nineteen-eighties when we had political correctness.‡

---

* I did honestly say something along these lines at this point, but even as I was saying it I passed a point where I was aware it had been an absurd decision to try and reason with the man, and so just went for broke, going on and on and on past the point of no return, enjoying the futility of it. These days I have utterly lost patience with cab drivers' nonsense. Last year, on finding out that I was a comedian, a cab driver started to explain to me how Roy 'Chubby' Brown was the best comedian in the world, and where once I might have agreed politely and waited for the encounter to end, I just said, 'He isn't, and anyone who likes him must be a moron.' And that was that. Enough is enough.

† The cab driver actually said this. I think it is one of the single funniest sentences of all time. Its implications are endlessly terrifying, and endlessly hilarious. I wish it had been meant as a joke, but it wasn't.

‡ The twisting of the idea of 'political correctness' into a soft, one-size-fits-all punchbag for the right-wing media and your nan is a personal bugbear of mine which I return to time and time again onstage, most specifically in the 2007 show, *41st Best Stand-Up Ever*. In 2008, Edward Stourton published *It's a PC World*, which explained everything I ever wanted to say on the subject far more

And people look back at that and they go, 'Oh, political correctness was shit, wasn't it? Being fair to people.' And I think, 'Maybe it was good, 'cause people wouldn't have said that, and you wouldn't have had happen what happened in May last year, right.' If you remember, er, Ron Atkinson, the football manager, he got in trouble for calling a black footballer a lazy, thick nigger.* Right? And loads of people complained about it, understandably. And then on May

---

eloquently than I ever could have, and used actual hard statistical facts to back it up. Because no one can imagine a remotely pro-political correctness book, Stourton's balanced account was, tellingly, misfiled by bookshops in the humour section, alongside Richard Littlejohn's *Hell in a Handcart*, those crappy politically correct fairy tales books and Al Murray's Pub Landlord annuals. Pundits on the Right like to imagine we live in a PC dictatorship, but the fact remains that in a high-street bookshop it is assumed that any book with PC in the title must be a hilarious attack on PC, rather than a book in its defence, because the only time you ever see PC mentioned is when people are complaining about PC. For money. And usually on the very publicly funded radio stations that these dicks believe are involved in a politically correct conspiracy to silence them.

* Even when you are using the word in inverted commas, quoting someone else unfavourably, there is an electric charge to saying 'nigger' onstage in front of hundreds of people. It feels utterly forbidden and wrong, as one would hope it would. Lenny Bruce, in his fantastic fifties routine 'Are There Any Niggers in Here Tonight?', argues that repeated use of the word robs it of its power. I don't know if this is the case, and it's certainly unlikely that this is a motivation that Ron Atkinson had in mind when using it in this context. Though in a world where the London *Evening Standard* has described Russell Brand as 'the closest thing we have to Lenny Bruce', I suppose it's possible that Ron Atkinson too may have been using offensive language and semantic shock tactics to expose our own inner hypocrisy. Or something. Anyway, here's hoping he dies face down in a toilet too.

the 17th, Jimmy Hill, the BBC-employed football commentator, came out in Ron Atkinson's defence. And he said that, in his opinion, it was a load of fuss about nothing. He said, 'What you have to understand', Jimmy Hill said in the papers, 17th of May, 'is that in the culture of football, calling a black man a nigger is just a bit of harmless fun.'*

And I thought, 'Call me old-fashioned . . . I mean, I know the culture of football has a very broad definition of harmless fun, broad enough to include carrying out a racial assault and still getting in the England team, er, gang-raping a teenage girl in a London hotel room, and yet perversely allowing Jimmy Hill to carry on living. But surely that can't be the case.'†

But Jimmy Hill went on to qualify his statement. He said that in his opinion, calling a black man a nigger was no more offensive than calling him, Jimmy Hill, 'Chinny', because he had a big chin.

And again, I read that and I thought, 'Call me a square from the past, but surely the word "nigger" is more offensive than the word "chinny"?' Because the word 'nigger' comes with a whole weight of cultural and historical significance that is not really there for the word 'chinny'. You know, there are not, um, there are not people standing for election now on the grounds that 'People with big chins should be sent back to wherever they come from – Chinland probably, I don't know, I haven't done any research into it, obviously.' And there were not vast swathes of humanity historically enslaved on the grounds that they had big chins. If there had been, all popular culture as we

* 'The culture of football'. What a ludicrous phrase! Listen to yourself, Hill.
† I hate football. And anyone that likes it.

know it would be entirely different. There would not be a blues root underpinning all the late-twentieth-century popular music that you love if the Mississippi delta had been populated exclusively by disenfranchised ex-slaves with big chins . . .

> 'Woke up this morning,
> Got a big chin.
> It's not that much of a problem to be honest.
> I won't base an entire musical genre on it.'

And you don't hear news reports saying, 'A man was beaten to death in Hull last night. The violence is thought to be chin-motivated.' Although in Jimmy Hill's case I'd be happy to see an exception made. Kill him! Kill Jimmy Hill! But kill him in an ironic way! Break into the Natural History Museum, steal the jawbone of a blue whale, the largest chin currently known to science, and beat Jimmy Hill to death with it, in an example of what sociologists are already calling chin-on-chin violence.

But we shouldn't be surprised, Glasgow, to find out that Jimmy Hill is evil and mad, right, because all people that are involved in the business of football or play football or go and support it or watch it on television, or even know anything about it, are filthy, reactionary scum, right. Er . . .*

Take Gary Lineker for example, right. Gary Lineker is a twisted, evil man. You're going, 'No, he isn't, Stew. He's nice. He's like a velvet owl.'† He isn't, right? Gary Lineker is evil.

---

* It was great fun taking a more or less arbitrary position against a whole bunch of people here, using football fans to stand for the new, post-Alternative Comedy consumer, and saying this show isn't for you, so go and watch something else.

† Each night I would change what Gary Lineker was like, but it usually involved fabric and some kind of living thing. Oddly, 'velvet

Gary Lineker chooses to advertise crisps, right, and with the benefit of early-twenty-first-century super-science, we now know that crisps, rather than being a life-giving health food as we previously thought, make little children fat, and then they die. Right?

Now, about six years ago, due to a tragic chain of events, I didn't live anywhere for about four months. I had to sleep on the floor of an office in West London. And I ate mainly . . . I couldn't cook anything, so I ate mainly crisps from the garage. And during that period, I put on about four stone. And someone said to me, 'Do you not know that a single packet of crisps contains your full daily allowance of saturated fats?' And I just thought that represented good value.* It was Gary Lineker looking out for

---

owl', the one that got recorded here, seems the most appropriate that I remember coming up with. If you were to see Lineker captioned 'Gary "The Velvet Owl" Lineker' on a sports show, you would probably assume it was a real football nickname. During the 1990 football tournament – I don't remember if it was the World Cup or the FA Cup as I don't like football – there was a goalkeeper called Peter Shilton, who my football-fan flatmates randomly christened Peter 'The Bee' Shilton. I know nothing about football, but I did find this funny.

* My former manager's personal trainer said this to me during a period when he was tasked to try and save my fat life, but my understanding of health issues was so low that I didn't immediately realise he considered the concentrated and convenient presence of the full daily allowance of saturated fats to be a bad thing. I just thought the crisps meant that all the saturated fats we needed were being delivered in a handy condensed form. Subsequently, I went running three times a week for five years, until my knees gave in, but went through a brief period of actual genuine fitness around 2005/6. That said, periodic bouts of the stomach illness that inspired the '90s Comedian set, coupled with months on the road eating Ginsters and drinking, have conspired to give me the

me. I trusted his velvet-owl face to look after me. And . . .

But he chooses to advertise crisps. Why does Gary Lineker advertise crisps? He can't need the money. He's on television all the time, isn't he, amusing us. His family run a fresh fruit and vegetable stand in Leicester market, Lineker's Fresh Fruit and Veg. He could advertise that. He could help save human lives. But instead he chooses to advertise crisps. Why does Gary Lineker advertise crisps? It can only be that Gary Lineker is sexually aroused by the idea of obese children dying.

Now . . . There's one person clapping over there. Of course, remember, for a comedian, the only thing worse than no one clapping is the sound of one person clapping, 'cause it suggests you're out on a kind of a limb.*

But to try and find out more about people who like football, I went on your internet, on your World Wide Web. And um . . . I went on Jimmy Hill's website, which is real. It's called, er, jimmyhill.co.uk, and there's a guestbook there where you the public, that's you, can leave your opinions. And, er, a bloke called Scott had been on it. Um. And um . . . I'm not allowed to read out what his actual email address is, but if you go there, you can find it. Erm, so, you know, do that. Anyway, he said . . . um, Scott says, in the guestbook of Jimmy Hill's website, he says, 'I agree with Jimmy's views that Britain is rapidly becoming no more a land which is populated by genuine British people born

---

fluctuating weight that means hostile posters on internet message boards are unable to decide if I am merely tubby or actually obese. As I write this, in 2010, I am approaching the weight where I will soon need to lose it, or change my act into one of those 'a cheery fat man looks at the world'-type turns.

* I love the sound of one person clapping, and inevitably use a rejigged version of this line pretty much every time I am onstage.

here. Please don't get me wrong,' writes Scott, 'I am no Nazi or xenophobe as the pressure groups or government would have you believe. I'm just someone who was born in this country and hates to see it going to pot now.' And it would be easier to take Scott's views seriously if he hadn't spelt the word 'xenophobe' Z-E-N-A-P-H-O-B, which of course just means someone who has an irrational hatred of Japanese Buddhism.*

But it is easy, Glasgow, right, in the current climate of paranoia to make a kind of race-based error, right. I've done it myself. Er, I'll tell you how it happened. I haven't been doing this for a few years, and one of the jobs I've been doing is working as a kind of arts journalist, writing about stuff. And last year I was really excited, 'cause I, I got to interview Ang Lee, the Taiwanese film director, um, about the Incredible Hulk film that he'd directed.† And I was really excited, 'cause I've read the Incredible Hulk comics since I was about, er, six years old and I still read

---

* I don't know if I'd do this material now. I am so politically correct these days that picking on someone because they couldn't spell properly would seem wrong. Mocking the uneducated, disenfranchised white working class for being uneducated probably isn't the best way to get them to feel less isolated and to stop being so racist. What is? I don't know, but I look back on bits of these routines from half a decade ago and sometimes I wonder who the person doing them was.

† I did do this. I did interview Ang Lee on the phone, but due to a bad line, my tinnitus and his accent I was barely able to understand a single word he said, and ended up having to cobble together the feature from nothing. That's the basis of truth in this story.

I have written two record reviews a week and the odd feature for the *Sunday Times* Culture section since 1995, and during the majority of my multi-award-winning *Jerry Springer: The Opera* years this was my only dependable source of income, and kept me afloat.

them now. And I will take . . . To prove that, I will take any question on the Hulk from you now, to prove that. Any question . . .

AUDIENCE MEMBER: What colour is he?

What colour is he? Have you asked me that because you know that's . . . there's a more complicated answer, than you . . .

AUDIENCE MEMBER: Er . . . no.

No. OK, well . . . Bad luck, because he was, er . . . You want me to say he was green and everyone will go, 'Aha, that's funny.' But actually, for the first, er, six issues of *Astounding Stories* in 1960 – there's a man nodding there, with a T-shirt saying KILL EVERYONE NOW on it, the kind of person who knows these facts – um, for the first six issues, he was of course grey. Of course. Um . . . But because of the dot-printing thing, the colours all used to run together, so it came out a blur. So they made him green after the sixth issue. And he's been green [*sic*] twice since then. Erm . . . once in a six-issue mini-series written by Jeph Loeb and Tim Sale called *Hulk: Gray*. He was grey in that. That came out last . . . year before last. Available in hardback now. And um . . . he was also grey in the comic strip between about 1989 and '94, when Peter David was writing it and he made him go in a nutrient bath and that made him grey.

I've lost you now as well. I've beaten you. I've beaten you, with your KILL EVERYONE . . . No, you don't claim to be an expert but you looked at me with a doubtful face, as if, 'This is going to get him.' But look, I know more about the Hulk than you, and I'm older than you. So!

No, that's fine.*

* I love comics, especially Marvel Comics, and I am not trying to be kitsch or clever when I say that buying a copy of Captain Marvel

off a revolving rack full of *True Detective* magazines and porn in the newsagents opposite the doctors in Shirley in 1973 changed my life, got me reading and made me who I am today. Nor am I trying to be provocative or wilfully offensive when I say that Peter Parker's mantra 'With great power comes great responsibility' means more to me than any religious creed.

When I was touring this show, 2004–5, I was still on top of the Hulk to the extent that I could answer pretty much any piece of Hulk trivia thrown at me, although in Melbourne in April 2005 I did get the issue number that Wolverine first appeared in wrong by one digit. I couldn't do this now. Since I had a son there's no time to read comics, and then Marvel restructured their continuity with the cross-title civil war plotline of 2006–7 and made it impossible for the casual reader and forty-something father to dip in and out of the stories, as everything was different now. It may not seem important to you that Elektra turned out to have been a Skrull secret agent, but depending on when exactly the substitution was made it would, for example, render rather hollow all the emotional investment I had made in her relationship with Matt Murdoch, aka Daredevil, in my teens and twenties.

But doing this routine had a lovely knock-on effect. When the DVD was shown on cable in the middle of the night in 2007, a comic-book artist called Gary Frank saw it, and subsequently drew me into the background of two frames of a fight between Doc Sampson and the She-Hulk in *Hulk* 106. He even sent me the original artwork for free. In his self-serving, egomaniacal and delightful blog, the comedian Richard Herring portrays his life as a continual succession of moments so superb that the young Richard Herring would not have believed they could ever have happened. Until fairly recently, my life was a succession of moments of which the young me would have been deeply ashamed or infuriated. But being in a *Hulk* comic would have been beyond my wildest dreams.

In the same month as I appeared in *Hulk* 106, I was asked to go on the radio show of Jonathan Ross, another split personality whose dark side leads him into destructive situations which destroy the lives of all around him. I did it gladly as it was always a great show. Ross is a high-profile comics nerd who once ran his own comics shop, and has made some great documentaries about

So, so I was really excited to, to interview Ang Lee about the Hulk, and um . . . 'cause he'd made the film. But, but when I interview, I try to make a little joke to put them at ease, you know. So I rang him up. He was in New York, I was in, er, London. And I said to him, 'Ang Lee, you have directed the Hulk film. You must be very excited and proud. But don't make me anglee. You wouldn't like me when I'm anglee.'*

———

comics' creators where he lets the endearing enthusiast in him come to the fore. I took along *Hulk* 106 to show him. 'Thanks for that,' Ross said, having perused it, and then put it into a sports bag beneath his desk full of promo DVDs, games, books, CDs and other stuff given to him that day by people plugging things or just bribing him. But that was my only copy of *Hulk* 106, the issue with me in it, and I had tried to get spares already but it was sold out. How could I tell Jonathan Ross that when I offered it to him, it wasn't for him, it was just to look at, without highlighting the embarrassing fact that a man of his status now just naturally assumes that anything put into his hands is for him to keep? He could have used some of his £18-million salary to buy his own *Hulk* 106. It's £2.50 or something. I bit my lip and let it go, and subsequently the comics nerd and writer Ben Moor gave me his *Hulk* 106 in compensation. For me, this Ross incident is worse than Sachsgate.

* I know this isn't funny. It's not especially meant to be. I can't remember when or how I thought of this joke, but I knew immediately there was ten minutes in it. Over the years this has become a routine of mine people always shout out for, but the truth is I could only really perform it on this tour. It was so complicated, and crucial parts of it needed to be so precise in the exact nature of the replication of extremely similar but subtly and importantly different words and phrases, that once it was gone out of my mind it was gone, and I could never remember how I did it again.

I suppose this is a perfect example of killing the punchline of the actual joke stone dead in the opening section of the routine, so that no one's waiting for the pay-off, and then trying to focus

Then there was a long, embarrassed pause. And then Ang Lee said, 'I'm sorry, what did you say?'

And I said, 'I said, Ang Lee ... you have ... you've directed the Hulk film. You must be very excited and proud. But, erm, don't make me anglee. You wouldn't like me when I'm anglee.'

And there was another kind of silence. And then Ang Lee said, 'I'm sorry, can you repeat that?'

And I said, 'There's no need, it was just a stupid joke.'

And he went, 'No. What did you say?'

And I said ... 'I said, Ang Lee, you've directed the Hulk film. You must be very excited and proud. But, erm, don't make me anglee. You wouldn't like me when I'm anglee.'

And he, he didn't say anything. And I said, 'I expect loads of people have made that joke to you.'

And he said, 'No. No one's ever said it before. Why did you say it? Why?'*   ·

---

the audience on the pleasure of the language contained within it. It didn't always work.

Every time I performed it I had to feel like I was doing it for the first time, like I was actually struggling through the argument in my head, in real time. I'd try to forget the exact words of any bits that didn't need to be exact, to surprise myself, to try and keep it fresh. I saw the avant-garde guitarist Fred Frith doing a solo show at the ICA through the London Musicians' Collective in about 1993, and someone was taking flash photos as he embarked on the opening salvos of an hour-long solo improvisation. In the end he asked them to stop, saying, 'I'm trying to forget where I am, but you keep reminding me.' In the end, I was no longer able to forget where I was in the Ang Lee routine. I knew every twist and turn and every blind alley, and there were no more new paths to explore and it died on the vine.

* This clearly echoes Monty Python's Mr Smoketoomuch, who, when he gives his name, is informed, 'You'd better cut down then,'

And I said, 'Well, Ang . . . You know the Hulk film?'

And he went, 'Yeah.'

I said, 'Well, in that, Bruce Banner – he's the Hulk – he says, "Don't make me angry, you wouldn't like me when I'm angry." And your name's Ang Lee and you directed it. So I said, um, "Don't make me anglee, you wouldn't like me when I'm anglee," um, because "Ang Lee" sounds a bit like "angry".'

And Ang Lee said, 'No, it doesn't.'

And I said, 'Come on, Ang, be fair. "Ang Lee" does sound a bit like "angry".'

And Ang Lee said, 'No, it doesn't. "Ang Lee" is a completely different word to "anglee".'

And I said, 'I'm sorry. Can you repeat that?'

And Ang Lee said, 'Yes. "Ang Lee" is a completely different word to "anglee".'

And I said, 'I don't understand the point you're trying to make, Ang Lee, because what I'm saying, if you listen, is that "angry" sounds a bit like "Ang Lee", so if you swap them round, people can see there's a slight change, there's some sort of joke there. Ang Lee . . . what you're saying is actually the same word as "anglee". If you swap those two words round, no one would notice the difference. It wouldn't work. But that's not what you're . . . What you appear to be saying is that "anglee" is a completely different word to "Ang Lee", but it isn't. They're the same thing. I can't understand . . . It's very simple, the joke I made. I can't understand how you've got into this kind of fix. I never . . .'

And then he went, 'Oh, I get it,' he said. 'Is this a joke about me having a Taiwanese accent?'

---

and then tells his embarrassed interlocutor that no one has ever told that joke to him before. I think I had this on the *Live at Drury Lane* record as a child, which I still probably know off by heart.

And I was mortified. I went, 'No, it never even occurred to me that you would think that. It's just a simple thing about the words, the syllables "ry" and "lee", sounding the same. My own surname is Lee, I've had thirty-six years of fun with that syllable. I know what I'm talking about. I can't see why you would begin to think . . .'

And he went, 'No! You're anti-Taiwanese.'

And I went, 'I'm not. I don't even know where Taiwan is. I've got no interest in it.' Which made it worse, to be honest.

And then he got, he got like a lawyer on from Universal, and I had to . . . Shouting at me, saying I was anti-Taiwan . . . I had to get my editor on from the paper to stick up for me . . . We ended up having this kind of four-way argument. It went on for ages. He was going, 'You're anti-Taiwanese,' he was saying. My editor was going, 'No, he isn't, he has no history of anti-Taiwaneseness at all.' And there was, like, this thing. And then Ang Lee started shouting at me about it. And I went, 'Well, I can't see what your problem is. Why don't you just listen to the joke? It's obvious.'

And then in the end he went, 'Don't make me anglee, you wouldn't like me when I'm anglee!'

And I said, 'You've proved my point, you fucking Taiwanese idiot!'

He said, 'Don't call me that!' He got another bloke, an adviser. I had to get someone else on, the publisher. There's like a six-way, two-hour debate going on. In the end, we argued for so long that Ang Lee missed his 2.30 dentist's appointment.*

---

* What time does the Chinese man go to the dentist? 2.30 (Tooth hurty). For me, the joke here is to dare to offer this seventies *Beano* joke up as the conclusion to all that has gone before.

That's the time he goes to the dentist, Glasgow! Don't let him tell you any different. He doesn't even need to write it down. They offer him an appointment card, he rejects it. He says, 'I'll remember it by thinking about my own pain.'*

I'm going to shout out some questions now. I need you to answer loudly to them. The answer to most of them is yes.† OK, one, two, three. Who likes alcohol?

---

* The subtext here is that the Chinese man in the 2.30 joke thinks the thoughts in his own head in English, in a bad Chinese accent, and that for him, this bad accent echoes the time of his appointment. I thought about elaborating on this live but it would, I think, have been adding insult to injury. That said, one of the things I love about proper jokes are mad assumptions of this nature: for example, the implication here that a Chinese man thinks in English in a Chinese accent and presumably because of that books his appointment at 2.30 as an aide-memoire.

† The sudden lurch into this Ben Elton bit is clumsy and clanking, but I found if I approached it with enough verve and gusto no one would notice, and often the change of pace out of the Ang Lee epic was welcome and necessary. It's also interesting to me, looking back at this now, that lurches between subject material like this aren't present in any of the stand-up shows I've written since, which all have either a narrative or a conceptual through-line, or ideally both. *Stand-Up Comedian* was cobbled together from material run in clubs in the nineties, which I toyed with at the odd benefit during my retirement, and stuff I wrote specially for it. Since then I have always written stand-up with its position in a full-length show in mind. The flip side of this is I have almost nothing left that stands alone, that I can do in benefits or little ten- or twenty-minute slots. Everything I write now is tied into these epic shows full of callbacks and cross-references or supporting shifts of mood or emotional gambits that induce sympathy to justify me being a patronising horrible arse later on, and so I end up falling back on bits I wrote often over twenty years ago. The head of BBC2 recently asked me about hosting a stand-up show for the channel, doing little bits in-between other acts. But I am no longer fit for purpose.

AUDIENCE: Yes!

Louder! Who likes sweets?

AUDIENCE: Yes!

Who likes cream cakes?

AUDIENCE: Yes!

Who likes their favourite food, whatever it is?

AUDIENCE: Yes!

Who likes Ben Elton? Oh, it's no one.

OK, here's another one. Who likes, er, who likes, er, *The Simpsons*?

AUDIENCE: Yes!

Who likes Spider-Man?

AUDIENCE: Yes!

Who likes their favourite fictional character from their own childhood?

AUDIENCE: Yes!

Who likes their own beloved mother?

AUDIENCE: Yes!

Who likes Ben Elton? Oh, it's no one again.

OK, here's another one. Who likes snowflakes?

AUDIENCE: Yes!

Who likes sunshine?

AUDIENCE: Yes!

Who likes the universal concept of eternal peace and happiness?

AUDIENCE: Yes!

Who likes Osama bin Laden? Yeah! Who likes Ben Elton? Oh, it's no one again.*

* I would change the exact detail of these questions every night, but it was always fairly easy to get the crowd to do what I wanted, namely to cheer Osama bin Laden and offer up nothing for Ben Elton, simply by varying the pitch and velocity of the sentences. And yet we still wonder how Hitler succeeded.

It's fucking weird, it's weird. That is weird, 'cause I must have done that thirty or forty times, right, and every time, without any element of manipulation, more people like Osama bin Laden, a multiple murderer, than Ben Elton. I think why, why would more people like Osama bin Laden than Ben Elton? And I think it's 'cause when you compare the two of them, compared to Ben Elton, Osama bin Laden has at least lived his life to a consistent set of ethical principles. 'Cause . . . Yeah, clap, let him hear you. So, er . . .

'Cause people hate Ben Elton, and every now and again a journalist has the courage to ask him why this is. I've seen it happen twice in print and once on *Parkinson*. Parkinson said to him, he said to Ben Elton, 'Ben Elton, why do you think everyone hates you?' And Ben Elton said – he did – and Ben Elton said, 'Well, Michael, it's 'cause in this country, people don't like success.' But he was wrong about that. The real answer is much more simple. It's just that in this country, people don't like Ben Elton.*

And they don't hate him through the kind of conduit

* Why don't people like Ben Elton? Admittedly, I was writing this material in the light of seeing Elton's Queen musical *We Will Rock You*. I was obliged to see it professionally, as the director of another musical, *Jerry Springer: The Opera*, but I found it profoundly depressing, even as an example of the largely futile genre of musical theatre (see Appendix I). It made me despair of humanity, but having seen it, Ben Elton's Queen musical is one of those things you can't unsee, like animal pornography or some especially horrible vomit in a gutter, and it haunts you for days, every time you close your eyes. There's bad art, and then there's corrupt art, dishonest art, art that lies and is made with nothing but contempt for its audience; *We Will Rock You* is all those. It is currently celebrating its eighth year in the West End. A film adaptation is in pre-production and a sequel is on the way.

I think the nature of my despair in Ben Elton is also

of the notion of success. They hate him entirely on his own terms, because of who he is and the bad things that he's done. And I think if you're my age, you can kind of understand why it is. 'Cause if you're, if you're over thirty-five, you'll remember before Alternative Comedy, when you'd watch comedians, and it had no kind of relevance to you and you didn't understand what they were talking about and who they were. And then *The Young Ones* came along, and all that, with Ben Elton, and you thought, 'At last, something for us.'*

------

generationally specific. Unless you can remember comedy before the Alternative Comedy boom of 1979/80, when for many people it seemed like no one was writing comedy that was relevant to them in any way, you probably can't imagine how much Ben Elton, *The Young Ones*, Alexei Sayle and co. meant. Of course, all of them have on some level betrayed the principles they espoused, or else the hopes that we plastered onto them, in the last thirty years. It's inevitable. Political and artistic ideals wither in the face of real-world choices. But few of Alternative Comedy's first wave have sold out with such spectacular glee and disregard for what they once stood for as Ben Elton, to the point where even watching his old material now he just seems like an opportunistic charlatan, working the system. Find the YouTube clip of Ben introducing the brilliant Kevin McAleer on *Saturday Live* in the mid-eighties and look how carefully the slippery snake chooses his words to disassociate himself from the risk of McAleer's brilliantly bizarre performance failing.
* This idea that a writer-performer would only criticise another because they are jealous of them is extremely irritating. In the last few years, I have been accused of being jealous of Ben Elton, Chris Moyles, Richard Hammond, Adrian Chiles . . . the list goes on and on, and no one on it is a source of jealousy for me. I have written material making fun of them because I dislike what they stand for, or what they are perceived to embody, or because they don't really stand for anything and so it's funny to be so furious with, or about, them.

98

Then, of course, over the years, Ben Elton's changed. He's worked with Queen, who were one of the British bands that broke the, er, cultural embargo on South Africa under apartheid.* He's worked with Andrew Lloyd Webber, who's worse than that. And, er . . . And a song that they co-wrote was performed at the inauguration of George Bush. And when questioned about it, Ben Elton said he didn't see it so much as a celebration of George Bush as a celebration of the President of the United States of America. But of course, they're the same thing. That's why that argument doesn't work.

But the problem is he's kind of been compromised by proximity to, to success. And, and if you think about it, all the great comedians are kind of outsider figures, commenting on society from outside. Kind of holy fools, shaman clowns, outsiders. Spike Milligan was able to remain an outsider by virtue of having long-term mental-illness problems. Um . . . Bill Hicks has been able to remain an outsider

---

That said, I wouldn't do ten minutes on hating Ben Elton today. When I wrote this, I was at a low ebb; I hadn't been getting audiences or good reviews. So there was almost something heroic about a pesky little outsider cocking his leg on the emperor's naked ankle. Six years later, Ben Elton has little critical standing left, but remains enormously wealthy and successful. Six years later, I have no obvious future, my DVDs sell poorly, the money for this book is less than Ben Elton makes from one night of *We Will Rock You*, but, wrongly or rightly, I'm accepted as a fixture of the fringes of the comedy establishment and there'd be nothing heroic today about me having a go at someone as obviously in slow creative decline as Ben Elton. The balance is all wrong.

* Of all the bands for Elton to work with he chooses the apartheid embargo-busters Queen, and then decides to impose onto their unwieldy frame the notion that they represent a political revolt. You couldn't make it up, as Richard Littlejohn will say later in this book.

because he died of cancer at the age of thirty-two. Michael Barrymore has been able to remain an outsider by becoming the subject of a murder investigation after a man was found dead in his pool. I admire Barrymore's commitment to this abstract notion of the outsider shaman-clown figure. And I think it's good . . . I think it's great to be on this late at night in Glasgow talking about this idea. But um . . .

But lately I have more sympathy for what we in the trade call Elton's compromise. And . . . 'Cause . . . In the last few years I, I directed a, a show and it was, it was kind of a hit in the West End. And I had to meet loads of famous people on, on press nights and, um, and opening nights. I met, er, Bonnie Langford. Yeah. I met her twice. I met, er, the tall one from the Three Degrees, Sheila . . . something, her name is. And one night, I found myself shaking hands before I realised who it was, with Michael Portillo, right? I looked up. I thought it was the little wooden goblin from the Cuprinol advert. But it was Michael Portillo, someone whose policies I had marched against as a student, or would have done if I hadn't been drunk. But theoretically . . .*

There was worse to come than Portillo. On June the 16th last year, I heard a rumour that Cherie Blair was going to come and see the show, right? And I thought, 'Well, I hope that's not the case.' You know, I don't want to have to meet her. 'Cause I'm one of two million Britons that marched

* The years pass. This meeting with Portillo was in 2003. Since then I've been on various TV shows with him and he seems nice enough. There are worse people, many of them members of the Labour Party. But again here, and throughout the Ben Elton-bashing bit, I am sort of in character as a smug, stuck-up, politically correct, holier than thou leftie, a character I have researched so fully I often feel obliged actually to behave like it in my own spare time, sometimes for years on end.

against her husband's war. I think it's unethical. I think it's going to come back and bite us in the arse and we'll be in trouble about it for decades, once the dust settles. And I, I don't want to have to be like some E-list celebrity New Labour apologist. I don't want to meet her, no way.

And then the next day, the woman from the public-relations company for the show rang me up. And she said, 'I've got some great news, Cherie Blair is coming to see the show, and she wants to meet the cast and the creative team afterwards.'*

And I went, 'I'm sorry. I can't do it. I've got . . . This is where I draw a line. You know. You d–,' I said. 'You don't even want me in the building. If I'm there, I'm going to get kind of political Tourette's syndrome and just do something like fly an anti-war banner off the stage, or make a speech at the end, or just do something to Cherie Blair that'll wipe that . . . whatever that is . . . on her face. You know, make it go.'

And she said, 'Well, that's a shame, because . . . Does this change your mind?' she said. 'She's not coming on her own. She's coming with her guest, who is the president of Scope, the Spastics Society.' Right, and this honestly happened. I was put in this weird position where you want to make some ineffectual gesture against Cherie Blair, but you don't want to snub a person from a worthwhile charity, Scope. You know, so . . .†

---

* This is another true story. On the rare occasions when I have been involved with anything that famous people want to come to, it does genuinely amaze me that the supporting PR people think you will want to meet them, especially when meeting them, as is the case with Cherie Blair, has political or ethical dimensions.

† Modern dilemmas. By snubbing the warmonger's wife I would also be snubbing the Scope woman. And yes, I know the Spastics Society

I thought, 'Well, I know what I'll do. I'll go down, and after the show I'll say to Cherie Blair, "I hope you're happy, Cherie. I hope when you look across at Tony every morning, you think of all those thousands of people killed in his war, and I hope you're happy when you think of all those little kids in Baghdad and Basra with their arms and legs blown off, maimed, crippled for life." Then I'll turn to the woman from Scope, and I'll go, "Maybe you can have a rummage around in one of your charity shops. See if you can find them some cardigans."'*

But in the end, I didn't do that. What I did was, I said that I would go, and then I just didn't. Yeah.†

But . . . We're back talking about the war again. Last, last bit. And er . . . Like I say, there's this kind of assumption I think from us here in Europe, where we look at, particularly in Britain, where we look at America's hysterical reaction to the 9th of November, and we think, 'Well, you know, that wouldn't happen here. We wouldn't do that, 'cause we're reasonable, sensible people here in Britain.' But we don't have to look very far back in our own cultural history to see an example of us losing the plot as a, as a nation. And I'm talking of course about the death of Princess Diana, the late Princess of Wales.‡ It was in the news again last summer

---

is now called Scope, and that they frown on the use of the word 'spastic', but I needed to use it here to give the moral choice involved more weight, to really hammer home what Scope is all about.

* This often didn't get a laugh. I don't really understand why. It's black humour, but it's not against the Scope beneficiaries or the victims of war.

† I just didn't go. Hurrah for me.

‡ Going over this show again it does seem like a bit of a ragbag of unrelated stuff. This must be the most contrived segue of the lot, as I limp into the Princess Diana routine, which I initially wrote in

because of the Princess Diana Memorial Fountain, which you'll remember was a rubbish fountain. And fulfilled very few of the job-description criteria of fountains.

But it's ongoing, it's ongoing. The story never goes away.* I remember when she died, um, 'cause about two days before the state funeral, I went down to Kensington Palace where Princess Diana had lived to, to look at all the tributes left outside, you know. And in amongst all the bunches of flowers and sympathy cards, and poems little kids had written, and drawings and paintings people had done, whatever . . . in amongst all that, I honestly saw, and this is true, I saw a life-size inflatable model of E.T.† It was honestly there, outside Kensington Palace, two days before the state funeral. And I stood there looking at the inflatable E.T. for some forty or fifty minutes. And I thought to myself, 'How did that get there? Who would have thought that that was an appropriate gesture?'

And I imagined a household somewhere on that awful autumn Sunday morning, where perhaps the wife had woken up first, and she'd watched the news and she went through to her still-sleeping husband, and she said . . .‡

1997, having elaborated on it over the years but never performing in a solo stand-up show. The new Princess Diana fountain was in the news, which was sufficient excuse to shoehorn it in.

* I am saying this as if to convince both myself and the audience that it is fine to do this routine about someone who has been dead now for the best part of a decade.

† I did not do this. I watched it on TV. Phelim O'Neil, a friend of my then girlfriend who is now a film critic, told me he saw an E.T. in the flowers.

‡ This was the first routine I ever wrote, I think, where I began to stretch the silences, the lack of laughs, the tension, to the point where I'd be worried about ever winning back the room. Since doing this routine a lot in the late nineties, and on the 2004/5

'Please. Please wake u– . . . I need you to wake up and be with me now. There's been a t– . . . Some terrible news. I need you to get up, come in the front room and watch it on the television with me, 'cause I can't be alone. So please wake up.'

But you know, he's asleep, he's asleep. He's going . . .

[*lying down, as though half-awake*]

'What? It's fucking . . . It's half past six on a Sunday morning. I am asleep. I know I'm speaking but I am asleep. I don't want to get up. I'm asleep. So . . . just . . . I know you're upset but just say what it is. What is it?'

And she'd have gone . . .

[*stands up*]

'Please. If you . . . If you love me, just this one time, just get up. And . . . Because it's an awful thing and I need . . . I can't be alone. I need someone to comfort me and share. Just . . . please. Get up.'

———

Stand-Up Comedian tour, it now seems easily manageable. There's always a clear end in sight, and lots of little handrails to grab onto in the midst of all the uncertainty, but at the time it felt like a nightly leap into the void, acting out the grief of the people in the story to the silent onlookers. Today, I'd go much further away from the shallow end.

I used to like doing this bit in theatres and bigger venues where there was a stage, so I could roll around the lip in imagined woe here, and even allow myself to fall a few feet on hearing the tragic news if the drop didn't look too great to risk, though I remember hurting myself quite badly dropping off the stage of the Hi-Fi club in Melbourne in 2000. Today, I love counter-weighting the apparent measured monotony of my routines with sudden bursts of possible physical jeopardy, and on the *If You Prefer a Milder Comedian* tour of 2009/10 I found myself in loads of nineteenth-century theatres full of ledges and empty audience boxes I could drape myself out of during moments of feigned mental collapse, to the distress of the panicked ushers.

[*lying down*]

And he'd have gone . . .

'Look, I was out late last night. I've got, I've got work at seven . . . tomorrow. This is my . . . this is my one day for sleeping in. I don't want to get up till about half past eleven, to be honest. And even then I'm not going to get dressed. I'm just going to be, like, in my pants and stuff, just sitting around. I kind of . . . I don't know what you . . . If you were just to say what it is . . . You know . . . What is it?'

[*stands up*]

She'd have gone . . .

'Princess Diana, Lady Di, has . . . she . . . has been killed.'

[*lying down*]

And he'd have gone . . .

'No! [*pounding fist on floor*] Not the Queen of Hearts! The Rose of England . . . and Scotland, and Wales, and bits of Ireland, no! How did it . . . There's no God! How did it . . . why? How did it happen?'*

[*standing up*]

And she'd have gone . . .

'It was in a car crash in Paris last night. They don't know the exact details yet. But she's dead.'

So presumably at that point, he'd have got up, got out of bed, tried to get dressed, you know, get some kind of grip on his emotions and his feelings. Calm down his grief. And then he'd have said . . .

'I'd better go out and get a life-size inflatable model of E.T. You know, for the gates of her home.'

And his wife would have said . . .

* There's another Lee and Herring echo here, as we would often write characters whose dialogue consisted mainly of them shouting 'Why?'

'Yes. But you'd better hurry, 'cause there'll be a rush on those now. We don't want to be the only people not putting one there.'

And I was talking about this onstage in Croydon at the time it happened, and a bloke shouted out, 'I was there! And I saw that! And it wasn't a life-size inflatable model of E.T., it was a life-size inflatable model of ALF!'*

I didn't even know what an ALF was, I had to ask him. He said, 'Oh, it's an American kids' TV thing. It's an alien – A-L-F, Alien Life Form. It's like a cross between a pig and an aardvark, from space. And it sometimes wears a nappy, and it says kind of wise-ass things.' And he said he'd seen one of those there. I didn't see an ALF outside Kensington Palace, before the . . . And I'm not saying there wasn't one there, maybe there was at some stage. But by the time I arrived, it had got covered up under flowers or carried away on a river of infants' tears. I don't know, I didn't see it.†

* This actually happened. I think one of the things I have consciously copied from Greg Fleet is to embrace talking in a routine about times that routine hasn't worked, and I think there's a direct relationship here to his bit about accidentally doing a routine about shark attacks to an audience that includes a couple who lost their son to a shark. We're comedians. Why do we pretend to be like you and do routines about everyday life? This is my everyday life, being heckled about an inflatable alien in Croydon, so I will talk about it, and it will be fascinating to you, because it is so different to your everyday life. Yes. You. In your suit and tie.

† Sometimes people complained to me about this routine after shows, but very rarely, and I could usually defuse the situation by showing how it was about the public response to the princess's death, and not simply personal mockery of her. But once, at the club on *The Tattershall Castle* boat on the River Thames, a woman came up to me crying about it, and I began my usual explanation. She stopped me and said she was upset because an AIDS ward

It never goes away, it's back in the news now, the Princess Diana Memorial Fountain.* Last year, people went, 'Oh, it's great, it's, it's what she would have wanted. It's a place where families can hang out, children can play. It's what Princess Diana would have wanted.' It isn't. What Princess Diana would have wanted would have been to have not been killed. And then in death, not to have become the unwitting receptacle of the hysterical, overemotional, shrieking grief of twats. That's what she would have wanted.†

It didn't even work! It didn't even work, Glasgow! Children were supposed to be able to play in it. They kept falling over, breaking their arms and legs. They made it out of slate, or sheets of ice, or something. They were getting dogshit-eye-blindness disease from the water. In the end, they had to close it down, fence it off, put warning signs on it like a decommissioned Chernobyl nuclear reactor. 'Don't go near the Princess Diana Memorial Fountain! It's

---

named after her father had been renamed after Princess Diana when she died, and she was just sick of hearing about her everywhere. It's impossible to guess what will upset people.

* How convenient for me.

† The material from here on in isn't really a good enough end to a show, but as the show didn't appear to me at the time to have a definite theme or through-line, it was hard to know how to end it. So I do what you'll see most comics do, when you watch the hour-long DVD of the unrelated series of gags they're touring off the back of a regular slot on a TV quiz show – I speed up and shout to give the impression that some kind of conclusion is being reached and then quit the stage on a roll, hopefully before anyone realises that choosing the material to close on was a largely arbitrary decision.

But in retrospect, the show did have a theme: extraordinary popular delusions and the madness of crowds. It was all there in undercurrents, but I never realised. One simple sentence could have tied everything together. But you can't go back.

dangerous! Don't even look at it! You'll get cancer and die! Run away!'

But it's ridiculous. There should be a memorial to her, there should be a memorial to her, because she did some amazing things. She worked, worked with charity and landmines. And she got one GCSE in domestic science. And to achieve that, and only that, when born into such a position of privilege and wealth, requires a steely determination of focus. You've got to know from an early age that you want to achieve next to nothing, and work hard at it, when all the odds are in your favour.*

And that's why there should be a memorial to her, the People's Princess, right. That's why I'm going to make my own, I'm going to make my own memorial fountain to the Princess Diana Memorial Fountain. It's going to be called the Princess Diana Memorial Fountain Memorial Fountain Fountain. But it's not going to be some state-approved, Viscount Althorp-subsidised architectural carbuncle. It's going to be simple, like she would have wanted. It's going to be me, lying on my back in Hyde Park, near the Princess Diana Memorial Fountain, naked, with a colander over my penis. Every hour, on the hour, I'll piss up through that. Children can come and play in it if they want, families can gather round, I don't mind. You can do it yourselves, Glasgow, do it yourselves. You don't even need a colander. That's gilding the lily, to be honest. Just do a piss anywhere you want. In the street, in your house, in a library, in an antenatal unit, in the face of a treasured family pet or an elderly relative.

And if a policeman says to you, 'What are you doing? What on earth do you think you're doing . . . madam?' just

* Irony.

say, 'I'm paying tribute in the only way I understand to the memory of Princess Diana, Princess of Wales.'*

I've been Stewart Lee. Thanks a lot for bearing with us tonight, thank you. Thank you very much. Thank you.

Now go.

EXIT MUSIC: 'QUEEN OF THE WORLD' BY LLOYD AND CLAUDETTE.†

---

* Is this an end? No. Pathetic.
† I chose this jaunty blue-beat number because it seems, subliminally, to tie in with Princess Diana. And because I liked dancing around to it backstage.

2

2004–5

Critical response to *Stand-Up Comedian*'s Edinburgh run was largely favourable, with the three major comedy reviewers establishing typically personal positions that they were to deviate little from over the next five years. The scholarly, but qualified, enthusiasm of *The Times*'s Dominic Maxwell: 'Lee's wilful sophistication will not strike everyone's funny bones. Like the avant-jazz that's playing as you file in, it relies on your knowledge of the rules it's toying with. But the self-reflexive playfulness never descends into onanism, because it's tethered to Lee's attack on a world dominated by half-truths. Form matches content. A stunning return'; the cautious, reluctant praise of the *Guardian*'s Brian Logan: 'Lee's technical excellence is driving him in directions I find easier to admire than enjoy. I appreciated his control while longing for the joke(s) to end. There are brilliant pay-offs, but he makes you work for them'; and the indecisive bafflement of the *Independent*'s Julian Hall, who reviews me suspiciously, as if he thinks some kind of trick is being played on him: 'Surly, arrogant and laboured, you either love or hate his on-stage persona . . . hit and miss.'*

---

* When I had returned to stand-up in 2004, it was not as a former and failed TV comic from the 'comedy is the new rock and roll' era,

Word of mouth was good, and two weeks in the 180-seater room at London's Soho Theatre followed in November, with a budget fixed at a level where I could not only break even, but actually make money. Then I got sick during the shows, shaky, feeble and hot, and my bright orange wee burned my shrivelled urethra on exit. I couldn't sleep or stand or eat. I'd get to the venue early and lie flat in the dressing room for hours to gather enough strength to hobble about for the length of the set. My GP agreed that my urine was a disturbing colour, but the sample I gave her got lost in the system, and eventually my girlfriend hassled my manager about my condition. He got his connected Notting Hill doctor, who knew which strings to pull, to check me out, and I was immediately admitted to the Whittington hospital in Archway. Between the three of them, they probably saved me from something more serious.

'Do you ever get rectal bleeding?' they asked at the hospital. 'On and off.' 'On and off for how long?' 'Ten or fifteen years, I suppose.' It hadn't really occurred to me that I had been ill for some time. But I'd had various ongoing bowel problems since getting ulcerative colitis as a teenager, which hospitalised me the day after I first saw The Fall live, the acidity of Mark E. Smith's onstage persona perhaps being too much for a young boy's stomach to take. And these problems had intensified since I first became

---

but as the Olivier award-nominated director and co-librettist of an opera routinely described as the greatest piece of musical theatre for thirty years. I benefited enormously from this change in the way I was perceived by broadsheet newspapers, and I think my then management deliberately exaggerated my role in Richard Thomas's idea with this aim in sight. I got highbrow credibility on the back of someone else's unassuming genius.

a full-time stand-up, to the point where I stopped even noticing that continuous rectal bleeding, the billowing clouds of flatus and the eternally unstable stools that made visits to the toilet during the nineties and the early part of this century such a constant source of amusement to me and others. The smell of farts hung around me perpetually as if it were, as Frank Skinner said in the most poignantly eloquent moment of stand-up he ever wrote, 'an ermine cloak'. In retrospect, it comes as no surprise that I should have been heading for hospitalisation. My diet from 1991 to 2004 consisted mainly of Diet Coke, beans on toast, crisps, Wheat Crunchies, margarine, lager and curry. To paraphrase the late satirist and crackhead Willie Donaldson, 'You cannot eat as I have ate and not end up like this.' It turned out I had a serious attack of an ongoing condition called diverticulitis, a step up from the ulcerative colitis I'd had as a teenager. I was rushed up to a vacant hospital bed and put on a drip and lots of drugs.

During the hours of darkness, the hospital experience had all the oddly comforting and hallucinatory grace notes that I remembered from childhood tussles with rare diseases and broken bones. Nurses at nursing stations in the night, lit by softly glowing desk lamps, their soft voices humming just at the edge of audibility. Croaks of pain in the dark from behind drawn curtains. Minimalist cycles of fluttering electronic bleeps and blips. Stomach gurgles and apocalyptic farts. One night, I remember, I staggered to the TV room with my drip to try and watch the first ever episode of *I'm a Celebrity . . . Get Me Out of Here!*. I was alone with a cup of tea and the telly, and things were momentarily normal. A thin man with a beard came in, wearing just pyjama bottoms and a brown leather jacket with a picture of a wolf on the back. He asked if he could join me. Then he stood between me and the television, pulled down his trousers, pointed out, one by one, the weeping wounds on his legs, and then started to rub petroleum jelly into them in a vivid ooze of blood, pus and the translucent gel. I had to go back to bed. I never did become an avid viewer of *I'm a Celebrity*. When you're hospitalised in a big city in the NHS system, you realise how many people are not especially sick, just lost and confused, alone and with no one to love them.

I lay awake at night, doped and thinking. People get ill. Then they die. I'd been ill and I hadn't known. Perhaps I might have died? This seems hysterical and banal now, and part of me knew it was hysterical and banal at the time, but that did not make it any less arresting. I did not want to die yet. I had things to do.

I was discharged with dietary advice. For the foreseeable future, try and eat lots of roughage, maybe a baked potato every day. And drink lots of water. No coffee, no carbonated drinks, and, the man suggested confidentially, if you *must* have alcohol, something flat and soft like Guinness. Guinness was my favourite drink and I loved baked potatoes. I'd be fine.

My mother was away, and she invited me to go and stay in her house to recuperate, so I unclipped my drip, rescheduled the remaining Soho Theatre gigs and drove west, to the new-build estate adjoining a once remote little village south-east of Worcester to which she'd retired. I pottered weakly about the empty house, all tidy and quiet, eating baked potatoes and sluicing myself with pints of Malvern water. I was still on a lot of painkillers. I tried to drink but it flattened me. I'd lost so much weight I felt like I was in a different man's body, or mine, twenty years ago, when I looked like the young Morrissey. I had to pee every twenty

114

minutes. If I wanted to smoke, I had to stand in my mum's garden. I was thirty-six years old. One day, I drove to Hay-on-Wye and looked for Arthur Machen books, staggering about in a half-dream in the shadow of the hill. One night, I watched *Master and Commander* on DVD, and I enjoyed it, which is unlike me. And from the window of the white fluffy bedroom, always open because the stifling heating was jammed on and no one has ever known how to turn it off, I looked out at the Malvern hills.

Everything was wobbly and trippy. The fields buzzed green and black. I felt ashen and pin-eyed, like an actor pretending to come down from a rave in an early-nineties ITV police drama. The skies out there seemed grey and enormous, as if they were coming to crush me into the floodplain of the Severn, deep down with the civil war dead in the flatlands all around Cromwell's, the insensitively named Indian restaurant, and Powick hospital, where a Dr Sandison dosed 683 schizophrenics and depressives with LSD in the fifties. I tried to go for walks, but the paths along the sides of the roads petered out or led nowhere, and lorries rattled past alarmingly, because the new-builds had been new-built where no new-builds should be built. I could just about make it as far as either a duck pond in the middle of a cul-de-sac, or an electricity substation on the edge of a sheep field, or a shop staffed by bleached women who sold pork rolls to lorry drivers who had stopped in the lay-by, or to the village pub, now a swanky restaurant, the die-hard drinkers crammed around what was left of the bar, trying to avoid eye contact. So, after a while, I went home.

In January, I set off to tour the cool hipster comedy venues the uncharacteristically sympathetic booker Charlie Briggs had scoped out. I was determined to downsize from the scale of the 'comedy is the new rock and roll' era, which was when I'd last toured a show, and to do everything myself, to see if, this time, I could make it worthwhile. I was booked into nearly thirty rooms of between one and two hundred seats, hand-picked by Charlie as a base to build from. Advertising was minimal, because suddenly there was MySpace and a website with a mailing list, new methods of direct mass communication that hadn't really existed last time I'd been on the road. I drove from Travelodge to Travelodge in my Mini Metro, listening to The Fall and John Lee Hooker albums from the fifties. And the blurb I wrote for the tour flyer and press release read like a personal manifesto: 'After an enforced lay-off from performing, and bewildered by critical acclaim in a world he never made, the "fifth best stand-up of his generation" returns in search of clarity, self-respect, and immediate sensual and intellectual gratification.'* (The 'fifth best stand-up of his generation' was an unattributable quote I made up, to combat the fact that everybody seemed to have similar things on their posters these days.) And after years in the slow, detached process of commercial theatre with *Jerry Springer: The Opera*, I was, genuinely, in search of 'clarity, self-respect, and immediate sensual and intellectual gratification'.

I asked Josie Long to open for me, a young comic who talked about paintings and the wonder of science onstage, swore loudly and pathologically in tea rooms, and appeared to make most of her own clothes. Josie was one of the acts

---

* The bit about 'a world he never made' is a nod to Steve Gerber's seventies *Howard the Duck* comic, a sacred text to reach for whenever you feel lost, like a giant speaking alien duck might if it found itself in disco-era Cleveland.

I'd been impressed by when I started back on the circuit. She hadn't toured before, and being away with someone who was interested in what Aldershot town centre would be like, for example, leavened the deadening effect of the driving. And there was an element of the miner's canary about her role in the proceedings. On the rare occasions when the crowd didn't go for Josie's open-hearted surreal spiel, I knew that despite Charlie's and my best efforts to book a tour that connected only with the hot freaks of alterno-Britain, we were in a venue full of sports fans and squares, and I was going to have to work hard.

It was a cold, harsh winter, and I was still shaky and weak. I sat at the wheel, gurgling back the prescribed bottles of water, necking painkillers, looking for baked potato stands in windswept city centres and stopping every thirty minutes to empty my distended bladder into any available space. In Glasgow, after I'd jumped out of the car in a traffic jam to piss up some wheelie bins by a multi-storey, a now soggy junkie crawled out from behind them, in the midst of injecting heroin into his forearm, and said, 'For fuck's sake, man!', but with an air of resigned and philosophical acceptance, as if we were both in this together.

The tour had a frosty, somnambulant quality. Before a lovely gig above a pub in the little Derbyshire town of Wirksworth, we walked to the Nine Ladies stone circle on a snowy Stanton Moor, through the tree houses and smouldering fires of frozen eco-protesters who were trying to prevent an American-owned quarry edging any closer to the stone circle. The locals left them food in boxes at the bottom of the hill. The Actor Kevin Eldon joined us for a non-cost-effective trek to the Isle of Skye, where we drew thirty people, still more than I'd played to in Dundee five years earlier. And in Lincoln, there was a heavy snowfall during the gig. I went back to my room, a monastic cell you could rent cheaply from the bishop in the actual cathedral cloisters, and Josie stayed and played snowballs in the grounds of the university with the audience. She was having enough fun for both of us, which was good, as I was perpetually shattered.*

The gigs, though, were great, and worked much better than they would have done in the partially filled municipal hangars I'd become used to. At the end of the tour, after I deducted all my costs, I think Josie's support fees of £100 a night added up to only a little less than I'd made myself. But I had made something. For the first time in fifteen years this was a wedge of live work that had been absolutely and incontrovertibly worth doing. 'Come back next time,' said the promoters of these real places with their hand-reared audiences who actually liked comedy. There was a whole world out there of enthusiastic comedy promoters and discerning comedy consumers that my management had never connected me with. And people liked the show.

* In February, while Josie and I were making a tourist stop at Worcester Cathedral, I received a text from Daniel Kitson saying that Malcolm Hardee, one of the progenitors of Alternative Comedy as we know it, had drowned. I was disproportionately upset, as I didn't know him well, but he had been one of the first people to book me, and represented the anarchic spirit that was slowly disappearing from the circuit. Malcolm's funeral, a euphoric variety show and rolling eulogy jointly presided over by Arthur Smith and a tolerant priest at St Alfege Church, Greenwich, was one of the greatest pieces of theatre I have ever seen, but I wonder if the sense of hysteria at the subsequent wake reflected, in some way, the fact that Malcolm's death symbolised the end of an era. Malcolm's signature act – the naked balloon dance he performed as The Greatest Show on Legs – was recently appropriated move for move by some scumbags on a Simon Cowell TV talent show.

After seeing *Stand-Up Comedian* in Edinburgh and wrongly imagining I would soon be huge, a DVD outfit called 2entertain paid my management company's production company to film *Stand-Up Comedian* for commercial release.* I saw enough from whatever fee my manager's production company were paid to make the DVD to pay off the mortgage on my flat. (I never thought to ask, or don't remember being told, what the actual fee paid to my manager's production company was, although I am sure this must have been discussed with me.) The DVD's executive producer tried to convince my manager, who he also was, to make me film it at the Bloomsbury Theatre to save money, and not to worry about spending any of the budget on making it good as all live comedy DVDs 'were always shit anyway'. But I managed to persuade both of him to let me film it in the more intimate

* Prior to the release of the *Stand-Up Comedian* DVD, TV's Jimmy Carr told me, over breakfast in Montreal, that my problem was that although critics and comics thought I was good, there was no commercially available filmed evidence of anything I had ever done to convince members of the public I was worth seeing. The sick funnyman kindly offered to put some of his own TV millions into filming my stand-up to help me, but as I then got the offer from 2entertain I was never required to see how much I could have stung him for. Peter Kay and Matt Lucas, who pretended to be physically handicapped and mentally and physically handicapped, respectively, and wiggled about to a Proclaimers song for Comic Relief, may seem more generous, but secretly Jimmy Carr is little short of a living saint. That said, of all the comics working in Britain today, I believe it to be I who am perhaps the most charitable, not in terms of the actual amount of money I give, but in terms of the time I give up for charity benefit shows. Richard Herring, of course, carries a bucket for Scope with him everywhere he goes, which also doubles up as a receptacle for his audience to be sick into.

and tense surroundings of The Stand, Glasgow, which worked perfectly.*

It was great to have the show filmed too. It drew a line under the material and forced me to move forwards. The problem now was how to follow it up. *Stand-Up Comedian* had been assembled from the best leftovers of a decade and the few ideas I'd had in my sabbatical. What was I supposed to talk about now?

In-between my discharge from hospital and the start of the tour, in December 2004 and January 2005, I went to Hanover with the composer Richard Thomas to help out on a piece he was writing for the Schauspielhaus there. I wasn't really switched on and felt like a passenger. I never really figured out what my role was, how to speak to anyone, or what to eat and drink. All the Germans we worked with evidenced a deep and dry humour. 'There are no old buildings here,' Richard said to a German actor. 'That is because you destroyed them all,' he answered. The

---

* A 2entertain executive later told me, in secrecy outside the first night of a terrible West End adaptation of *Steptoe and Son*, that they couldn't do a follow-up as the price charged by my manager's production company had been too high considering their possible sales, which I had repeatedly told them would be the case whenever I met them. As with my management company's telesales live department, while one was grateful for a large and life-changing one-off payment like this, these smash-and-grab ram raids never seemed to build towards return bookings or long-term relationships. I still felt, perhaps naively, that a better way forward would be to do worthwhile work at a cost-effective level at which no one lost out, in the belief that it might ultimately be rewarded on its own merits. On the other hand, shifting my mortgage in one fell swoop was an amazing thing to do, and even what I saw of the fee for the *Stand-Up Comedian* DVD was three times more than I've ever earned for similar work since.

120

Weihnachtsmarkt by the station glittered pleasingly, and I finally found an Irish pub where I could drink halves of Guinness all day. But the flat we were billeted in was freezing and we ended up spending too much time there, sitting up, dealing with phone calls and emails and mass panic when, suddenly, out of nowhere, the *Jerry Springer: The Opera* shit hit the born-again Christian evangelist fan.

Because the show was now on its last legs as a live West End proposition, the producers had decided it was time to auction it off to the BBC, who had long been seeking a transmission, and then send it out to tour the provinces. The TV director Peter Orton, who had played sax for the sixties mod group The Attack, was contracted to film it, and caught a great performance with the sublimely subtle David Soul in the lead. I was happy the piece was going to be out there, for anyone to see, for free. And then a right-wing Christian pressure group decided to use objections to the show's religious content to catapult themselves into the public eye, causing 65,000 people to complain in advance of the broadcast, their vociferousness eventually leading the police to advise some BBC executives to go into hiding on the night of the programme.*

It was odd to be in Germany and to know that 65,000 people wanted your work banned. The Germans found it funny, and mocked us for being enemies of society and makers of '*Entartete Kunst*', the Nazis' demonised 'decadent art'. When we had first heard about them, I had looked at Christian Voice's website and assumed the whole thing

* An early attempt by the BBC to get the opera on BBC2, which we were able to resist, saw the then controller Jane Root advising me to learn about how to present it using the example of *On the Hour*, a show for which I had been one of the four main writers.

121

would soon blow over. They were obviously small-time shock merchants, who even suggested that Hurricane Katrina was God's punishment on New Orleans for having a gay parade. Matters soon escalated, though. On the night of the broadcast, we sat, in defiance of Christian Voice's homophobic agenda, in a gay bar in Hanover, drinking gay drinks nervously until we were sure the show had gone out without anyone being killed.*

Christian Voice's head honcho, Stephen Green, had quickly mastered the art of the inflammatory soundbite, and the press lapped his comments up without really doing any background checks on him or his organisation. Acres of angry newsprint were generated, much of it about things that weren't even in the show – the supposed nappy-wearing Jesus, the 6,000 swear words that never were – and frightened white people who imagined immigrants were getting an easy ride whenever their faiths were mentioned joined the queue of incoherently angry people eager to see the show closed. In December, Gurpreet Kaur Bhatti's play *Behzti* had been closed by furious Sikhs at the Birmingham Rep, and on a not unrelated note even the national treasure Billy Connolly had recently been censured for a routine about the British hostage in Iraq Ken Bigley. But Stephen Green managed to mobilise the non-specifically miffed on a previously unseen scale. Then he started to close in for the kill. Green's creative interpretation of the legal implications of the proposed and pending new laws on the incitement of racial and religious hatred meant that a whole slew of venues that were lined up to take the show on tour pulled out after he wrote to them and said they'd

* A gay bar in Germany is the same as a normal bar here. Whereas a normal bar in Germany is like a dentist's waiting room with beer.

be prosecuted. Our final chance to make some money on the opera faded away.

Over the next few months, as the fuss rumbled on endlessly and Christian Voice began to make plans to prosecute us for blasphemy, in-between smashing my head into walls in rage I began to wonder whether there might be a stand-up show in it. Becoming part of the news itself ought to offer the comedian-victim interesting creative possibilities. Would it be possible to comment, satirically and objectively, on a story, or a scandal, in which you yourself were a character?*

* Out of professional curiosity, I would like to have seen the TV personality Russell Brand's 2009 stand-up show, *Scandalous*, in which he talked about his role in the Sachsgate scandal. A BBC producer had mistakenly broadcast a recording of the hairy corncrake telling the elderly character actor Andrew Sachs that he had enjoyed sexual intercourse with his granddaughter, who is one of these Goths that they have nowadays that are sexy. (In a grainy film of the phone call Jonathan Ross can be seen touching himself mysteriously in the background, in an act of magical transference, ingesting psychically the energies of his young buck.) As I say, I would have liked to have seen Brand's stand-up show, but pretty quickly it became possible to sum up the whole story thus: two overexcited middle-aged men make stupid comments and are then persecuted by a slavering right-wing media to fulfil its own anti-BBC agenda, mobilising 'decent people' much in the manner of Christian Voice. And the thought of watching Russell Brand drag this out for an hour, whilst girls threw their bras at him, and then having to read him being described as the 'closest thing we have to Lenny Bruce' by Bruce Dessau of the London *Evening Standard* free-sheet made me, to be honest, bitter and resentful. I would also like to remind you all that despite the fuss about Sachsgate, the most-complained-about broadcast ever remains *Jerry Springer: The Opera*. I am not proud of this. But if this is a competition, and I have chosen to see it as one for now, I am still on the winning team.

In mid-February, I took a week off the tour to go to America and perform *Stand-Up Comedian* at the invitation of the Aspen Comedy Festival, which is basically a trade fair for the American TV comedy industry, hosted by HBO. As noted, my show didn't really work, though Janeane Garofalo and all the cool teeth-grinding radicals liked it, which pleased me no end. The American comics in Aspen were mainly terrible, as usual, and luckily I managed to wriggle out of hosting a showcase full of acts whose worthless material, it turned out, would have made it very difficult for me to introduce them with any degree of enthusiasm and sincerity. But I did get to meet loads of my favourite underground American comic-book creators, who were doing a panel there, and I was smuggled into a rich man's party, high in a mountaintop mansion, by the persistent and perverted writer Jonathan Ames, whose work I admired enormously. And the festival offered one of the last opportunities to see the brilliant Flight of the Conchords baffle an unprepared American crowd before they broke big, as they silently died in a tent in the afternoon.

But the single best thing about the Aspen festival was a film screening I attended, out of sheer boredom, of a documentary about stand-up called *The Aristocrats*, by Paul Provenza and Penn Jillette. It features clips of over a hundred principally American comics telling variations on a joke known as 'the Aristocrats', which concerns an obscene vaudeville act. Gradually, the film becomes a hilarious and often moving treatise on shock, surprise, taste, humour, the art of storytelling and the creative imagination. I became an evangelist for *The Aristocrats*, writing lengthy pieces on it for the *Sunday Times*, cannibalised below, and *The Wire* (see Appendix III).

Apparently, the Aristocrats gag, though never repeated

onstage and unknown in Britain, had been a dressing-room staple of American comics for decades. It begins with a man entering a showbiz agent's office to pitch him a nightclub act comprising a man, his wife and their two children, whose performance is then described in as much pungent, pornographic and scatological detail as possible, limited only by the imagination and scruples of the teller. The horrified agent then asks what the act is called. The man replies, 'The Aristocrats.' The humour arises from the contrast between the repellent nature of the act and the polite, gentle title it has been given. The lure of the Aristocrats gag for the film-makers appeared to be the infinitely extendable central section, which pushes boundaries of both endurance and taste, and has, on occasion, been stretched out for as long as an hour and a half.

I interviewed Paul Provenza, himself a stand-up, about his film later that year for the *Sunday Times*.

> The editing process reflected a conscious decision to make the movie about ideas. In fact, we ended up doing some comics a disservice because we didn't necessarily use their funniest bit, but the bit that best helped to illustrate the ideas of the movie clearly. The movie starts repetitively, but if you listen to each version of the joke, hearing the same gag again and again shows how people take off with it and create different things. In the first six minutes George Carlin does a version that's totally grossed-out and scatological, then we move on to Drew Carey teaching us how to do the joke, then into a riff constructed entirely of little sound-bites until, I think, your moral judgment is suspended. You've been bludgeoned. Boom! And then you can concentrate on the absurdity of the thing, the structure of the gag, and the

different layers of offence. It's about the singer not the song. *Repeating the same joke actually allows us to get over the issue of content and concentrate instead on the thorny issue of aesthetics.*

For me, hearing Provenza say this last sentence was like a cartoon lightbulb appearing over my head. This was what I had been trying to do in comedy for nearly twenty years, but I'd never heard the idea expressed with any degree of clarity.

Sometime around the mid-point of the film, after an especially hilarious sequence in which a clown-faced mime acted out the gag silently on Venice Beach, there was a twenty-minute section where, for me, the joke wore thin. I began to feel as if I was being dragged through a trench of filth. The violence against women in the various versions of the story became so relentless that when Bob Saget described one of the male performers smashing his penis repeatedly into a drawer, I was almost relieved because at least it offered some respite. That said, other sections of the comedian-packed cinema were still splitting their sides.*

Seen in public, *The Aristocrats* becomes a living object lesson in the fact that a one-size-fits-all approach to mak-

---

* There can be something utterly hysterical about imaginatively framed obscenity. One of my all-time-favourite routines remains one which Sean Lock performed, I think only once, in about April 1990. Sean, today a popular TV personality and consequently able to play the crowds he always deserved, pictured himself sitting on a toilet, defecating, and looking down to realise that the first stool to emerge from his anus has splashed down into the toilet bowl in the shape of a penis. A second stool emerges. To Sean's delight it is in the shape of a vagina. The penis-shaped stool and the vagina-shaped stool begin bumping into each other in the water of the toilet, at which point, aroused by the activity of the genital-shaped

ing decisions about what is acceptable just won't fit. It doesn't even work in one room full of people who all do the same job. It could be used as a tool to refute Christian Voice's claims that *Jerry Springer: The Opera* was, *in and of itself*, offensive.

In its closing section, *The Aristocrats* transcended its base subject material to become genuinely profound and emotional, and I think I took this unlikely transition as a challenge, eventually borne out in the closing stages of the *'90s Comedian* set. Viewers were softened up for the final sequence of *The Aristocrats* with a specially made *South Park* short, in which the animated toddlers describe a version of the vaudeville act where the perverted family run around impersonating the victims of the 9/11 disaster whilst covered in various bodily fluids. Next we go to a charity event filmed in New York three weeks after 9/11 itself. 'The shock of hearing the *South Park* bit makes us close to the state of the room when Gilbert Gottfried takes the stage at a Friars' Roast,' Provenza said. 'Inadvertently, we had somehow created our own third act of *The Aristocrats*. We had already shot Gilbert doing the Aristocrats joke in private three or four weeks before 9/11, so the joke was in his mind.'

Onstage, Gottfried's gag about taking an internal flight with a connection at the Empire State Building died. Someone shouts, 'Too soon.' 'You can see him stall,' remembers Provenza,

---

stools, Sean falls to his knees at the bowl and begins to pleasure himself. Sean must have made this story last ten minutes, and I was weeping with laughter, admittedly alone. Whenever I see him I always ask him about this bit and tell him it was the best thing he's ever done, apart from his BBC2 sitcom, and that he should do it again one day, which seems to irritate him no end.

and his fingers twitch, and then he decides to start the Aristocrats gag. He didn't plan to do it. There were no paradigms. But if you look at his face you can see him doing the math in the moment. He chose it for a reason. The room was full of comedy pros busting his ass for 'crossing the line'. And all around town the comedy clubs were closed and club owners were asking when it would be time for people to start laughing again. Gilbert was proving a point. The Aristocrats gag became a kind of safety rope. It was all about crossing the line. And he knew an audience of comedians would intuit the subtext. He was asking us when it's OK to laugh. The transgressive nature of the piece was the cathartic relief that everyone wanted after the confusion of 9/11.

Cutting between Gottfried's grinning face and the sight of people literally falling off their chairs laughing and gasping, in pain, for breath, *The Aristocrats* made a convincing case for absurdity as a logical response to tragedy. I wept, not tears of laughter, but tears of joy. I wept tears of joy watching a tiny man describe a family of four sexually and physically abusing each other, and any animals in the vicinity, in the name of entertainment. And after an hour and ten minutes of *The Aristocrats'* surgically precise analysis of how we are made to laugh, and why we laugh, I think I almost understood why.

In my mind, Provenza and Jillette's extended essay on the mutable nature of offence synced up immediately with all the spurious debates unravelling at home about the offensiveness of *Jerry Springer: The Opera*, which until now had been universally praised, even in the religious press. The nature of offence was not objective. It was essentially subjective. We are offended. You are offended. I am offended.

But is anything offensive *in and of itself*? In short, if a tree says 'fuck, cunt, abortion, piss' in a forest, and no one is there to hear it, is the tree offensive? And could there be any circumstances under which those words could even convey the opposite of offence, whatever that is? What delighted me about *The Aristocrats* was watching material which, on paper, should have been indefensibly obscene transformed by context and performance skills into something funny, something sometimes even moving or cathartic. There needed to be something of the flavour of this approach in whatever I chose to do onstage about the *Jerry Springer: The Opera* debacle.

Added to this, my bleeding arse, my orange piss, my contorted stomach, watching my blood bubble around the needle in the drip, feeling the cool saline fluid in my veins, suddenly losing and gaining and losing weight, feeling like a tube of screaming meat whose only purpose was to process the muck I ate and crap it out the other end, eating only potatoes, feeling the burn on my left side if I strayed to coffee or whisky or soft drinks, the mildly hallucinogenic vibe of my recovery period, the Scottish junkie I urinated on, the endless pressure on my weakened bladder through all those long car journeys on tour, and the wolfman's weeping sores, had made me acutely aware of the physical world, the pungent world, the world of flesh. I was poised to make something of it.

When the tour with Josie wound up, my good Edinburgh reviews wafted me away to four months of work in festivals and touring in Australia and New Zealand. In Melbourne no one really came to see me for a month, and I struggled to keep the set alive. But I did get to know the marvellous Mike Wilmot, whose show I went to see repeatedly because it moved me, and it shouldn't have done, being an evening

of dirty jokes capped with a very long routine about licking someone's anus. Just when you think you can't stand
hearing another middle-aged male comic moaning about
his marriage and how he can't please his wife any more,
along comes this Falstaffian Canadian, who can invest an
hour on these tired old subjects with unexpected levels of
humanity, surprise and inventiveness entirely absent from
the work of more self-consciously original comics. Mike's
act was knee-deep in filth, and every night he pretended
to need an extra beer because the gig was going so well at
exactly the same point, but all the time he was really talking,
from the heart, with utter sincerity, about what it meant to
be in love. On the bills of the pathetic Nasty Show, at the
Montreal Comedy Festival, Mike, a great artist, is annually
misfiled alongside the usual predictable American racists,
homophobes and misogynists, and yet this good-natured
honey-bear of a man seems not to mind at all, and just gets
on quietly with the business of rendering their noisy whin-
ing irrelevant.*

In Auckland I played a full 150-seater venue every night
for a month, The Classic, arguably a tie with The Stand in
Edinburgh for the world's most perfect stand-up room.
Late at night the same space was used for a club gig, where,
one evening, I was suddenly seized by the spirit of Phil
Nicol, who was out front hosting the show to a room full
of enthusiastically oiled punters. Phil is a total performer
who thinks nothing of beginning his shows naked and
screaming and then trying to move forward from there.

---

* Wilmot's been touring the same hour for about a decade now, on
and off, but it seems to me to be one of the all-time great routines.
It's not even on DVD anywhere, but anyone who thinks they love
comedy as an art form needs to see it.

He does not understand the notion of peaking too early. That night he was improvising wildly with the public, his shirt pulled up over his head so that he looked like a kind of stunted Weeble, swinging his arms, singing hillbilly folk songs, and gesturing repeatedly at his bottom. I forget why. Far away from home, cut adrift, if you like, I suddenly felt that everything I did seemed tame and trite and safe, and that it was my duty to just walk out and try to do something I had never done before, without a safety net. I had nothing to lose. No one knew me here anyway.*

I tried to jam an old routine I wrote in my early twenties about coming home drunk and being sick at my mum's house onto some kind of scatological encounter with Jesus, without any real planning. I don't really know why I decided to do this. I suspect I was subliminally under the influence of *The Aristocrats*, but I don't really remember what I did, or how I did it, or how it was received. It was late and I was probably drunk. But when it came to assembling the new stand-up show, I remembered that I had tried it, and suddenly it seemed that with some careful thought, it would be the perfect way of exploring the idea of religious offence.

After the Auckland festival was over I went on the road in New Zealand for a week in a package show, flying over vast forests and mountain ranges in tiny tin aircraft, and sweating in Maori hotsprings. I learned at the feet of the Australian Zen master of everyman observational comedy, Carl Barron, scored an out-of-print Penguin of Algernon

---

* That same week I had jumped off the highest building in the southern hemisphere on a rope, a decision which has since caused me to develop vertigo at the slightest hint of a drop. I was behaving with uncharacteristic daring and have regretted it ever since. That'll teach me.

Blackwood's *The Centaur* in an Oxfam bookshop on a deserted beach, and had a transcendental moment watching a psychedelic trio called Jakob in a student dive somewhere on the South Island. Then I travelled for a further two months in the same kind of set-up in Australia, backed by some kind of bung from the Australian equivalent of the Arts Council, which is just one woman in a floral-print headscarf, crying alone in an empty room. By the time I reached the Great Western Desert I felt like I was completely off the grid. We watched a Little Feat covers band in a Chinese gambling den somewhere in the middle of nowhere, genuflected to a statue of the Red Dog of Dampier, and played towns inhabited only by miners and strippers, where no live entertainment ever went and the only places you could get a drink were topless joints. Near Kalgoorlie we saw the biggest man-made hole in the world. 'This place is a hole,' said the cat impersonator Sam Simmons, with hilarious inevitability. Again, I felt far away and disconnected.

During a week of the package show in Perth, in a sold-out 1,000-seater variety theatre, I did my whole half-hour set from behind the curtain, with just my feet showing, as I improvised as many variations as I could think of on an old routine I had written fifteen years ago about arguing with a Jehovah's Witness. I was reckless. What had caused it? The threat of prosecution for *Jerry Springer*? Starting stand-up again and loving it? Jumping off the Auckland Sky Tower? Seeing *The Aristocrats*? Filling a bedpan with my own blood? Wondering, if only for a night or so, about dying? Being far from home for so long? Or eating only potatoes for five months? Whatever, I was not quite myself.*

* My onstage confidence was also increased dramatically by a pair

On a west coast layover at a little town called Exmouth, staying in a deserted American air-force base abandoned at speed after 9/11 and now a motel, we jumped out of a spotter boat to go swimming with forty-foot-long whale sharks as they migrated north. The eco-tourism guide got in the sea with us and shot footage on an underwater camera. The antipodeans, Frank Woodley and Jesse Griffin, were confident and graceful deep-water swimmers. I, our tour manager Edwina Lunn and the American comic Jackie Kashian weren't entirely at home. But I splashed alongside a whale shark all the same, even if I was spluttering through my snorkel. Months later, I received a DVD of the edited footage of us all cautiously trailing the mottled giants, set to a soundtrack of dance music and ambient house. That wasn't what I was hearing in my head. At one

---

of trousers I had found in Wellington in New Zealand. The Lee jeans company were experimenting, in the deep southern hemisphere, with a new trouser product, which sadly never made it out to Western civilisation as a whole, called the Stovepipe Jean. They looked like a kind of cross between power-pop skinny keks and a renaissance fool's leggings, and were made of a stretchy denim–rubber polymer. I was able to squeeze into the largest size, a 34-inch waist. Contrasted with my thickening belly and a pair of big boots, these superb trousers had the effect of making me look as if I hadn't realised I couldn't quite carry them off, and seemed, in my mind, to allow me a greater arrogance in my performance, as any supposed superiority was being undercut by my subtly inappropriate and quietly ridiculous trousers. The Stovepipe Jeans saw me through the whole '90s *Comedian* tour until my mother, taking it upon herself to sterilise my presumably smelly trousers in a hot wash without my permission during a weekend visit, somehow managed to dissolve them, and the already weakened gusset irreparably disintegrated. It proved impossible to replace the Lee Stovepipe Jeans, the production of which had been discontinued, but I think these trousers played a crucial role in helping me consolidate my clown.

133

point, I accidentally got above a whale shark in the water, which you're not supposed to do, and he just sank, as they warned us the whale sharks would, slowly, slowly, deeper and deeper, until he had disappeared into the dark. All I heard was a cold and beautiful silence.

On my last week on the road, like the sinking shark, I'd finally had enough of Australia. In Perth, I went to a record store to get the new album by Oasis, who I had never previously liked, and then I went to a British novelty shop and got some Bovril, which I had never previously drunk. I am sure there were things I should have been visiting in Perth – museums of genocide and islands full of rats. But I stayed in the hotel, listened to Oasis, drank Bovril and dreamed of England, where my heart lay. There was work to do at home.

At some point while I was away my management asked for a name for the show for Edinburgh. I called it *'90s Comedian* because it made me laugh, it being 2005, but as the set started to come together I wish I'd been able to give it a better name. *'90s Comedian* was looking like being one smooth through-line of a single story, drawn from the physical and mental traumas of the previous few months. If I fudged the dates of my stomach illness, I could blame it on the stress caused by persecution by the Christian right. Then I could use the invasive probing of my anus in the colonoscopy I was subsequently required by the hospital to endure as a way into the second half of the proposed show. And the second half of the show would be a version of the drunken religious encounter I had improvised under the influence of Phil Nicol and *The Aristocrats* onstage in Auckland, during which I planned to describe vomiting repeatedly on Christ, in an attempt to explore genuine limits of expression, rather than the imagined ones the

Christian right had extrapolated from exaggerated reports of the content of *Jerry Springer: The Opera*.

I did not conceive these two sections of the show as a Rorschach mirror image of each other, but I doubt that the second half of the show, in which I am invited by Jesus to use him as a receptacle for my vomit, would have worked so well, if at all, had I not chosen to show myself suffering my own rectal invasion, due to an illness exacerbated by pressure from the religious right, in the early stages of the piece. The gruesome subject material would also give me a chance to experiment with an aspect of *The Aristocrats* I'd enjoyed enormously, namely the notion that the piling up of obscenity might reach a point where it became transcendental, or even beautiful, and reveal the objections to our opera for what they were – subjective opinions about material which was inevitably altered by context and intent. But I also liked the fact that *The Aristocrats* was about comics talking about jokes, and I wanted to give people the same pleasure the film gave me, of letting us see behind the scenes of how a joke works. Even if the show was formed as one massive overarching idea, I still wanted it to be just a joke. I was newly proud to be a comedian once more. And whatever meanings might be laid on top of the show, I wanted to end it by reminding everyone that I was a stand-up comedian and this was a piece of stand-up comedy. Not a piece of theatre. Or an opera. Even if the arts editors of the *Guardian* and the *Independent* were suddenly fans.

It was a chance remark by the nurse who gave me that actual colonoscopy, soon after my return from Australia, which provided the structural device that allowed me to do all that I hoped to.

The behaviour of the doctor and nurses performing my

135

colonoscopy was so strange anyway that I was already filing it away for further use, but when the nurse said I couldn't possibly be a comedian, because a comedian should look funny, like Tommy Cooper, I realised I could lead into the stomach-illness story via the real colonoscopy story, and crank in a whole wedge of material I'd been sitting on for a decade, if I just pretended that, instead of Tommy Cooper, she'd said Joe Pasquale. For, if I could just crowbar my dormant Joe Pasquale bit into this story somehow, then I would have a show.

I'd been thinking about Joe Pasquale since 1995, ever since I wrote the following article for the *Sunday Times* Culture section.* But be warned: it describes a different and long-forgotten world, a world I described at the beginning of the book, where the possibility of 'alternative' comics crossing over to the mainstream was largely undreamed of, and where the idea of 'one of us' appearing in the Royal Variety Performance was ludicrous. Today, Michael McIntyre, Rhod Gilbert and Steven K. Amos have all achieved serious career boosts by doing just that, as has the Queen herself, who remains as popular as ever. Joe Pasquale, however, has just been fingered by Frank Skinner for stealing his roller-coaster routine on a poor new ITV stand-up show called *Comedy Rocks*.

> It is 1988 in some underground, underlit London comedy club. A prematurely aged Irishman stands onstage, dressed in a shabby long brown mac, all bloodhound eyes and a droopy Wild West moustache, and utters another in a beautifully understated seam of immaculate

* See also here how the twenty-six-year-old me, flattered to have been asked to write for a proper grown-up newspaper, is struggling self-consciously to write in a respectable journalistic voice.

one-liners. 'A lot of people say to me, "Hey you", pauses, makes almost imperceptibly small gesture of dismissal, '"what are you doing in my garden?"' The audience takes a couple of seconds to catch up, and then dissolves into hysterics.

The man is Michael Redmond. The joke defines him perfectly as an odd, outsider character and hints at a host of other weird situations as yet unrealised. For once, the audience is made to use its own imagination. There are no clues, or helpful pointers. The line has little in common with most of the material of the other 'alternative' stand-up comedians of the time; it doesn't ask us to share an experience, as when three of the same bus come at once; it doesn't contain any easy cultural signifiers, such as references to 1970s television or the forgotten play-ground rituals and newsagent confectionery of childhood; it isn't 'about' anything. The everyday phrase, 'hey you', is disrupted and made bizarre by being followed by the unexpected 'what are you doing in my garden'. It is, to invoke a now wasted phrase, a moment of pure comic genius. Of course, appearing in print does no justice to it; it relies on the nuances of performance.

I first heard the 'what are you doing in my garden' joke in 1987, when I was 19. My friend Terry, who had been to see a proper London comedy gig, did it in a student show and cheekily let everybody think it was his own. The next time I heard it was when I shared a bill with Michael Redmond himself, in 1989, trembling with nervous admiration. And I heard it for the last time just last month, when mainstream comic Joe Pasquale told it for the delight of the Queen and the Duke of Edinburgh at the Royal Variety Performance.

Pasquale's act that evening was a triumph, the

undoubted highlight of the show, and he worked the Dominion Theatre audience with a skill that made the huge venue seem intimate. Despite learning his trade on the mainstream circuit and working with scriptwriters rather than producing all his own material as most of the Alternative Comedians do, Pasquale feels he has more in common with the Goons than with the 1970s club acts such as Mike Read and Ben Elton's bête noir, Bernard Manning. He's looked past them to rediscover a delightful and engaging brand of Tommy Cooper-esque silliness that stretches way back to the last days of music-hall tradition. But Pasquale did use some material that seemed familiar, with lines and visual jokes similar to a number that have been performed by 'alternative' acts such as Martin Soan (a balloon-modelling bit involving a catwalk-style wearing of an uninflated balloon), Boothby Graffoe ('My girlfriend said, "I can't see you any more." I said, "I'm behind the settee."'), Arthur Smith (the 'I Know a Song That'll Get on Your Nerves' song) and, of course, Michael Redmond.

Soan, who says Pasquale also does a routine with a tiny voodoo doll of himself that's like one Soan made up in the 1980s, finds this upsetting. 'Thinking about it gives me the shivers. Not because I don't think Pasquale's any good, but because it's just depressing when you see him up there. But he may have done it entirely innocently.'

Historically, so-called 'alternative' comedians, with their post-punk aspirations towards some vain ideal of artistic integrity, have been as quick to demonise the old club-scene comics as amoral thieving magpies as the club-scene comics are to paint them as humourless middle-class lefties who wouldn't know a decent joke if they saw one. But now hostilities are ceasing and both camps sit comfortably alongside each other on *Gag Tag*, *Jack Dee's Saturday Night*, *Fantasy Football* and *Have I Got News for You*.

Traditionally, mainstream acts aren't precious about material in the way that their Alternative Comedy cousins are. To them, jokes are just jokes, naturally occurring phenomena, like wind or rain, resistant to the abstract notion of ownership. When London circuit comedian Nick Wilty found himself doing warm-up for Granada TV's special of the old mainstream show *The Comedians*, in 1993, one of the performers gave him a lift back to London. Entering the Blackwall Tunnel, the comedian said to Wilty: 'You had some good lines there, I can't wait to put them in my act.' 'He wasn't trying to hide anything,' remembers Wilty, 'he just genuinely had no idea that I'd be pissed off. He didn't appreciate that my material was written by me.' Backstage on *The Comedians*, the acts bicker about who is going to do which jokes and flip coins for the honour of performing any new gags that they've all heard.

The gag-writers who supply mainstream acts with their jokes obviously share this outlook. London clubs are regularly full of bit-writers and researchers scribbling down notes, and last November Stan Nelson, the floor manager of The Comedy Store, actually ejected a man who was surreptitiously taping the evening's performances. Pasquale, of course, uses writers, but said that he wouldn't wittingly use someone else's act. 'It's impossible to know where to stop, though,' he adds, 'you get so many people telling you jokes.' Ideally, routines as told by comedians, as opposed to jokes told by blokes in the pub and cab drivers, will reach a stage where they are impossible to plagiarise. In the year 2525, the futuristic supa-comedian in his silver suit will have developed an act so distinctive and steeped in his own individual specialised world view, that his lines would be incomprehensible in the mouth of anyone else, and we can see the beginning of this evolution in the work of Harry Hill, Simon Munnery and, er, Eddie Izzard. In the meantime, most jokes are still viewed as part of the public domain.

On the 'alternative' circuit the obvious fallacy of the spontaneous generation of material, authorless and fully formed, out of thin air, is vilified, and any duplication of material is seen as theft, even when it could realistically be mere coincidence. This is especially true of topical humour, dealing as it does in a limited range of personality or news-based observations. Most satire has a crushing air of inevitability about it. A member of The Comedy Store's 'Cutting Edge' team, a weekly news-events based show, told me *Spitting Image* had stolen his idea of Frank Bruno doing pantomime routines in a boxing ring. But there are thousands of people making a living out of topical humour in Britain today, and Frank Bruno is only known for two things: pantomimes and boxing. It wouldn't take an infinite number of monkeys to think of these two elements and come up with the same result. In fact, it would take two monkeys, perhaps sharing one typewriter.

Musical comedian Jim Tavare says he can remember the exact moment of the birth of 'what are you doing in my garden?' In the summer of 1987, he and Michael Redmond had been performing at the Screaming Beavers comedy club in Macclesfield and were staying at Tavare's parents' house in Prestbury. Looking out of the window while they were sitting in the lounge drinking tea, Jim, Michael and Jim's brother saw a distressed man running around in Jim's parents' garden. According to Jim, they rang the local mental hospital, who sent someone around to pick up the escapee. Later that evening, Redmond wrote his legendary gag. Redmond himself, however, has no memory whatsoever of this peculiar incident, which made such an impression on Tavare, but recalls the thought processes by which he arrived at the line. 'I'd been worrying at the idea for ages. I thought of "Hey, you, what are you doing in my kitchen?"' he says, 'but that seemed like too much of an invasion of privacy, too threatening. I changed it to "garden" and it worked.'

In contrast, Pasquale's manager Michael Vine says that, as far as he is concerned, 'a new gag is only a gag you haven't heard before'. With regard to 'what are you doing in my garden?', he says he 'associates the line with the public domain', and that it seems to suit Pasquale's bumbling innocent persona perfectly. It is true that when Pasquale and Redmond both tell the joke the image conjured up is quite different. On seeing Redmond in your garden you would think: 'Wow! A tired Jesse James is in my garden. Why?' On seeing Pasquale, you would think: 'Hey! There's Joe Pasquale from Thames TV's *He's Pasquale, I'm Walsh*. And he's in my garden! Whatever can he want?' As for Pasquale himself, he has an innocent explanation for how 'what are you doing in my garden?' found its way into his act. In 1993, he was playing Silly Billy in *Jack and the Beanstalk* in pantomime. Phil Nice, the former double-act partner of playwright Arthur Smith, was the pantomime dame. On discovering Silly Billy planting beans alone onstage, Nice would shout: 'Hey you! What are you doing in my garden?' The following year, Pasquale had the idea to use this line of dialogue as an actual gag in his Black-pool summer-season stand-up set. Coincidentally, the sound technician told him it was his favourite joke, and he had been entertaining his mates in the pub with it for years already, although even he didn't know where it had come from. And, after a day on the phone, vainly chasing the flickering spark of the creative imagination, I, too, was none the wiser, and what has become perhaps one of the most compelling mysteries of the 20th century must remain unsolved.

For me, hearing 'what are you doing in my garden?' for the first time opened up a vast world of potential comic possibility, of things that could be funny without really relating to anything, bypassing logic and satire, and crudity or stereotyping, and kitschy cultural references. Even Vine is moved to admit: 'It's just one of those lines, so simplistic. You think, "Why couldn't I have thought of that?"' Indeed.

And so, to any young comedians reading this, a warning. If you are sitting at your window at night, trying to find a better word than 'kitchen', and you see a figure in the garden, do not allow them to look at what you are writing. Just tap the window and say: 'Hey you . . .' (*Sunday Times*, 1995)

I realised that the structural framing device for this show, a single hour-long shaggy-dog story about anal investigation, religious persecution and a blasphemous physical encounter with Jesus, would be that the whole thing had been conceived as the joke that Joe Pasquale could not steal.

Now I had two months or so to write it and learn to try and perform it.

Pretty early on in the process I realised that it was crucial, despite the show climaxing in a long and explicit encounter with Jesus, not to use any swear words. It was too easy for critics of *Jerry Springer: The Opera* to use its language as a reason to attack its ideas. I would not be giving anyone that satisfaction. Also, I wanted to focus the audience on the thoughts and the images in the show in their most pure sense, not to try and smooth the path to laughs by using crude words for the things I was describing. In the closing section of the show I maintain that 'I vomited into the anus of Christ', and it was very important that I did so using those exact words, rather than any slang expressions. I wanted to focus the audience on the act and its meaning, rather than distracting them with rude words.

There was also sound creative logic in adopting this approach, for, as Cicero said, 'an indecency decently put is the thing we laugh at hardest'. Thus, I was disappointed when an unfavourable review of the show in the Brighton *Argus* in October 2005 said that I 'spent most of my time talking about puking into the arse of Jesus Christ', as I had deliberately gone out of my way not to do this and, moreover, had succeeded. 'Lee is supposed to be a groundbreaking comedian and writer, but I found little entertainment value in his material,' continued the writer.

> It was not funny. It was a sad and deliberate attempt to see how far he could go. This was the ultimate in sick humour, and if anyone thought it funny, they must be sick as well. Some members of the audience found it too much and walked out, including Brighton actress Carol Cleveland of Monty Python fame. She quipped: 'I am running out to find a doctor. This guy is sick and needs help.'

143

It wasn't a struggle to keep the work clean. On the whole I don't swear onstage anyway. That said, I am happy to use 'cunt', for example, as a swear word, as long as there is no risk of confusing the use of the word with a reference to a vagina, i.e. 'Richard Littlejohn is a cunt.' Sometimes I might say cock, as in 'wee out of a cock', if I were momentarily and obviously switching the register of my performance, and adopting the persona of a normal comedian, to try and get a normal joke to work, but on the whole, despite being the co-author of an opera supposedly containing 6,000 swear words (which it didn't, and the 170 that it did contain were all put there by the composer Richard Thomas anyway, who has turned his obsession with genitals and faeces into an art form), I prefer to use the scientific names for these things and avoid profanity. It also means people who want to complain about you have to work a bit harder to figure out why it is they are annoyed. I am sick of reading on *Daily Mail* message boards that I am 'one of these foul-mouthed modern comedians' when I am absolutely not. Honestly, who are these cunts?

My other worry with swearing onstage, in the most general terms, is that it is, creatively, something of a spent wad. Jerry Sadowitz, *Viz* comic, the composer Richard Thomas, Peter Cook, *The Thick of It*'s profanity consultant Ian Martin and the folk singer Beans on Toast, for example, are poets of swearing, and use the foulest of language with creativity and conviction. Peter Cook and Dudley Moore, playing critics discussing obscenity, satirised the belief in acclaimed artists' right to swear, a right denied to scummy comedians and other lowlife: 'An arsehole in Ralph Richardson's mouth comes out as pure gold . . .' they extemporise on Derek and Clive's *Ad Nauseam* album, 'and a prick in the hands of Pinter is a punctuation point, an epithet, a marvellous moment, the end of an extremely witty line . . . but a prick or a cunt in the hands of Cook and Moore is just a gratuitous prick or cunt.'*

I have no opposition to swearing in principle, though in recent years it has become fashionable amongst respectable comedians of a certain vintage to dislike it. In 2008, it appeared that Frank Skinner, the foul-mouthed Brummie comedian, a Rabelaisian alchemist of filth, had come out against swearing, inadvertently making him the subject of approving headlines in the worst kind of newspapers. Skinner is clearly gripped here by the same anxieties about his legacy that trouble Tony Blair, his chat shows being the equivalent here of Blair's decision to go into Iraq. But the TV millionaire's position on swearing was actually considered and nuanced. One would expect nothing less from a man whose belated and evangelical enthusiasm for the art form he once abandoned at the first opportunity has earned him, amongst younger comics, the nickname of 'The Old Wise Monkey'. As Skinner told the *Independent* newspaper in December 2008, 'I am a great champion of swearing, but I don't want Gordon Ramsay to spoil it for comedians. That would be terrible. Used properly, swearing really can be a beautiful thing.' Sadly, finely nuanced

---

* Ironically, the posthumous canonisation of Peter Cook has made him an artist fit to file alongside Pinter in the arts establishment, rather than the representative of the low culture of comedy he would perhaps have preferred to have been, so the satire here is skewed somewhat. And to be honest, even a 'cunt' in the hands of a cunt like Roy 'Chubby' Brown can still sometimes be a pretty funny cunt. But the chef-driven swearification of modern life does mean that these marvellous words have been robbed of some of their power now, and can sound lazy and desperate.

positions don't have a habit of translating over to the mass media very successfully, so Skinner's equivocal and thoughtful statement arrived in the collective conscious-ness transformed into a blanket opposition to swear-ing generally. 'Even Frank Skinner says there's too much swearing now,' summarised saloon-bar bores all around the country.

Skinner's 'Profanity Repudiation', a handwritten docu-ment The Old Wise Monkey famously nailed to the door of the BBC in full view of the ashamed heads of comedy and light entertainment, has since provided further ammuni-tion for the forces of evil to gag freedom of expression all over the world, silencing artists who speak out against oppression and crushing creative thinkers beneath the iron jackboots of censorship. As the gate clangs behind another prisoner of conscience in some repressive totalitarian regime, Frank Skinner's irresponsible comments on swear-ing mean he could not be more culpable if he himself were the jailer, laughing and delivering the final kick as his vic-tim is beaten senseless behind closed doors and left to rot in the dark.

I'm joking of course.

But having realised that I needed to eliminate all the bad words from the shocking story I was planning to inflict on the paying public, I was soon made to realise that I also needed to bleed out any bad feeling. The bruising encoun-ter with Jesus, it transpired, needed to happen, as in the transcript in the next section, 'at His insistence'.

The first time Bridget, my future wife, a practising Catholic and fellow comedian, saw me do this routine was after we had only known each other for a short while, at a club downstairs in a pub in Putney in July 2005. It was the second or third time I'd tried it. She didn't like it, and neither did a load of other people, who walked out. But we were supposed to be going out for some food, and she is nothing if not greedy, so she stayed. Afterwards, over a plate of hot offal, Bridget collected her thoughts enough to explain, rationally, what she didn't like about the material, saved me from making a terrible professional mistake, and handed me the keys to the most well-reviewed show I have ever written.

In my early passes at the piece, the encounter with Jesus was like an assault. And sometimes I even dragged His mother into it. I vomited on him, presumably against His will, as His complicity in the incident was never addressed. In real life I was furious with the religious right for messing up my life, professionally, emotionally, physically and financially, and I wanted to take it out on their spiritual figurehead. The early attempts at this bit were just me in a bad mood, trying to wreak a hollow revenge and losing sight of any artistic discipline in a splurge of scatological abuse.

But Bridget pointed out that the real Jesus would help me in my distressed state, because that was the kind of guy He was, and that He and I had to meet each other half-way. If I was attacking Jesus, the story wouldn't do what I wanted it to do. Thus, the Jesus in my story invites me to make use of Him, as if taking upon Himself the sins of those who have driven me to this state of drunkenness, and in so doing He proves Himself a better Jesus, a better God, than the vengeful tyrant posited by the religious right who had taken issue with our deeply humane opera.

Was it possible to write something which, when reduced to its content alone, would be impossibly offensive, featuring as it did a urine- and vomit-fuelled encounter between a drunk comedian and a holy figure in a cramped toilet, and yet to write and perform it in such a way that it became tender, moving and meaningful over and above the supposed taboo nature of its content alone? Where notional ideas of offence were concerned, could one conceive a piece that proved that intent and tone and context could make something more uplifting and ennobling than it was offensive and gratuitous, despite the apparently irredeemable nature of the events it portrayed? In short, if you felt our careful, theologically rigorous and kind-hearted opera was blasphemous, well, try this on for size, you twats, and – you know what? – I will still win on points. I will make meaningful religious art out of toilet filth, just to beat you. I will give you the Word made flesh.

Having got comfortable onstage again doing *Stand-Up Comedian* the previous year, and having made the odd bold stage move during my trek around the deserts of Australia, I also started to think more about how I could bend the physical parameters of the performance of stand-up, and yet still have the new show remain, recognisably, a stand-up show. The influence of many different performers and styles of performances had been nagging at me in my period off, and now I was ready to put them into practice.

In the autumn of 2003, I was taken on holiday by my then partner to the Corbières region of south-east France. We went for sun, sea and sand. But we got more. A whole lot more.

Having read nothing beyond a website about beaches, we didn't know that the Corbières, and the Cathar region further south-west, were rich in history, myth and folk culture. The French spend a lot of money preserving their rural traditions and national arts identity, and cinemas and radio stations are heavily loaded against English-language content. Both times I've visited the Corbières I've stumbled across some astonishing site-specific musical or theatrical performances of clearly commercially non-viable shows, propped up financially by regional government in the belief that they are culturally necessary. In 2004, I saw a show by a big burly man, who looked like Julian Barratt from The Mighty Boosh, playing a bagpipe made out of the untreated carcass of a pig from the pulpit of a church in an isolated mountainside village, while his female partner clowned around in the aisles, Noel Fielding style, in a red hat, which was by turns hilarious and moving. In 2003, despite my initial reservations, we followed a troupe of state-subsidised drama-student types pretending to be the mentally and physically handicapped outcasts of medieval French society, as they loped through the labyrinthine alleyways and squares of a tiny mountaintop citadel, causing licensed mischief in the twilight. The event was called Bouffinades en Circulades and was staged every night for two weeks in September in different little rural villages, and appeared to recreate a medieval tradition where the village's social rejects were allowed, for one night only, to run free and mock the core values of their superiors. The French clowning master and revered theatrical theorist Jacques Lecoq, whose shadow hangs heavily over loads of polo-necked types who studied physical theatre in the eighties anywhere in Europe, repopularised the forgotten term 'bouffon' to describe the physical embodiment of 'mockery' in clowning and theatre in the early sixties.

In the village we followed the bouffons from house to house, from square to square, from business to business, and outside each one they would stage a semi-improvised sketch, an especially beautiful one being something to do with animals in the stable of a farm building, where they were all lit by flickering candles. Outside the butcher's the bouffons mocked the butcher, outside the baker's they mocked the baker, and outside the town hall they mocked the mayor, all in a variety of costumes, declaiming comic verse in French which we were unfortunately too ignorant to understand. But outside the church, even the licentious bouffons were cautious. A circle was drawn in the dirt before the church and the performers huddled inside it, dressed as bishops and priests, waving crucifixes, and an audible frisson rippled through the audience.

I was thrilled, not in some adolescent way, about to enjoy a gratuitous mockery of religion, but because something essential about what stand-up was had suddenly, by association, become clear. The bouffons were in a charmed circle, perhaps under the protection of serpents, in a sacred and clearly delineated space where they were free to work their magic without interference. The director of *The Aristocrats*, Paul Provenza, once told me he saw the stage of a stand-up club as a giant pair of inverted commas, framing the performer, saying 'what is being said here is only being said, not actually done, so judge it accordingly'. Could there be any clearer image for the special privileges of the comedian than this moment, where the clowns marked out their own unassailable territory in the very shadow of the church, the great forbidder that binds with briars our joys and desires?

I'm eternally grateful for the combination of chance, coincidence, French regional-arts funding and my then girlfriend's instinctive theatrical good taste that allowed me to witness that moment. It made me certain of something, convinced me that I was on the right track, and I'm not sure what I'd be doing now had I not encountered it. Like seeing Ted Chippington open for The Fall in 1984, this was, twenty years later, an absolutely key moment for me as a comedian. I could do anything I wanted. I was in a charmed circle.

But as well as the supposed intellectual theory behind the bouffons' show, the spatial relations of the performance also excited me. Like the Native American Pueblo clowns of the Hopi, the Zuni and the Tewa, of whom I had read much but never been fortunate enough to see, even these drama-student bouffons broke through the safety barriers between audience and performer, using the whole village as their stage. You never knew where they were coming from next. Because they were actors, not the anointed clown mystics of the Hopi or the genuine outcasts the medieval French bouffons would have been, it never felt truly dangerous, but the performance did have a relationship, I realised, with moments when I'd seen performers closer to home blur the edge of the space. And the periods when I left the stage and wandered around the room in *'90s Comedian* were perhaps most indebted to the influence of a strange incompatible trio of a roly-poly funnyman, an acid-fried archaeologist and a Russian physical-theatre group.

Johnny Vegas, for me, is a massively misunderstood talent. I love him (see Appendix IV). In August 2003, Vegas had been given a budget to make a live DVD, but instead got me to direct an attempt to improvise a story about the Edinburgh Fringe, with live stand-up comedy inserts, called *Who's Ready for Ice Cream?*. The cast, by their own admission, all had mental problems. And the only one who didn't wasn't an actor. He was an ice-cream man that Johnny had met in a park, though having been cast as an ice-cream man, he delivered a consistent performance. The crew seemed to hate me, imagining that I thought I was above them because I had recently worked at the National Theatre, and my time on *Who's Ready for Ice Cream?* is honestly the only occasion in my career when I have failed to win the confidence of the team working under me. And, because most of the people involved were from St Helen's, the entire catering budget was spent on chips and gravy and fags, so that everyone had scurvy by the end of the week's guerrilla-style shoot. That said, the live footage is great, and I used it as the template for all the live footage of myself subsequently shot for DVDs and BBC2 as I became more popular.

When Johnny would leave the stage and wander around the tiny rooms we filmed the live shows in, begging for affection and attention, close-up and personal, it created a crazed panic and tension. The literal boundaries of the stage itself had been abandoned, so were there any rules left? I met the American theatre director Peter Sellars at a theatre conference in Limerick in 2006. He said he had enjoyed *Jerry Springer: The Opera* because of the way 'it introduced air into an airless room', and he felt that this was a key to making theatre. Stand-up is already a fairly well-ventilated form. Was it possible to open the windows a little wider?

The following year, I saw the rock-star survivor and sometime archaeologist Julian Cope play a psychedelic hard-rock set with his band Brain Donor at the Hammersmith Lyric. Cope, clad in full face paint, camouflage fatigues, flying helmet and platform boots, left the stage for around twenty minutes to patrol the auditorium, stalls, circle and balcony, singing on a radio mic during one extended two-chord drone, often entirely invisible to the majority of the audience and largely unlit. But just knowing that he was in the room, not on the stage where the performer should be, made the whole performance terribly and terrifyingly exciting. At any moment, the madman – and Cope often seems genuinely mad – might creep up behind you. I wondered if there was some way of mainlining this manic thrill into stand-up, and now that I get to play theatres with circles and balconies I am always on the look-out for the opportunity to make a Julian Cope-style foray into the audience. In the little rooms and on the low stages I was playing with '90s Comedian, making this conceptual leap into the dark usually meant just stepping 30cm downwards.

And in the summer of 2002, I went to see a show called Inferno by the Russian physical-theatre group Derevo. It was in a circus tent in a meadow in the north of Edinburgh, and in amongst a series of beautiful set pieces there was a sequence where some deranged hobo figures, not unlike the bouffons of the Corbières or the Pueblo clowns I'd read about, worked their way around the crowd, singing to them in Russian, sharing bread and wine with different individuals and communicating with wordless grunts. I became obsessed with the free nature of this section, within an otherwise tautly choreographed piece, and of the breathing space it seemed to provide. I went five times in all to try and see Inferno from every angle, to try and fix it and nail it in my mind and decode it. But I couldn't. It was different every night, as different as the responses of the people Derevo approached to join their crazy party could make it. I realised this was what it meant to attend a genuinely live event, and the off-mic improvisations that have been in all my subsequent shows were an attempt to bleed a little of this, and Johnny's unpredictable artistry, and Julian Cope's panic-inducing presence, into the airless rooms I perform in.*

Again, on some level, I think this approach was a reaction to my experience of the world of commercial theatre. 'Let's see the money on the stage,' the financiers of the West End say, meaning massed ranks of tap-dancers, holograms of Laurence Olivier and gigantic swinging chandeliers. But stand-up's strength, it seemed to me, was in its power to suggest, by spoken word alone, the most vivid pictures. So, how about not even being on the stage at all and giving people nothing to look at? The communal experience of being in the room was still exciting, because somewhere I was crouched down, hidden in the dark, mumbling, crying and masturbating.†

* It's also worth mentioning that the fourth stand-up I ever saw live, after Peter Richardson, Phill Jupitus and Ted Chippington, was Oscar McLennan. In the early days of Alternative Comedy, McLennan was a minor player on the circuit, and I saw him at Warwick Arts Centre in 1985, touring a confrontational and compelling, but largely laugh-free, stand-up show about a dysfunctional family, before he finally abandoned comedy and recategorised himself as a performance artist, having produced much fine work since. I remember McLennan, thin and wiry, rolling on the floor at the edge of the studio space, lit by a low-level light in semi-darkness, snapping at the feet of the front row, while a song by the psychobilly band Turkey Bones and the Wild Dogs blared. Looking back at some of my recent stand-up, I think the memory of McLennan was simmering inside all along.
† I had become a great fan of the idea of the empty stage, having always liked the empty frame in television and film. When I script-edited Harry Hill's three Channel 4 series in the late nineties, our director was Robin Nash, a bow tie-sporting septuagenarian who had been producing and directing classic BBC light-entertainment shows since the war, and who was a perfect fit for Harry's faux vaudevillian aesthetic, approaching it without any sense of hipster

*

Reading *'90s Comedian* again, with the benefit of hind-sight, the repetition of the phrases, the language and the measured tone in which it was performed give it an almost liturgical quality, and I suspect this is not just coincidence. First of all, it makes sense to address the subject material, Jesus, in a manner in which He is normally discussed. And secondly, I was in a church choir from 1975 to 1980, a posi-tion which enabled me to go to the local C of E school with all the proper middle-class children and become educa-tionally privileged, and during this time I sat through at least three services a week of High Anglican ceremony,

---

irony and just doing the best possible job he could with the mater-ial. Now, we loved an empty frame, a sketch that ended with the protagonists leaving the set, but Robin simply would not have it as it flew in the face of everything he held dear about television. 'Tele-vision is about moving pictures!' he would insist. But, in a milieu like television where you are supposed to be looking at something happening, or in a stand-up gig where you expect there to be some-one on the stage, sometimes the most powerful thing you can do is nothing.

Robin's rules of light entertainment were an education in them-selves, and having worked with him for three years I felt that I could now break them in future with the full knowledge of what I had chosen to do, and I am very grateful to him for that. Another one of his pet hates was any item longer than three minutes. He had been schooled in variety and simply would not have it. 'But', I countered one day, throwing one of his own anecdotes back in his face, 'you were the producer of *Top of the Pops* when Queen were number one with "Bohemian Rhapsody", and they all slept at your flat, and that song is about six minutes and presumably you let them do that.' 'I did,' admitted Robin, 'but I allowed them to perform half of the song each week on subsequent weeks.' As far as Robin Nash was concerned, this milestone of pop history was, quite simply, 'too long, dear!'

sometimes more. To this day I can remember the exact into-nation of the respective priests as they struggled, week after week, to inject meaning into the words they were obliged to repeat again and again. Canon Raymond Wilkinson, the oldest priest, was the best, and sometimes the choirboys in their pews would tear themselves away from their Michael Moorcock and Isaac Asimov paperbacks to enjoy the high drama of the ceremony. I must have listened to the Com-munion ritual at least five hundred times during my sen-tence in the choir. It wouldn't be too much of a stretch to suggest that some of it went in and shaped the way I look at the world, despite some sour experiences.

I suspect, reluctantly, that the actual business of being a priest isn't that different in some ways to the business of being a comedian. My wife took me to her church in Gloucester. I always listen to the way the sermons are pitched with interest. It was a mixed audience – old Irish fellers, lots of displaced Filipinos, Poles, general Catholic diaspora, many without English as a first language. Tough crowd. And the Father's out of the pulpit, down in the aisle, shouting, jumping around, working the room. The priest that did our marriage course in Stoke Newington faced a similar problem of playing to an incredibly varied demo-graphic. His approach was to speak softly and calmly about some incident or personal story that seemed a million miles away from religion, then, having drawn the punters in, to clobber them with a theological right hook. Most priests are rubbish performers, though, and one wonders how an organisation as wealthy as the Catholic Church, for example, can't spare some money to school the poor sods in a few basics of stagecraft. That said, the good ones are an inspiration, and let's not forget a lot of them are turning over a new twenty minutes every week, which makes even the stalwarts of The Comedy Store's Cutting Edge team look lazy.

Comparisons between comedians and priests are a cliché of comedy criticism. 'Bill Hicks was more than a comedian, he was a preacher,' offers some fuzz-faced pothead loser on every documentary you've ever seen about the self-styled 'Shiva the Destroyer' of stand-up. Why is a preacher 'more' than a comedian? Why are comedians regarded as being so low in status that the most flattering thing you can do is compare them favourably to almost any other form of performer, public figure or artist? Out in the provinces, beyond the citadel of theatre, the stand-up comedians that pitch up to council-funded venues round the country are actually the closest thing punters there get to experiencing real art. In the first three months of 2010, when I was on the road, the only shows in places like the Beck Theatre, Hayes, or the Millfield Theatre, Edmonton, that weren't hypnotists, mediums or tribute bands were me, Rhod Gilbert and Jo Caulfield: comedians. The only shows that contained original material, any form of authorial voice, had anything to say or explored on even the most basic level any degree of theatre practice were the stand-up shows.*

When I was working on *Jerry Springer: The Opera* at the National Theatre, Nicholas Hytner called Richard Thomas and me in to discuss his anxieties about the end of

---

* The comedian Simon Munnery, who invented top-selling computer games for the ZX81 whilst still a teenager, was reviewed, favourably, by the *Guardian* recently as 'the closest stand-up comedy gets to art', and has pointed out himself that this suggests that however good stand-up gets, it can never really be art. There is an impassable canyon between the two. Munnery has since decided that rather than it being good comedy, he now wants his work to be categorised as 'shit art'.

the first act, which he didn't feel was working. 'You have to stop thinking like comedians,' he said, his apparently endless patience finally exhausted, 'and start thinking like theatre practitioners.' It was a slip of the tongue that serves as a reminder of our status. In the world of the arts, a comedian, despite all the skills they pick up in the harshest environments, is never more than 'trade'. But by the time I'd finished *'90s Comedian*, I realised I was more than happy with that.

'90s Comedian debuted at the Edinburgh Fringe in August 2005 and became the show that gave me a career and convinced me that, while stand-up's sandy coastline was clearly mapped, its uncharted interior still hid vast swathes of fertile territory. There was a lifetime in this. Thinking like a comedian meant, as The Goodies told us decades ago, you could do anything, anytime, anywhere. Leave me here, all you legitimate artists, at the tradesman's entrance, with my can of lager and my notebook. I can draw a magic circle all around myself and do whatever I want. I am a stand-up comedian. You can't touch this!

3

'90s Comedian

A transcript of the show recorded on 10 March 2006
at Chapter Arts, Canton, Cardiff

PRE-SHOW MUSIC: MILES DAVIS'S *KIND OF BLUE**

* For all performances of *'90s Comedian*, the music played in the venue before the show was Miles Davis's album *Kind of Blue*. The flamboyant composer Richard Thomas, of *Jerry Springer: The Opera* infamy, and the insolent comedian Simon Munnery, from Watford, got me to listen to this album in the mid-nineties, when they used it as walk-in music for our Dadaist Edinburgh Fringe cabaret show, Cluub Zarathustra. Richard would argue that anyone, from any-where in the universe at any point in time, would find *Kind of Blue* beautiful, and tried to employ it as a yardstick of objective artistic values. Simon, on a more practical level, just used to keep playing it, The Clash's 'White Man in Hammersmith Palais' and Bob Dylan's 'She's Your Lover Now' over and over again, late at night, when I tried to sleep on his filthy floor during a lengthy period of sporadic homelessness, until I accepted that all three were masterpieces just so as to stop his damned dancing.

The *'90s Comedian* set culminated in a half-hour section which, on paper, seemed deliberately and unjustifiably shocking, but my aim, as explained in the previous chapter, was to offer this mater-ial up, not brayed at full volume as if it were intended to horrify, but calmly and quietly, without any apparent gloss, as if for your contemplative consideration. Thus, *Kind of Blue*'s narcoleptic calm seemed utterly appropriate, hopefully chilling the audience, rather than working them towards a frenzy. Also, the album has this air about it – sometimes it seems sinister, sometimes romantic, some-times cold and deathly, other times warm and fuzzy – and you realise Miles Davis and company somehow created this variable emotional space, ready to be shaped in infinite ways by the ear of the beholder.

I wanted the last half hour of '90s *Comedian* to have the same kind of take-it-or-leave-it, unforced emptiness, so that what you chose to carry away from it – offence, comfort, shock, warmth, hate, love – was up to you. Don't imagine for a moment here that I am arrogant enough to be making a case for '90s *Comedian* being a masterpiece of the calibre of *Kind of Blue*. I am not. That is for others to say, such as the cyber-critic Steven Bennett, head honcho of the Chortle website and the Val Wilmer of the London open-mic circuit, who named it the greatest stand-up show of the noughties. But he is merely an expert.

Again, it was probably a reaction against aspects of the commercial staging of *Jerry Springer: The Opera* that lodged this take-it-or-leave-it approach in my subconscious. When Richard Thomas's songs were arranged and underscored by professional, commercial musical-theatre arrangers, hot from *Mamma Mia!* and such like, they necessarily made interpretive choices about the intent of the material, scoring a lyric that could have been taken as ironic, sincere, delusional or triumphant with a musical-theatre texture, such as kitsch strings or jolly staccato guitar. *Kind of Blue* allows and encourages you, in its glacial space, to decide for yourself how you are going to respond to it. For me, it was an antidote to the shouty certainties of musical theatre and mainstream stand-up, with its funny faces and jokes.

The Go Faster Stripe recording of the show had no money to clear existing music, but we needed something on the titles for the DVD. What you hear there is a recording of a little jam I'd done on bass and guitar, with Al 'The Pub Landlord' Murray on drums, in about 2001, when we were toying with reconvening my vain sub-Dream Syndicate guitar-drone band, which had played all of three gigs more than a decade previously. Jim Version, of the groups Delicate AWOL and Tells, dubbed it up with some spot effects on a desk at Moat Studios, Stockwell, where the free-jazz improviser Derek Bailey recorded and where various shoddy *Doctor Who* audio dramas were produced. He and Al allowed us to use it as intro music on the DVD for no charge. The choice doesn't mean anything. It was simply the cheapest music available.

160

VOICE OFF: Please, ladies and gentlemen, welcome onto the stage Mr Stewart Lee!*

Thank you. Ah. It's great to be back.†

Um. Now, I'm going to, I'm going to tell you a story, right, it'll take about, um, an hour and fifteen minutes, er, which is sort of a bit too long for a show without an interval. But it's also not long enough to split into two halves. It's kind of disappointing either way. But it is a little bit too long, so if you need to go for a wee during that, you can do that and I'm not the sort of person that picks on anyone. Also, if you become bored or irritated, er, you can also go. Likewise, if you're watching this at home on a DVD and you need to go for a wee, you can just pause it and you can go and I'll have no problem with that. I

---

* Most times I performed this show I would come out in the dark and, before speaking, draw a bouffon-style circle, as described in the previous chapter, around the stage in chalk, which I would then not refer to until much later in the show. Then I'd bring the lights up and try and launch into the show in an upbeat showbiz style entirely at odds with the borderline performance-art gesture we had just seen. The show transcribed here was recorded in a venue where the angles of the stage and the seats meant no one would have seen the circle if I'd drawn it at the beginning, so I had to wait and make a point of doing it in full view later on. Strangely, as I entered the more uncomfortable areas of the show I did feel safer for having the circle around me, and sometimes I would dare myself to step outside it at key moments, as if to test my invulnerability.

† This gets a laugh at the Cardiff taping. I'm not sure why. Maybe, as I said, it's because it was an odd, *Sunday Night at the London Palladium* thing to say having just drawn a chalk circle in the dark. Or maybe it's because this is a transcription of the second run at the recording, and the audience knew I'd already done the same set in the same venue once that day already.

won't even know that it's happening, literally.*

Um, so. This is a story about a load of stuff that happened to me last year. Now, on, um, Thursday 7th July – 7/7† – I woke up in London . . . at about midday, and already I can sense people going, yeah, course you did, Stew, you slept through that major news event because you are a lazy stand-up comedian, right, but that's not strictly true. What happened was I didn't get in till about half past three the night before because I'd been driving back from Lincoln, where I'd been doing what was optimistically billed as an Edinburgh Fringe warm-up gig, right? And what happened in Lincoln was I went out in this little club, about sixty people, and before I could say anything a guy down on my left had made the noise of an animal, which I correctly identified as being a sheep, right. To try and nip that in the bud, to try and stop it from building, I said, 'A sheep there. And any other noises of any other animals you want to make, I will be able to identify correctly.' But what happened was that the people of Lincoln took that as an invitation to spend the next thirty-five, forty minutes

* This is a terrible introduction to a show, but looking back on it, there's a sort of point to it. Received wisdom says, 'Open with your best line,' but this waffle has the effect of putting the audience at their ease and saying that this isn't going to be a laugh-a-second, or a confrontational, set. I wanted to relieve the punters of the obligation to laugh, I suppose, and hope that they'd laugh anyway. This tour was booked into some comedy clubs, some arts centres and some theatres, so you had to flag up that it was a long piece in case people were expecting a club-paced set, and I wanted to try and stake out the space as mine.
† In the vapour trail of the 7 July bus and Tube bombs simply saying '7/7', like the phrase '9/11', had a chilling effect on a room, which created a real tension and focused the audience, especially off the back of the deliberately sloppy opening.

162

making the noises of increasingly complex and obscure animals, all of which I was able to identify correctly. Until, by about half past ten, I'd started to wonder if I'd perhaps been wrongly advertised as being a man that would come from London, the city, and correctly identify the animals of Lincolnshire from their sounds alone, in case the people of Lincoln didn't know what we called them.*

But eventually all that subsided, and I thought, 'Right, I'll get on with my ace new stuff now.' But before I could do that, a guy down on the right with long curly hair and little round glasses, he started shouting out catchphrases from a television programme I did eleven years ago that as a rule most people have forgotten, right.† So I had to

---

* This story is entirely true, except that the animal-noises section of the evening probably lasted about twenty minutes, not forty. I exaggerated for comic effect. Again, I am indebted to Australia's Ned Kelly of comedy, Greg Fleet, here, with his brilliant ability to make up routines about the telling of routines, such as the shark-death routine mentioned earlier. But I'd also been listening to Lenny Bruce's 'The Palladium', a twenty-minute bit in which he tells the same story three times to three different audiences under three different sets of circumstances with three different results. Bruce is, sadly, remembered only for his superficially shocking subjects, but his restless formal experimentation also prefigures every supposed advance we've made in stand-up since.

† The catchphrase was 'Moon on a stick!' from the second, disappointing series of BBC2's *Fist of Fun*, from 1996, nearly ten years earlier. In *Fist of Fun*, in which I was very much the Syd Little of the Lee and Herring double act, I was always described by Richard Herring as wanting the moon on a stick, a metaphor for having unreasonably high explanations and a phrase that is still often yelled at me out of passing cars to this day. In the last episode of the series I was given a huge moon on a stick by Herring, about fifty feet in diameter, which I denied ever having wanted.

Soon after this, *This Morning*'s Judy Finnigan, clearly grumpy at

explain to the other confused fifty-nine people in the room that I used to do this thing in 1995 that used to get two million viewers, and then they started to feel like they were watching a performer in decline. OK, so, that's why I got in late on Wednesday the 6th of July, woke up late Thursday the 7th of July.*

And the first thing I did on 7/7 when I woke up was I checked all my emails, right. And the first one in was from an American comic called Jackie Kashian that I'd worked with in Perth in June. And it was just one line, it just said, 'Are you all right?' So I emailed back, 'Yes, fine thanks, how are you?' And the next one was from a New Zealand comic called Ben Hurley who I'd worked with in Auckland in May, same thing, one line, 'Are you all right?' So I emailed back, 'Yes, fine thanks, how are you?' There

---

being forced to have us on her show, was obligated to introduce a clip of this sequence during a TV interview. With hollow and weary eyes, Finnigan turned to us, looking sickened and bored like a hot and bothered polar bear in a rundown Soviet zoo, and said, 'It's comedy about nothing really, isn't it, your stuff?' – a quote we subsequently and delightedly used on posters.

* Being a sometimes beloved but essentially obscure cult figure has enough drawbacks to make me realise I would never be able to cope with actual fame. Even in 2005, there'd always be a tiny minority of an audience who were audibly thrilled to see me, and their excitement made the people who were in the room but didn't know me at all feel resentful, as if they had been judged for not being up to speed. To this day, in a pub, for example, someone will very occasionally come out of a dark corner and ask me for my autograph. Then other people, usually men at the bar, become enraged somehow that they do not know who I am, and begin to say, 'Are you famous then? Why haven't I heard of you?' in a threatening way, as if I have deliberately orchestrated the whole embarrassing encounter just to annoy them.

was about fifteen more, all saying, 'Are you all right?'
Then I checked my text messages, there was about twenty
there, from all over Britain, all over the world, from Roger
in Canada, Graham in the Philippines, Jess in New York,
all saying 'Are you all right?' 'Are you all right?' 'Are you all
right?' 'Are you all right?' 'Are you all right?' 'Are you all
right?' 'Are you all right?' 'Are you all right?' 'Are you all
right?' 'Are you all right?' 'Are you all right?' 'Are you all
right?' 'Are you all right?' 'Are you all right?' 'Are you all
right?'*

Now, as you may or may not know, I did have quite a
difficult year. Um. I had to go into hospital in February.†
I've also been going a bit deaf.‡ And in January, because
I was the director of the controversial theatre piece *Jerry
Springer: The Opera*, I became the co-focus of a hate campaign led by 65,000 right-wing born-again Christians . . .
resulting in the threat of prosecution in the High Court
for blasphemy and the collapse of four years of work into

* All these enquiries were true. I found if I repeated 'Are you all
right' enough times, with enough conviction, then the switch into
the sentence 'Now, as you may or may not know, I did have quite a
difficult year' would get a big laugh. I think this was mainly because
elements of my life, namely my harassment alongside *Jerry Springer:
The Opera*'s composer Richard Thomas by the religious right, had
become a top national news story, and one that most comedy audiences were aware of. Thus, the laugh here is coming from an understatement, from what isn't said. When your life becomes a news
story that everyone knows about, you can use it as an unspoken
punchline.
† Diverticulitis.
‡ Tinnitus. Hyperacusis. The specialist said, 'Some frequencies are
gone. You may experience difficulty hearing the voices of women.'
If I were a different kind of comedian, there would definitely be a
routine in this unintentionally ambivalent sentence.

financial non-viability. So it had been a difficult year.* And while I was touched that all of my friends had chosen to enquire after my welfare, it did seem strange that they had all chosen the same morning to do that, right.†

So like I said, I had to go into hospital in February, right. I had this thing called diverticulitis, right. That's where your stomach starts to kind of poison you. Normally, only very old people get it, but if you've been a stand-up comedian for seventeen years, drinking heavily and eating mainly Ginsters pies in the night, erm, that can move it on, right. So I had to go into hospital in North London, and while I was in there, I had to have an endoscopy, right. That's where they insert a camera on a fibre-optic tube into your anus.‡ Now, on that occasion, Cardiff, it was my anus. But it would be your anus§ if it were you that were under-

* Understatement.
† This is true.
‡ This procedure is actually called a colonoscopy. But 'endoscopy' always seemed to work better onstage, perhaps because it didn't include the telegraphing prefix 'colon'.
§ Here I stress the words 'your anus' so that it sounds as if I am going to make some old wordplay gag about 'your anus' and Uranus, the celestial body. But then I don't do that, so there's a suggestion of a set-up for a feeble joke that is never even delivered. As I was saying these words I always had at the back of my mind an incredible and bizarre geography lesson, which I was not even in, but which had become legendary at our school.

A beloved but slightly camp geography teacher asked the class wag, a tall and beautifully eloquent black boy, to identify a South American country on the blackboard. 'Uruguay,' said the boy, but pronounced it 'You're a gay.' The class laughed. 'I think you'll find it's Uruguay,' said the teacher. 'No, sir,' said the wit, 'I think you'll find you're a gay.'

This is an example of the pathetic genius of teenage boys, for whom no situation is too contrived to serve as a launch pad for

going the endoscopy, right, because in medical science as a rule there's a direct relation between who is the subject of a procedure and the information that the doctors are trying to find out. That's why you can't send a friend along instead. OK? Even if they really love investigative surgery, er, it has to be you. So . . . It's frivolous, anything else . . .

So I was being wheeled in there, and I was lying on a slab, and I was naked except for this kind of third-length, floral-print hospital gown, right. Goes down to about there. Now, I've never understood the design of them, because as a man, right, I'm not ashamed of my breasts, OK? What I want concealed are my genitals: my penis, my two testicles.* They're the source of my shame. But the design of

---

some idiotic and offensive piece of wordplay, and it is a mindset I continually try to channel in order to offset my natural tendency towards incredible comic sophistication and maturity. Remember when you were thirteen and you ran as fast as you could just because you could run fast? Remember when you were thirteen and your first pint of cider tasted of all your tomorrows yet to be? Remember when you were thirteen and you always pronounced Uruguay as 'you're a gay', just for the sheer pleasure of it, just to show that you were free from Their Rules?

* I enjoyed saying 'penis' and 'testicles' here, instead of 'cock' and 'balls'. Sometimes I would say 'my testicles. My *two* testicles', but only if the room was cooking, obviously. Now that even children's TV presenters are free to say 'cock' and 'balls' with impunity, or at least imply them with their tight figure-hugging garments, it seems much funnier anyway to say 'penis' and 'testicles'. And how much more vulnerable do the stringy 'testicles' and the floppy 'penis' sound than the consonant-crowned 'cock' and 'balls'? There's no shame in having a cock, in having balls. But having a penis and some testicles sounds awful, like an ailment, or as if a deep-sea eel and some dangly pasta have been unceremoniously stapled to a man's groin, before he is forced to dance naked in front of a Liverpudlian hen party in a subterranean Greek restaurant.

the third-length, floral-print hospital gown makes it look as if I've chosen to expose them. In a coquettish fashion.* Which I would never do, I wouldn't do that.

So I was being wheeled in there, I was lying on a slab, and I was naked except for this kind of third-length, floral-print hospital gown. And I had a fibre-optic tube inserted into my lubricated anus. And then suddenly out of nowhere, and this is true, the doctor said, 'Oh, I see from your notes that you're a famous comedian.' And I said to him, 'There's a problem with that sentence, isn't there, Doctor? Which is that if the phrase "You are a famous comedian" is preceded by the qualifying phrase, "I see from your notes . . ." then I'm not, and I'm not anyway, really.'† And then the nurse interrupted rather aggressively. She went, 'Well, I've never heard of you,' as if it were I that had arrogantly introduced this vain notion into the endoscopic procedure, which was

---

* What a great word 'coquettish' is. I wish I could claim to have thought of using it myself, but I think I have leeched it from Richard Herring, whom I seem to remember using the word in an unexpected context in one of his shows, and who has a great feel for the untapped comic value of such unusual words, as befits a man who spent most of the nineties playing Scrabble against himself and weeping.

† The doctor did say that my notes said I was 'a famous comedian', but I didn't make the witty reply above. I just said I wasn't. Comedy is all about timing, and sadly my witty responses to things are usually thought of days, weeks, even years later. As John Hegley concludes in his poem 'The Stand-Up Comedian Sits Down', 'the comedian comes up with the line so apt and incisive/ that any further heckling is redundant/ unfortunately he comes up with it on the bus home'. I hope that asking someone undergoing a colonoscopy if they are a famous comedian was a deliberate attempt to distract me from the pain in my small anus, rather than just being an incredibly inappropriate thing to do at a very personal moment.

not the case. I hadn't done.* So I said to her, 'Well, I am a comedian.' And she said, 'Well, you don't look like a comedian.' And I said, 'Why?' And she said, 'A comedian should look funny.'†

Now, at the time I was lying naked on a slab in a third-length, floral-print hospital gown, with a fibre-optic tube inserted into my lubricated anus. If I'd seen that, I would have laughed. But I suppose if you work in endoscopy, you run the risk of becoming jaded.

So I said to her, 'What do you mean, a comedian should look funny?' And she said, 'A comedian', she said, 'should be the sort of person', she said, 'that as soon as you look at them,' she said, 'it makes you want to laugh,' she said, 'like Joe Pasquale.'‡ So as I lay there naked on a slab, in a third-length floral-print hospital gown, with a fibre-optic tube inserted into my anus, looking at live video-footage relay of my own rotting and bleeding internal organs, I thought about Joe Pasquale. And I've thought about Joe Pasquale once before in my life. They say that you think about Joe Pasquale twice in your career: once on the way up . . .§

* 'Vain' is, I think, another word which Richard Herring became fixated on and which I now find hugely useful. When we first lived together in London in the late eighties, on subsistence rations unknown to today's credit-card laden generation of would-be artists, Rich would, for example, accuse me of being 'a vain man' if I had a sausage with my baked beans, rather than just eating the naked beans alone.
† This conversation is recorded verbatim. Even as it was happening, and even though I was in some discomfort, this was a rare example of being aware that a routine was writing itself before my very eyes, and anus.
‡ As noted earlier, she said 'Tommy Cooper'. But I didn't have a bit about Tommy Cooper, I had one about Joe Pasquale.
§ You don't even have to finish this joke off. People get it. I love

it when you don't even have to finish a joke off. But perhaps one reason I didn't need to finish the joke was because people already knew it in its original form.

Back in the late eighties and early nineties, when I was starting out on the circuit, I'd always be doing try-out spots on bills with the great Irish comedian Ian Macpherson, a spindly and romantic figure whom I was quite in awe of, and who is already mentioned in the notes to *Stand-Up Comedian* for the line 'It is not for me to draw parallels between my own life and that of Christ,' which I did not copy off him, as I have already explained.

However, Ian also used to open all his sets with the line 'They say you play [The Balham Banana, for example] twice in your career. Once on the way up. Once on the way down. It's good to be back,' which this joke consciously echoes. To be fair, as an opening line Macpherson's Gambit, as it is known to scholars of stand-up, is so perfect and classic I assumed it was an old music-hall lick or an American Catskills comics line from the fifties. One almost expects to hear a snare drum and a cymbal crash after it. It is such a wonderful joke, not least because of its fatalistic optimism. The declining comedian knows he is on the way down and yet he says, 'It's good to be back,' and is still grateful for the gig.

The comedian Simon Munnery, who got the highest A-level results in the country in 1985, pointed out to me that the joke is obviously relatively modern because (a) it contains within it the notion of upward and then downward career progression for an 'alternative' comedian, which he maintains is a relatively new possibility, and (b) it sees the comedian step outside his act to comment on his own role as a comedian, rather than as a pretend ordinary member of society, which is a post-modern device. As usual, Simon is, I think, very wrong here, and there are so many examples of very ancient comedians employing similar devices that I am not going to do him the honour of even bothering to think of any and list them here.

Also, I'd heard the late, great Malcolm Hardee, the unheralded godfather of Alternative Comedy who built a three-decade career on two jokes and his willingness to expose his unfeasibly large testicles to paying customers, do it, and assumed it was a standard opening. But it turns out there's a superb article on the internet about the genesis of this very line, by the comedian Robert Wringham, on the website the British Comedy Guide. I stumbled across it whilst trying to find any versions of the joke that perhaps pre-dated Ian's by typing the phrases 'they say you play' and 'twice in your career' into Google.

In the piece (http://www.sitcom.co.uk/features/ian_macpherson.shtml) Macpherson says the joke was 'an ad lib born out of terror. It just popped out. It was a great opener at venues like the Red Rose Club, The King's Head in Crouch End, Banana Cabaret and so on, and for some time afterwards it carried some of my – how to put it? – more esoteric stuff. It used to fool them into thinking I was funny while I spent the next 30 minutes tinkering with their brains.'

According to Ian in Robert's revealing piece, Malcolm Hardee came to use the joke

by nicking it. Simple as that. And, as he'd done it on some pap-for-the-masses TV programme, it looked as if I'd nicked it off him. So I had to drop it. He also put it about that he'd bought it from me. Which he hadn't. He then offered to buy it retrospectively. 'Fuck off, Malcolm', I quipped. So I fined him a pretty modest sum for theft. I was pretty furious about it at the time, but he had his eye on other stuff I'd written, so I was also warning him off. He ignored the fine at first, but he was just about to open Up The Creek, so I gather some comedians refused to play there till he paid up. Which he grudgingly did. I also made it plain in words of one syllable that I was not, repeat not, selling the line. He muttered something about 6 seconds of material but, as I pointed out, 'It was 7½ seconds, Malcolm. You should have nicked my timing.'

My own assumption is that part of the reason the audience laugh at the version of the joke in '90s Comedian, where playing the venue twice is replaced by thinking about Joe Pasquale twice, is because they recognise it may be true. Macpherson tells Robert Wringham in the interview:

Arthur Smith told me I'd written the most stolen line in British Comedy. Not bad for a middle class white boy from Dublin. I was told that Simon Fanshawe did it on radio. I wrote to his agent at Noel Gay Artists three years ago but he must be a slow typist. No

And here's why I first thought about Joe Pasquale, right. It was in 1995 . . . and when I started doing the, er, comedy circuit in, in London in about 1989, there used to be this Irish comic on the circuit called Michael Redmond. He was great. He lives in Glasgow now. But he had big bushy hair and a kind of long, droopy moustache, and deep-set bloodhound eyes. And he always used to wear a long brown mac and carry a little plastic bag. And what he used to do was he'd walk out onstage and he'd stand still in silence for about a minute and a half looking weird, and

---

response as yet. I've now got back to the standup after some years of writing the obligatory books, and it seems that various people have been paying homage to my more accessible stuff. I mean, how much homage can one man take?

I like to think that my rewiring of Macpherson's joke was homage, but his comment 'how much homage can one man take?' is telling. Whether something is a homage or an act of theft depends on the relative fame, status and wealth of the homager and the homagee. When advertising scum rip off Bergman or Wenders or some obscure Brit artist for a campaign and say that it was a homage, the real effect is that simply by virtue of the mass audience their adverts achieve as opposed to the minimal audience enjoyed by most actual art, it immediately renders the subject material a cliché by association, rather than validating it in some way. Or do advertising 'creatives' imagine it is some kind of homage, as I did when I pilfered from the greats?

That said, 'They say you think about Joe Pasquale twice in your career' doesn't work as a joke unless you already know, or at least can intuitively guess, the Ian Macpherson joke that informs it. But it did work. So people either knew it or guessed that something else that made sense of my line predated it, like astronomers that approximate the position of unknown suns by the evidence of their gravitational pull on smaller and less significant, yet more visible, bodies. So it is a homage. And not a theft. And in a single bound I am free.

then he would say, 'A lot of people say to me, "Get out of my garden!"'*

Now I think that is the greatest opening line ever. Um . . . not just for a comedy set either, for anything. I don't think there's a book or a film or a poem or a play that couldn't be improved by having 'A lot of people say to me, "Get out of my garden!"' as . . . The Book of Genesis would be a lot better . . . You feel it would, it would kind of cut to the chase of what it was really . . . It would save a lot of faff if you went straight in there.

And it always used to get a good laugh, that line. But it got a much better laugh, Michael's joke, in 1995, when Joe Pasquale did it as one of his jokes in his Royal Variety Performance set of that year. And there's always been a kind of tradition of the mainstream acts stealing our jokes.† In fact, you might remember at the end of 2004, er, Jimmy Carr had to take Jim Davidson to task for stealing some of his material, right, although to be honest, if Jim Davidson can steal your material, maybe it's time to think about dropping it. Although to be fair to Jimmy Carr, it was kind of a sexist, woman-hating bit that he'd written with a sense of irony that Jim Davidson was able to appropriate at face

* Michael is best known for playing Father Stone in *Father Ted*. He used to write the most brilliant little gags. 'Do you ever notice how nervous people get when you follow them up a ladder?' There's a clip of him, in his mac-wearing era, on *Saturday Live* in the eighties, on YouTube. Young hipsters creaming their twenty-first-century pants about some American space-cadet one-liner merchant from the New York alterno-scene need to realise it was all done before, better, and with less self-conscious, look-at-me artifice.
† Note that I'm not saying Joe Pasquale definitely stole Michael's line, as it's impossible to prove that is the case. I am merely implying it.

value. One of the kindest things you can say about Jim Davidson as a fellow comic is he's not a writer-performer who's troubled by the notion of duality of meaning.*

There's always been this kind of material-theft tradition. So I rang him up. I did an article for a Sunday newspaper in 1995, and I rang up Joe Pasquale about this idea of stealing material. And I said to him, 'Joe, how did you think up that joke about the garden?' And Joe Pasquale said, and this is true, he said, 'Well,' he said, 'I thought if someone looked out of their window and they saw me in their garden, they would say "Get out of my garden!"' Now, that's not quite right, is it? Because if you looked out of your window and you saw Joe Pasquale in the garden, you'd just go, 'Is that . . . Joe Pasquale in the garden? What can he possibly want?'† You might even be frightened, right. 'Cause that joke only works if a kind of anonymous weirdo is saying it. As soon as you introduce a celebrity into it, it's kind of structurally compromised, so . . . I said to him, 'Well, are you sure you thought that joke up?' And he said he couldn't remember

* No one cares about this sort of thing any more. To the average punter there's no difference now between Jimmy Carr and Jim Davidson, between irony and intent, except that Jimmy Carr is much better and more original. And does secret work for charity. But ethical and political questions are largely irrelevant to today's comedy consumers. Comedians are little more than content providers.

† Pasquale's comments here are a mixture of his actual comments and things his manager said on his behalf. The pause between 'Is that' and 'Joe Pasquale' has become a stylistic cliché of my routines, which now bores even me, as I am sure it does you. My hope here is that the second part of the phrase has a feeling of inevitability and predictability about it that means the audience, ideally, laugh once in anticipation of it, and then at me having the audacity to have actually bothered saying it, even though they've all guessed what it was anyway.

if, if it was his idea. And it is sometimes difficult to remember if you've had an idea, especially when they occur as thick and fast as they must do in the mind of Joe Pasquale. And under duress, he admitted one of his writers might have written it. Turned out what he meant by writers was not so much people that wrote for him, as people that went around writing things down that other comedians had thought of. So I said to him, 'The thing is, it's Michael Redmond's joke, you shouldn't be doing it.' And he said what a lot of the mainstream acts say. They say that they don't think it's possible to own a joke. They say they don't think you can copyright a joke. So bearing that in mind, I've tried to write a joke that Joe Pasquale won't be able to steal. And it goes like this.*

[*reading*] 'Joe Pasquale goes into a bar. He says to the barman, "I'd like a pint of beer please." And the barman says, "Why don't you just come around the bar, help yourself to the beer, and then walk off without paying for it? After all, you are Joe Pasquale. Or perhaps send in someone else to steal the beer for you and then deny that beer can actually be owned. Say that you find the very concept of the ownership of beer hard to understand. Or better still, insist that it's your beer and that you brewed it at home. In your house. Even though your home lacks the most rudimentary of brewing facilities."'

Ah, someone nearly clapped alone there. But then they stopped, because of course for a comedian the only thing

* The act of getting a piece of paper out to read a prepared statement accurately is something I have done in all my shows since. People seem to laugh as soon as you get it out of your pocket. Maybe it's to do with bringing a deliberate and obvious piece of artifice into a performance that strives to give the illusion of spontaneity that makes it funny.

worse than the sound of no one clapping is the sound of one person clapping alone, as it indicates that what you have is a very specialised appeal and no commercial future. As if I didn't know that.*

Right, um . . . So . . . I got home late on, er, the 6th, woke up late on the 7th of July, got all these emails, text messages, I thought, 'Something's up,' right. So I put the television on. And by now, it was about three hours after the London al-Qaeda bombings. And on TV news, there was all these kind of insensitive news journalists running around trying to get statements out of bomb survivors that weren't really in a fit state to give statements. And I started writing them down, right. This was, um, a guy that had survived the King's Cross bomb and he said to camera, he said, 'The rescue workers have been amazing, really amazing, I mean I take my hat off to them. I'm not wearing a hat, obviously, but if I was, I would take it off.'† And laughs over here, a

---

* As previously mentioned, I usually end up doing a variation on this once genuine ad-lib at least once during any show, but it is especially important in '90s Comedian. I was aware it would be difficult to get the average audience, in its entirety, onside for the supposedly scatological and obscene half-hour section that closes this show, and so throughout I was trying everything I could to isolate individuals in the audience, or pockets of people in the audience, and make them think about their responses. By dividing the audience into those who 'get it' and those who don't, eventually, usually, the 'don't gets' wanted to be part of the 'do gets', and gradually a strong enough coalition of the willing was formed to support the unacceptable stylistic and narrative thrust of the last half of the show.

† This actually happened. I did see this interview. Since then, other comics have told me they saw it too, and wanted to write stuff on it, but I was in there already, the very next day, and claimed the territory with my big flag first. My wife is a comedian. Sometimes

smattering of applause, and then doubt spreading towards the back corner.*

Now. Don't judge me for this, OK? Don't be uncomfortable, I am a human being like you, I am a member of society. I watched that news report, I thought, 'I hope these people are OK and things don't pan out too badly, er, for the world situation.' But on the other hand, I'm also a comedian, so I was thinking, 'Mind you, it's quite funny, I should write it down.'†

Then on the radio I heard a woman, I heard a woman who'd survived the number 30 bus bomb, and she said, 'After the bus blew up, I saw people lying outside the British Medical Association headquarters. Ironic,' she said, 'but

---

something funny happens to both of us together, and we have to decide who gets to talk about it onstage. I got the rats-in-the-park routine for my 2009 show. She got the story of our honeymoon, the misguided trip to Shetland in December 2006 that ended earlier than scheduled after an incident involving a pizza and almost perpetual darkness. The smart-arse show that is waiting to happen, surely, is one where we both describe the same experiences from our very different perspectives. Men are from Mars and women are from Venus, as I am sure you know, so I expect the results would be hilarious! That said, I am pretty sure that, as usual, Greg Fleet has already done this show, with his then partner Janei Anderson, in 1996.
* Here I am again, breaking down the audience into conflicting fragments with a view to shaping them into a whole further down the line. I want them to realise I am not laughing at the man who said he would take his hat off if he had one, but at the desperate hysteria of live news gathering. But the public, they are nervous, bless them, and need to be groomed for their new responsibilities.
† I am asking the punters to suspend their innate squeamishness by inviting them to see the world from the comedian's perspective. Yes, it's terrible, but imagine if your job was to try and see the funny side . . .

if you're going to do this kind of thing, that's the place to do it, I suppose.'*

But, Cardiff, who are these inhuman bombers that strike, they strike at the very heart of our society with no respect for human life, without even the courtesy of a perfunctory warning? It makes you nostalgic, doesn't it, for the good old days of the IRA. 'Cause they gave warnings, didn't they? They were gentlemen bombers, the finest terrorists this country's ever had. We'll not see their like again.† Let's . . . let's have a little clap for the IRA. Come on, give them a little clap. Give them a clap, right? 'Cause the IRA, they were decent British terrorists. They didn't want to be British. But they were. And as such, they couldn't help but embody some fundamentally decent

---

* Again, this is a genuine quote. Everyone interviewed is clearly in such states of shock that everything they say has an edge of the absurd.

† Once again, in a show that appears threaded through with deliberate questions about where ideas come from, here's an accidental echo of that anxiety. By the summer of 2005, Patrick Kielty, Andrew Maxwell and I were all doing routines on this idea, all of which featured the phrase 'gentlemen bombers', entirely independently of each other, having never heard each other's bits. Had there been a news story, or a think piece, somewhere which had used the phrase 'gentlemen bombers', and which we had all remembered without realising it? Subsequently, the rock star and archaeologist Julian Cope included a line about the 'gentlemen bombers' of the IRA in a song about Islamic terrorism on his 2009 album *The Unruly Imagination*, which means he'd either heard one of these routines, heard the same source for the phrase which we'd all forgotten, or that the phrase suggests itself to anyone thinking of the way the Western media portrays Islamic terrorists as motiveless fundamentalist psychopaths, as opposed to the more finely nuanced forms of terrorism and terrorists we have here in the civilised world.

British values. We'll miss them now they're gone.*

And another great thing about the IRA, I always think, apart from the warnings – and the uniforms, which were stylish but also practical – is that they had achievable aims, didn't they? What do they want? Er, a united Ireland. And of course it's possible to imagine getting round the table and negotiating towards that. What do al-Qaeda want? Al-Qaeda want to see the destruction of Western Judaeo-Christian civilisation in its entirety. And it's harder to imagine getting round the table and negotiating towards that, isn't it? 'Obviously, you'll appreciate we're unable to meet all your demands. But here are some areas of Western Judaeo-Christian civilisation that we'd be happy to let go.' Like Splott.† I don't even know what that is, I just saw it

---

* It was always tremendous fun doing this bit onstage, especially, say, in Derry, where republicans in the audience didn't know if they were being flattered or insulted. One of the few good things about being an English, as opposed to British, comedian, is that you can play with the expectation that you ought to be ashamed of your history when playing the previously oppressed parts of the UK. No one expects an English comedian to go to Derry and praise the IRA for having decent British values, and the audience there at least have to give you a grudging respect for doing so.

† Splott is an area of Cardiff with a funny name. It is onomato-poeic. It sounds like porridge falling onto a red-brick, terraced-house doorstep. Splott used to be a student zone when I was young and had friends there. I was performing the show this text is tran-scribed from in Cardiff. I always cranked in some local reference at this point, wherever I was, as the thing that we in the West can afford to sacrifice to Islamic terrorists. These days, I try not to make this kind of local gag. Having said that, when I was last in Liver-pool, the local paper reviewer hated the whole evening, apart from an obvious, off-the-cuff joke I made about housing quality in Tox-teth, which seemed to her to be the only evidence I offered all night that I even deserved to be called a comedian.

on a map. Splott and Joe Pasquale, he could be sent out as well.

But there's lots of good stories from the war against terror, though. I mean, I was reading this, um . . . I hate it when comedians do that as a kind of intro, 'cause basically the link between what I've just said and this bit is a bit contrived. So I go, 'Yeah, there's a lot of good stories from the war against terror, though, but I wasn't actually talking about that then, was I, no.' But I would have got away with it, no one would have noticed. But. There *are* a lot of good stories from the war against terror, apropos of nothing.*

And, um . . . I was reading this great book of, of trial transcripts, of American soldiers accused of human-rights abuses in, in Abu Ghraib, which was of course closed today.† And, um . . . I don't know if you remember Charles Graner, he was a fat American soldier but he had a moustache, so you could identify him. And he was the guy that organised the photographing of a naked, hooded, bound Iraqi civilian being dragged out of a cell, er, on his hands and knees, er, on a dog's lead. And, um, in his defence, er, his lawyer, Charles Graner's lawyer said that the naked,

---

* Deconstruct and do it anyway. The first place I ever noticed the phrase 'apropos of nothing' being used outside academic circles was in the surprisingly subtle 1994 Sheryl Crow song 'All I Wanna Do', where it is tossed away with grace and ease as if part of a casual everyday conversation. Since noticing this I too have tried to use the phrase in the same way wherever possible, but I am aware that in doing so I am stealing a little bit of Crow's linguistic genius. Or paying homage to it anyway.

† By sheer coincidence, the American prison camp Abu Ghraib was closed on the day this recording of me doing a routine about Abu Ghraib, which I'd been doing for nine months, was made. See how professional a comedian I am, in that I mention that here, to give the routine a feeling of absolute, cast-iron relevance.

180

hooded, bound Iraqi civilian wasn't being dragged out of the cell but was actually crawling of his own free will. And I just wondered how many other lines of defence they rejected before they settled on that one. And also what the naked, hooded, bound Iraqi civilian might have been crawling of his own free will towards? And I like to think he was crawling towards the notion of Western democracy. But obviously he was having some difficulty knowing which way to crawl, er, because of the hood, er, and because of the fact that he was approaching a palpably abstract concept.*

OK? And so there's good laughs for that over here in this area, and those tail away towards that corner there. When it's late at night, there's a long set to get through, as I said, there isn't going to be time for me to work a mixed-ability room tonight. No offence, right, but time's money, you know. Now. So. Everybody over here, for the rest of the night, you're on board, you're going to be Team A, OK? And you won't mind if I don't play over here too much,

* There are few things as inspiring for good stand-up as utter disgust, as genuine utter contempt for a person, an event, a point of view. But there are also few things as unattractive in a comedian as appearing to occupy, deliberately, the moral high ground, especially with the degree of smugness I am prone to, even though I sometimes attempt to disguise this repulsive characteristic as a deliberate artistic choice, as if I were inhabiting a subtly crafted role rather than just being an actual wanker. That said, when I was in Aspen doing this bit, I didn't really care what the people there made of it, such was my self-righteous hatred of Amerikkka, which you will notice I have spelt with three 'k's, despite the fact that its current president is black. Of course, within a few months, when evidence of similar British abuse of detainees emerged, it wouldn't have been possible to go over there and take this tone with them. They should have all stood up, as one, and spat in my face.

I'm going to be mainly concentrating on Team F in that corner. Don't cheer that you are better than them, right, Team A, for some of you it's just the luck of random seating, isn't it, right? I don't want you . . . Don't laugh at them or cheer yourselves, right, we must do everything we can to make them feel comfortable and we will bring them along with us. Don't laugh at them, don't even look at them, right? Look at me, Team A. But if you're sitting next to an F and they laugh at a clever bit, right, you can just reach over and give their hand a little squeeze, and we will bring you along. I will not leave anyone behind, I swear. All these jokes have worked before at some stage, they are about things in the news and people who exist, so you have . . . Don't laugh at them, Team A. There's Team . . . you are . . . right? And I know it's weird, what's happening now, 'cause you've thought, 'Ooh, let's go out and sit in the dark and judge someone,' right? But now you're being judged and it feels strange, right, but don't worry, you will . . . I will . . . you will not be . . . look, it's fine, OK? You'll be all right. There'll be a point in about eight minutes when you'll be . . . when you'll laugh at something. You won't know why. But you will laugh. And it will all be fine, right? Sometime . . . I've, I've done this before when there's been a kind of split in the room. Usually it creates an atmosphere of bonhomie. But tonight, it's made it worse, hasn't it? It's made it worse. There's a tension in the room that's now 'the gig is lost', right? It's lost.*

---

* This breaking down the room into groups didn't always happen at this point, and it didn't always play out exactly like this – this is a transcript of what happened on one occasion – but I'd always need to do this at some point in the first half hour of this show to soften up the ground for the heavy aerial bombardment of toilet-related blasphemy in the second half. By the time I gave up stand-up in

OK, Team F, I'm going to put you at your ease, right? It's OK to not like all of this. It has sometimes happened before. Will that relax you, madam? Good. Um. It's OK to not like some of this, right? People have not . . . I've done this show about ninety times. I did it for three weeks in a little theatre in London and I had some walk-outs. And one of the walk-outs was the pop star Robbie Williams, who left about halfway through. Yeah. And on the way out, the woman from the Soho Theatre said to him, 'Oh, are you not enjoying it?' And he said he was, but that he had just remembered that he had to go to a wedding in the morning. Do you think that's true? Do you think that's true? If it was true, I hope he'd already bought them a present, and he didn't just get something from a garage on the way . . . And then he said that he thought that I was all right, but that my voice – and this is true – Robbie Williams said my voice would be better suited to meditational relaxation tapes. That's what he said. And the weird thing was that when I saw him in there, I thought, 'Oh, I hope he doesn't come backstage afterwards, I won't know what to say.' What positive thing could you say, you know? But, like . . . 'I liked it when you dressed as that skeleton,' you could

_____

2000, one of the few things I still enjoyed onstage was trying to lose a room and then win it back for my own amusement. Now, instead of it being an act of self-indulgent self-sabotage and wire-walking, I was able to use these skills for some purpose, as I attempted to forge the audience into a group that will go with the heavy stuff ahead, proving to them that they need not find supposedly offensive subject material offensive. Form and content, finally, had a relationship. And, with an eye on the cohesion of the evening as a whole, I encourage the stronger and quicker sections of the room to help the weaker, slower members of the audience, and encourage those weaker, slower punters, in turn, to feel no shame in accepting this aid.

say it was good. But I didn't know when he'd gone, right?*

But it is . . . But there are people in Team F – there's A people are . . . Team F are going, 'Yes, Stew, that's very funny isn't it? But in Cardiff Robbie Williams plays in the stadium, not in this small room, like you. So maybe you should look at him and learn something about what entertainment means. And what it means is not talking in a monotonous voice, dressing as a luminous skeleton. That is what people want.'

So all I'm saying is, if you're . . . It's OK to not like this, but if you don't like it, that means that you are the same as Robbie Williams.

Lynndie England was a female American soldier and she was photographed pointing and laughing at the naked genitals of hooded, bound Iraqis. And in her trial the judge actually intervened, rather unusually, and he said that he

---

* This story is entirely true. R. Williams, formerly of the group Take That, was in the company of his showbiz friend, the tiny satirist Matthew Lucas, of *Little Britain*, who was laughing alone, both of them on the right-hand fringe of my vision in a balcony over the stage, Williams's boredom visible to the crowd. Sometimes I elaborated the story, explaining that I was going to tell Williams that I had gone with a crowd of people to watch him onstage at Glastonbury in 1997, hoping it would be awful so that we could all laugh at it, but actually his performance had been entirely adequate.

A few years later, the gossip column of the *Independent* ran a story saying Robbie Williams had walked out of my show because he was offended by the religious content. I wrote back and pointed out that he walked out before the religious content, and that he left simply because he was bored and thought I had a boring voice, a clarification that the newspaper was happy to publish.

I expect it is hard to concentrate on a long monologue by a speaking man if you are from the world of pop, with all the flashing lights and fast music. And cocaine.

184

wasn't convinced that Lynndie England knew what she was doing. Now, I don't believe that, 'cause in my experience, when a woman points and laughs at a man's genitals, she's normally fully aware of the effect that will have. In my experience. Especially if he's hooded and bound. In my experience.

The laugh spreading into the, the Team F region for that, because it's a kind of bit of satire about the news, but it's got cocks in it as well. So that helps to bring the whole room onside.* Come on, come on in, Team F, come on. It's a bit like, kind of, at the moment, I feel like we can get there, and I know it's a bit early in the evening but . . . At the moment, it feels like over here, there's loads of nineteen-fifties American teenagers splashing around in a lake in little shorts. And there's some other nineteen-fifties American teenagers, and they're going, 'Oh, that looks fun. I wish we could go in that lake. But we can't. 'Cause we've got orthopaedic shoes.' But you can! Throw them off! Take them off, throw them away, you will float in this lake. You will float.†

---

* Here I am having my cake and eating it. I set up the audience to laugh at a pathetic cock joke, and then berate them for doing so. It is I that have trivialised the Americans' sexual abuse of Iraqi detainees by using it as a platform for a cock joke, and yet I choose to shift blame onto the audience for enjoying the very food I have force-fed them, like some French pâté manufacturer berating geese for being gluttons. Sometimes, going back over these transcripts, I hate myself for my hypocrisy. Shame on you, shame on you, Stewart Lee.
† This wouldn't always happen at this point, or in this form, but a riff on cheery American teenagers would usually be applicable to the crowd response at some point, and however long it went on there was always the funny phrase 'orthopaedic shoes' to get a laugh at the end. The phrase feels like it belongs in that Baby Cow production company school of post-Alan Partridge comedy that aspires to combine an illness and a brand name in one sentence

And there was another story from that war, it was, er, it was discredited but it was true. Which was, apparently in Guantanamo Bay, um, the Americans threw a copy of a Koran into a toilet. Now, I'm not a religious person, but I don't like the idea of a Koran being thrown into a toilet. Especially when bookshops and libraries are full of millions of pristine copies of Dan Brown's new novel. Which you have to stop reading, right, because . . . You have to stop reading, because Dan Brown is not . . . It's not literature, right? And you should know this in the land of bards, right? Um . . . Dan Brown writes sentences like, 'The famous man looked at the red cup.' OK? It's not . . . And intellectuals like

---

as the ultimate in northern realist humour: i.e. 'He fell down in the aisle of Morrison's when he had a sudden attack of pancreatic cancer. Well, there was tins of alphabet spaghetti everywhere. One smashed and it spelt out a racist word on the lino. I didn't know where to look. My sister-in-law is Turkish, as you know. It's not the same, you're right, but she's very dark-skinned and their little boy is half-caste . . .' etc., etc.

The phrase 'orthopaedic shoes' is not in my natural vocabulary and so I feel it must have been brought to my attention either by some Mancunian Steve Coogan character that I and Rich Herring perhaps wrote for in *On the Hour*, or by a graduate of the same eighties Manchester drama-school gang as Steve Coogan, or else by Rob Brydon in thrall to this particular idiom in the early noughties, or else by the acclaimed playwright and 'new Shakespeare' Patrick Marber when attempting to write in this style for profit in the mid-nineties. I can also picture the delightful Caroline Aherne, aka Mrs Merton, sitting before me in her tiny Manchester flat, when we toured student shitholes together in 1993, saying 'orthopaedic shoe, orthopaedic shoe', or something very like it, in-between playing me New Order's 'Love Vigilantes' and making me watch *Pretty Woman* on video, and the words burying themselves deep into my brain. I know this isn't a phrase I would have arrived at naturally. It's not from my realm. But where did I rip it from? Someone must know.

me have tried to explain to you why Dan Brown is a bad . . . and it's not working. So I'm going to have a big poster campaign, a big, anti-Dan Brown poster campaign. It's going to be a massive picture of a toilet, right? And there'll be all pieces of shit floating in the toilet. And in the middle of the pieces of shit, there'll be a copy of *The Da Vinci Code*, with a speech balloon coming out of one of the pieces of shit, saying, 'Ah, there goes the neighbourhood.'*

And I don't know if you know, but the Catholic Church are very worried about you all reading *The Da Vinci Code*. And in fact, in January last year, the Vatican actually issued an official statement reminding Dan Brown readers that the books are largely fictional and full of historically unverifiable information.†

---

* Today, the literary critics of quality broadsheets define themselves in opposition to Dan Brown, while populists, or people like Dylan Jones of *GQ* trying to have surprising opinions, say we should stop being so snobby and appreciate his ability to spin a good yarn. Whatever, this Dan Brown riff was four years ahead of the mass acceptance of the fact that he is abysmal, and was later recycled for my 2009 TV series, *Stewart Lee's Comedy Vehicle*.

I first read Dan Brown in the flat of my future wife, Bridget Christie, in July 2005. She was swotting for an act she had in mind, where she would be Dan Brown being a stand-up comedian, telling old pub jokes in breathless, dramatic prose, to the bewilderment of audiences. It was hilarious and I wish I'd thought of it. But I only do me. And the smug-wanker version of me.

† This joke is calibrated to fail. Nine times out of ten it wouldn't get much of a laugh, and if it did it would only be from a minority of hardcore, atheist, intellectual pseuds, predisposed to equating the stories of the Bible with the idea of 'fictional and historically unverifiable information'. But it did the job of further dividing the audience just as they were usually starting to become a workable unit, and thereby cranking up the tension, amplifying the sense of unfolding drama in the room, the narrative of my own failure to

[*Long pause.*]

Six minutes' time, I tell you, you'll be fine, right? But you're right not to laugh at that, it's not a proper joke, right, it's just based on a shared set of assumptions, it doesn't work.

Um . . . Now I was talking about the Vatican there. I don't want anyone to think, anyone to think I'm, I'm anti-Catholic. I'm not. I actually love Catholicism. It's my favourite form of clandestine global evil.

What I really like about Catholicism, my favourite thing about it, is the way that it combines a search for profound spiritual meaning in the universe with a love of kind of inane seaside tat. And you don't often see those two things working as a team, do you?*

I'll give you an example of what I mean, right? I was in the Vatican at the start of last year. And outside the big church there, in the square, there were these little carts selling souvenirs, little souvenir stands. And outside the Vatican at the start of last year, you could buy – and this is true – you could buy lollipops about that big, with the face of Pope John Paul II on them, you could buy Pope John Paul II's face loll– . . . I bought about ten and brought them home, right?† And I was just wondering if, in the light of

---

master the entire audience that plays along underneath the actual through-line of the material. It also allows me, in the next sentence, to appear totally in control by not being fazed by the failure of this joke, and to assure them that they have nothing to worry about and that they will all be onside again soon.
* Again, I am in thrall to Harry Hill here. 'Working as a team' is very much a Harry Hill phrase, although in his world it would be applied to foodstuffs and animals, rather than abstract concepts.
† This is all totally true. After the furore surrounding *Jerry Springer: The Opera*, and my subsequent involvement in the politics

his death early last year, whether sales of those lollipops went up or whether they went down, you know. Whether good Catholics thought, 'Ah, the Pope's just died, it would now seem inappropriate to lick a sugar effigy of his face.' Or whether they'd go, 'Ah, the Pope's just died, but what better way to pay tribute to his memory than by licking a sugar effigy of his face.' To eat that, swallow it, digest it, shit out a kind of enchanted papal shit. I don't know if whatever spiritual properties those lollipops have would survive the digestive process. I'm neither theologically nor medically qualified to do anything other than speculate on that, right? We can't know.*

But I did ask my girlfriend, she's Catholic. I said to her, 'If you drink holy water and then you do a wee, is the wee then magic?' And she said, 'No, that would be ridiculous.' And it would, wouldn't it? It'd be stupid.

Now, I don't know if you remember, when the Pope died, the Catholic Church put out this story about his last words. They said that the Pope's last words on his deathbed were addressed to God. Apparently, in his closing moments, the Pope said to God, 'I searched for you, you found me, I thank you.' That's the story they put out. Let's call it what it is, an obvious, made-up lie. 'Cause even the cardinals in

---

of blasphemy, I have learned to moderate my atheism, and always try to give the impression of being as reasonable a person as possible, and to respect people's religious beliefs unless they impinge upon generally accepted human-rights norms. But some religious things are just hilarious, such as Catholic gift-shop culture. Greater love hath no man than to fashion his God into an ashtray or a cigarette lighter.

* The last pope died in April 2005, while I had a run at the Melbourne Comedy festival, and this piece came together over a couple of nights during the run, basically written onstage.

the Vatican admitted that the Pope was in a coma for the last two weeks of his life. And that does seem to me like a very eloquent and profound statement to make in a coma.*

And I'm suspicious of that story for personal reasons as well, right? Because I actually nursed two friends, right, um, an elderly relative and someone I'd known from school. And they were both people that I loved. And I nursed them both, and I visited them both through very long illnesses, not dissimilar to the late Pope's. And I can assure you that in their closing moments, neither of them were in a fit state to say anything as eloquent or profound as that. Although admittedly I was holding pillows over their faces at the time.†

---

* I was able to play this with a steely calm just by thinking about what an incredibly offensive story this is for the Vatican to distribute when it is obviously not true, and by how, on the rare occasions I have been awaiting the death of someone I love after some protracted suffering, the messy chains of events never resolved themselves with a similar moment of clearly fabricated closure. The most memorable and heartbreaking last words I ever heard were, 'God, oh God, let me die.'

The Australian comedian and inventor of all Australian comedy Greg Fleet has a superb routine about how his father wished to emulate Oscar Wilde, whose last words were 'Either that wallpaper goes or I do,' to the point where he arranged to be sent home in the final stages of a terminal illness to a specially prepared room which he had already gone to the trouble of having decorated, at great expense, with an appropriately unpleasant wallpaper. In the event of feeling the hand of death upon him, he sits up, clears his throat to deliver his witty final epithet, and says, 'Either this wall ... ah fuck this really hurts ... agggh ... ah fuck ... ah ... Akkh ... Ugh.' And dies. It's all in the telling, of course.

† The trick here was to play this with bald-faced conviction, summoning up memories of visiting dying loved ones, to the point where it looked like I nursed an honest and terrible grievance about

But, you know, it was an act of love, right? It was an act of love. The first one was, the second one in retrospect I feel ambivalent about. But you're in the moment, aren't you? You have to act in the moment. It's the kind of split-second decision London anti-terrorist officers have to make every day.*

I don't know if you remember, but the Pope's . . . The scheduling of the Pope's funeral actually caused some problems for the royal family because it ended up being arranged for the same weekend as the wedding of Prince Charles and Lady Camilla Parker Bowles. So they actually ended up moving that wedding to avoid a clash of interests. Now, I don't think they should have done that, right, they should have left that wedding where it was. 'Cause for me, that's what split-screen television technology was invented for.† Although it is hard, isn't it, to imagine which one of

---

the way the Vatican had lied in the light of the appalling deaths I had witnessed, and then flip it. It was a good way of testing the water for the second half, which basically extends this method of po-faced sincerity as far as it will go.

* The final few shows of *'90s Comedian* took place soon after the police had shot Jean Charles de Menezes dead, in Stockwell of all places, mistaking him for a suicide bomber. This is another proper joke, albeit a black one. Within a few years these 'jokes', as we comedians call them, will have been entirely purged from my work in favour, exclusively, of grinding repetition, embarrassing silences, and passive-aggressive monotony.

† This was just a throwaway comment made in an email from my friend, the notorious bluestocking and radio comedy producer Louise Coates, which I asked her if I could have. Louise wrote me a facetious email while I was in Australia, keeping me up to date on world news events which she felt I might have missed. Louise is a natural and caustic wit whose arrival in a room spells either delight or disaster, but is always certain to bring about an exciting change

those two events would have been the most distressing to watch, you know? The public veneration of a wrinkled old corpse . . .*

You all right now?†

---

of some sort. So much of what she says could be strip-mined for laughs that were I ever to face total artistic block I would secretly follow her around, writing down her indignant expressions of outrage at facets of modern life which I would have placed in her path to provoke her. Then I'd have her killed by a hit man and pass them off as my own.

* I added this bit to the bluestocking's bon mot, and it relies on the audience's innate understanding of the way stand-ups usually structure this kind of gag. The implication, of course, is that the wrinkled old corpse is Camilla Parker Bowles, and not Pope John Paul II. Ideally, I wouldn't have to finish the joke, as the whole crowd would anticipate the end, and this would be the point at which I would be able to congratulate them at having begun to work as a unit, where there were no stragglers. I needed them pleased with themselves and confident by now, as this is the last possible point to try and get them on my side before we launch into the difficult second half.

Sometimes, if the audience hadn't anticipated the correct ending to the joke, and hadn't laughed ahead of it, I would deliberately spoil it by saying, 'The public veneration of a wrinkled old corpse . . . or the wedding of Prince Charles and Camilla Parker Bowles.' I don't know why I would do this. I don't know what I was trying to achieve. In the cold light of day, it seems extremely self-indulgent and futile.

† In April 2000, in an Australian wildlife park, I saw the raspy-voiced American comedian, rancher and renowned horse whisperer Rich Hall bring a fully grown bull kangaroo to its knees by talking calmly to it and gently stroking its furry face. He was on the horizon, some distance from us, and the sun was behind him. Perhaps he had positioned himself there on purpose, aware of how the mythic status of his kangaroo-mastering abilities would be magnified were he to be backlit by the sun. Talk softly and sweetly to a

OK, the problem we've got now, right, is that there are . . . There's a section of the room are ahead of the punchlines. You have to be up to speed now. 'Cause the first half of the show, this is the kind of fun bit. And the second half is awful. Right? So you have to . . . And if you, if anyone had anticipated that joke and was holding back from laughing out of kind of politeness to me – thinking, 'Oh, he won't like it if we guess his jokes,' right – I don't care. I would welcome it. I think it's good, right. 'Cause if you think about it, I have to write about an hour and a half of jokes every year, that's quite hard, right?* But what's just happened suggests that with the correct encouragement of audiences, I wouldn't have to write any jokes. I could just come out with a list of topics and read them out. And you could think of something amusing about them in your own heads.† Then if you didn't like the show, that would be your fault, 'cause you hadn't been very funny. It's about the apportioning of blame, I think.‡

Now I was talking about religion there. Um . . . And it wasn't something I really wanted to talk about, 'cause I was one of a bunch of people that got in trouble with religious

_____

confused and frightened audience, like Rich Hall would to a kangaroo, and do not threaten them, and soon they may submit. Or not.

* I meant this genuinely. It is quite hard to write ninety minutes of jokes a year. But the audience would always laugh, as if I were being sarcastic and admitting that my job is much easier than theirs. But it isn't. Comedy, as Jimmy Tarbuck once told the young Richard Herring, is the hardest job in the world, a comment which, as Herring has noted, managed to be both encouraging and nakedly territorial.

† Here I flatter the poor fools. I make them think they are as clever and funny as me, so that we are all in the game together come the difficult second half.

‡ Back at ya! See how I toy with their affections!

people, er, last year. Er, but I am going to talk about religion for about twenty minutes and then I'm going to run away. Um, but before I do that, I'm going to draw a little circle on here in chalk, right. People are going, 'Oh, why are you doing that?', right. OK, what this is, is . . .

About four years ago, I went to, er, Languedoc in the south of France, right. Because I wanted to see this week when they recreate medieval clowning techniques, the 'bouffons' they were called. And what they do is they, they run through all these French mountaintop villages. And outside the baker's, they make fun of the baker. And outside the town hall, they'll take the piss out of the mayor or whatever. But before they did stuff about the church, right, outside the church they drew this kind of shape round them in the dirt, so they were kind of protected from prosecution, if you like, under the kind of magic spell of comedy. So that's what I've done here. Now, it doesn't work at all, OK? But it is a kind of concession to theatre, and this building receives some arts subsidy, so I have to do this. Otherwise you'd be just watching a piece of stand-up comedy, which is of course of no value.*

So, um . . . So, yeah, like I say, I, I worked on this opera about Jerry Springer. And, um, we got accused of being

* I flatter myself and I flatter them. Of course, we all know, the audience and I, that comedy can be art. It's the others, the others out there, beyond our circle, who don't get it. Re-reading this makes my skin tingle. I am not religious or superstitious, but it always felt great stopping to draw the circle, engaging in the briefest nod towards ritual magic. I shared a dressing room with Ram, a Haitian voodoo band, for a month in Edinburgh in 2000. Before every show they poured rum on the floor, set fire to it and danced over it, as a good-luck charm. How I envied them the certainty of their belief. Before I go on I just have a cup of tea and go to the toilet.

blasphemous, which was, came as a genuine surprise, 'cause it honestly had had really good reviews in the *Church Times* and the *Catholic Herald* when it first went out in the theatre.* So it was kind of weird, it all came a bit out of nowhere. We got 65,000 complaints when it went on television. The BBC executives that commissioned it had to go into hiding, with police protection. And me and the composer were going to be taken to court and charged with blasphemy. But at the end of June, the High Court threw the case out on the grounds that it isn't 1508.

But . . . It is . . . Hey, and before you all write in, I know that the first blasphemy prosecution was 1628, right, but there's something rhythmically pleasing about 1508.†

---

* This is true. Proper Christian academics are, by necessity, comfortable with the idea of using an untrue story to tell a truth. Meeting them, one sometimes suspects they admit, privately, that they're involved in propping up a great big metaphor, which they doubt the reality of, whilst at the same time thinking it's the best hope we've got. It's the angry Christians in their sheds, with their laptops, who struggle with the slippery meanings of words and ideas.

† 1508 is funnier than 1628, isn't it? I don't know why. In the end, in 2007, a blasphemy charge was brought by Christian Voice, not against the composer of *Jerry Springer: The Opera*, Richard Thomas, and me, but against the producer, who was also our manager, and the head of the BBC, which broadcast a version of the piece. Even Christian Voice, it seems, realised that prosecuting writers doesn't play as well with the public as prosecuting the BBC, which was then, as it is now, the tabloid whipping boy for everything that's wrong with the world. Christian Voice lost their case, and soon after this, in July 2008, the Blasphemy Law was scrapped, though there is currently the threat of the UN's so-called 'Global Blasphemy Law', which would muddy the waters once more, and the Republic of Ireland is also in the process of doing something very stupid.

By the time it went to court, I couldn't have cared less about the whole case. Christian Voice wanted to use the opera to publicise

So, um . . . But it was kind of weird. 'Cause I've got a web-site and whatever, so I was getting all this kind of hate mail all the time. And, er, it was – it still goes on now – it was quite distressing. But there was . . . I did get one funny one in March last year where someone wrote to me and they said, 'I enjoyed listening to you defend your work on Radio 5 yesterday. You seem like a very intelligent and thoughtful young man. What a pity you'll be going to hell.'*

And you have to admire that, don't you, the kind of construct of it, you know, it's beaut– . . . It takes you one way, and then it goes the other. It's a classic Pasquale move. We thought he was at home in his bedroom, naked. Turned out he was on a bus. So . . . That's how that works. We got to the end of the sentence, we found out he was on a bus. We thought he was in his house, naked – he'd given us no reason to believe he was on a bus till he got to the end of the sentence. Then we realised the nudity was amusing.†

------

their own reactionary agenda. Our manager and producer wanted to make loads of money out of it or, to be fair, to try and make back some of what he claimed to have lost, much of it on behalf of other people. Neither party reflected the spirit in which the show was conceived and devised. The court case felt like a bar-room fight in a silent comedy, and Richard and I were Laurel and Hardy, crawling out of the bottom of a brawl we'd begun, but which had now taken on a life of its own irrespective of our absence.

* Ah! He got me. There were usually hate letters waiting for me wherever I played, but they tailed off as nutters found new people to berate.

† This riff, which was played out differently every night, is clearly indebted to an old Lee and Herring routine which we called 'And Then I Got Off the Bus', broadcast during the second series of BBC2's *This Morning with Richard Not Judy* in 1999. It is not com-mercially available but can be downloaded illegally and free from

my website without the consent of the BBC. Young upstarts that we were, by the age of twenty-five Richard and I had of course swiftly seen through the entire apparatus of all comedy and quickly and brutally set about dismantling it, arrogantly proving our innate superiority to thousands of years of existing comic traditions, with no thought for the pleasure of future generations.

There is a classic joke mechanism, called the Pull Back and Reveal, of which audiences never seem to tire, the fools. The first half of a sentence creates a certain set of expectations, concerning the location, age or social status of the participants in the story, which is then reversed in the second half of the sentence as the frame of the picture, so to speak, widens to include details which, had they been evident initially, would have clarified the situation immediately: e.g. 'Every day at school I used to get bullied, kicked, spat at, and pushed into a urinal . . . so after a while I resigned from my job as headmaster.' If it had been clear that the speaker were a headmaster at the start of this sentence, the joke would not have worked: i.e. 'I am a headmaster at a school and every day at school I was bullied, kicked, spat at and pushed into a urinal so . . . so after a while I resigned from my job as headmaster.' Or, 'So, I was lying there, stretched out on the seat naked, masturbating . . . and then I got off the bus.' If we had been aware, at the beginning of the scene, that the masturbating, naked speaker was on the bus, then we would have realised immediately that he was a sexual deviant, rather than simply a man masturbating, harmlessly, alone at home: i.e. 'I was lying there, stretched out on the seat on the bus, naked, masturbating . . . and then I got off the bus.' Why not try writing your own Pull Back and Reveal jokes? And then why not try smashing yourself repeatedly in the face with a claw hammer?

These days I love a good Pull Back and Reveal. Not in the way you are thinking, madam! I just wish I could still write them. I don't do Pull Back and Reveal any more. Instead, with painful slowness, I raise a ratty curtain that was covering something which we had already seen quite clearly anyway through holes in the tattered fabric, and display it shamefacedly, with an air of crushed inevitability, as if to say, 'Here you are. Is this what you wanted? Are you happy now? Do you feel entertained?'

So . . . But it is weird, getting accused of blasphemy. I don't know if any of you have ever been formally accused of blasphemy* . . . but . . . And I'm always relieved when people laugh at that idea, because everywhere round the country . . . when I say . . . 'Hey, I don't know if any of you have ever been accused of blasphemy,' people go, 'Ha ha, no, it would be ridiculous.' Except in, er, in Builth Wells, I don't know if you know that. It's kind of . . . I said that, there was kind of silence of people going, 'What have you heard about here? What have you heard about this apparently normal market town with a stone circle on the rugby pitch? What have you heard?' But it is, it is weird, right, joking apart, to be accused of blasphemy, right, because I'm . . . I don't, I don't . . . I don't believe in God, thousands of people do, they might be right. OK? But even if you don't believe in God, the idea that you have offended a super-being is quite intimidating, right. It makes the idea of having made Robbie Williams bored seem inconsequential. Do you know . . .? That's, that's water off a duck's back to me. 'Oh, were you bored? Oh, are you God? No.' Right, so . . .†

* The joke here, of course, is that it is rare to be accused, formally, of blasphemy. Now, hopefully, in this country at least, it will never happen again.

† As someone who doesn't believe in God, I wasn't really worried about the idea of having offended God Himself. But for this whole forthcoming section to work dramatically, I needed to be in jeopardy. I needed to entertain the possibility of God for this half hour to work, and every night I would try to rephrase this section, to keep it sounding real, so that I could scare myself at the enormity of what a charge of blasphemy might mean, if there actually were a God, or if one were prepared to consider the possibility of there being a God. And by the end of doing this show, I'd played this part out so many times that I think that whilst onstage I was actually

But also I'm not a religious person but loads of people are, and they might be right. And even if you aren't religious, I suspect like me you entertain the fact that it's your right to change your mind, and you might want to go back towards faith. But the idea that you've been cut off kind of legally is quite a frightening idea. So that, and the threat of prosecution and the threats and whatever, it did kind of really stress me out, this idea of being cut off . . .*

---

afraid of God and what He might do to me. I made Him real to myself.

In the same way, in the late nineties Johnny Vegas performed a routine about being a Redcoat at a fifties Butlin's holiday camp so many times, and with such conviction and depth of local colour and period detail, that when I asked him about it in 2002, he seemed uncertain whether he'd actually been a Redcoat in the early days of rock and roll, until we worked out that this would have meant he would have to have been born in the forties at the latest. Johnny did not look especially well at the time, but was clearly not of pensionable age.

* I don't really imagine making the journey back to the religious faith that I had briefly in my teens. But it was dramatically necessary for me to have something at stake here, and it was easy to extemporise something convincing every night when I put myself in the position of an agnostic, or even a faltering believer, rather than an atheist, worrying that they might be shut out of God's light for ever. The visible Stewart Lee onstage in this show needed to be more uncertain of his beliefs than the Stewart Lee inside his brain controlling him, so that the charge of blasphemy had an emotional impact for him and for the audience.

I also wanted to make the piece relate to everyone, irrespective of their religious beliefs, and to invite believers to put themselves in my position. After all, the issue that I was seeking to explore here was a human-rights issue about freedom of expression that everyone should be able to support, regardless of the red herring of their actual religious beliefs.

In the six years since I wrote this, atheism or agnosticism has

And so in February, I . . . I left London where I live and I went to stay with my mum, where she lives, in a little village in Worcestershire, right.* This is the kind of little village it is. I got there early to see her once and she wasn't in. So I walked round to the village shop and I bought a muesli bar and I ate it in a lay-by, right. And about four hours later, my mum said, 'Oh, the woman next door said she saw you eating a muesli bar in a lay-by earlier.'† That's the kind of little village . . . This is the kind of little village it is, right. The house opposite my mum's, on the lawn the guy's got a white flagpole and occasionally he runs the Union Jack up it.‡ And if he does, you know that British

-----

become the default setting for many more performers, writers and audiences, probably as a reaction against the rise of religious fundamentalism. It's no fun preaching to the converted, even when you agree with them. Recently, the comedian Marcus Brigstocke toured a show, *God Collar*, which examined the emotional limitations of atheism, the piece being an alternative to a glut of rationalist comedians currently making a progress round the mid-scale art-centre circuit. As the comedian Simon Munnery once quipped, 'If the crowd gets behind you, you are facing the wrong way.' Luckily for Simon, this is not a situation he has ever had to deal with.

* I did not go to stay with my mum during this phase of the *Jerry Springer* blasphemy scandal. I was actually in Germany at the time. But I had been to my mum's two months previously, in November and December 2004, after I was discharged from hospital with diverticulitis, and it was this period, as explained in the previous chapter, and this memory of my mother's home and the landscape around it, that I used as the basis for the rest of the show.

† This happened.

‡ It would be nice if you didn't assume anyone flying the flag might be a BNP voter, but they usually are. Especially west of Birmingham. A chain of bed-and-breakfasts run by frightened racist Brummies stretches as far south-west as Land's End, where they in turn are hated by pureblood pirates as unwanted incomers to the

troops have committed an atrocity abroad, OK? That's . . . that's the kind of little village it is, right.

But as it turned out, running away to Worcestershire was a mistake. What I didn't know was that the New Labour MP for Worcester was one of the New Labour MPs that was calling for our opera to be banned and for us to be prosecuted, so it was in all the local papers. My mum's friends would keep coming round with clippings of me and the composer, with a thing saying 'BAD MEN DUE TO GO TO HELL' or something . . . And my mum would go, 'Oh, you look a bit fat in that one. Never mind, I'll put it in the scrapbook. With all the other clippings of people calling you a cunt. Going right back to your school reports. And your adoption certificate.' [*turns back on audience*] 'Reason for abandonment of infant.' 'Infant is a cunt, clearly.' 'I expect this early childhood rejection will lead to him spending most of his adult life travelling the country in search of the approval of ever-dwindling groups of strangers.' [*turning back*] Yeah, laugh it up. Um . . .*

But those women in that shop . . . The women in the shop that I mentioned, right, they really like me in the

---

republic of Cornwall, taking our jobs, buying our cottages, gobbling up our cream.

* Obviously, as an adoptee, I reserve the right to do this material about myself being adopted, but I don't know if I'd do it today, as a parent myself. I suppose the joke enabled a valuable moment here, creating a jarring shock laugh in the middle of this meandering set-up, and it was fun to play with the set of assumptions made around adoptees, such as them being attention-seekers looking for approval, that dovetail with similarly glib assumptions made about stand-ups. And perhaps the brutal line 'Infant is a cunt' was also an important hinge in the whole show's shift of tone. 'Infant' is also one of the great comedy words, an especial favourite of the shadowy satirist Chris Morris.

village shop. And from what I can work out, it's 'cause I've got a long black coat that I sometimes wear. And that's kind of enough, you know. They go, 'Ooh, he came in, Mrs Lee, in his coat.' Whatever next. It's like Keanu Reeves in *The Matrix*. It's like Gary Numan had come round. Batman.*

And so they really like me. So they used to cut these things out of the newspaper slagging me off, laminate them, stick them on the wall in the shop and get me to sign them, right. Like I'm an outlaw, you know. So if you ever go past there, you'll know what that is.†

But again, joking apart, the blasphemy things did your head in, the legal threats, the collapse of the work and everything, it did kind of stress me out. So I did what anyone would do under the circumstances, which was to drink heavily every day. Um. But it's difficult to drink in the countryside, right. It's not like here in Cardiff where the streets are thronged with revellers all the time.‡ Nothing going on, you know. I used to have to walk about two miles

---

* I once owned a huge, long, swishy leather coat and I wore it in Edinburgh in August 1999. I was of no fixed abode at the time and I could sleep in or on the coat, wherever I ended up, and keep pants and deodorant in the massive pockets. Because I wore this coat, the *Guardian* Photoshopped my head onto a picture of Keanu Reeves in *The Matrix*, dressed in full leather cyberpunk mode, and appended an unfunny caption.

† It's all true. In the corner shop, on the road near the village where my mum now lives, I was asked to sign a clipping of a newspaper article in which the local MP slagged off *Jerry Springer: The Opera*, which was then put on the wall by some bus timetables above the takeaway-pork-roll counter.

‡ Whatever town I was in I would use its name here. People either seemed to think it was funny because the streets often were thronged with revellers, as in Nottingham or Newcastle, or because they weren't, as in Malton, Yorkshire.

to the nearest pub. And I'd get in there and there'd just be the same three old blokes every night. And they'd go, 'Ooh the blasphemer's arrived, cross yourselves lads,' you know.* And they'd make me drink stuff without telling me what it was. They'd go, 'Have some of this.' And I go, 'All right, I'll have a pint of that.' 'A pint?' 'Yeah.' I'd have about four pints of this stuff. I thought it was real ale, it turns out it's this thing called barley wine, right. And you're only, you're only supposed to have an egg cup of it, basically. But no one told me that, 'cause I wasn't from there. I was from a town, right.†

So I went out at about half – I was trashed – about half eleven at night. I could hardly stand. I was mad anyway, and paranoid 'cause of all this blasphemy stuff. Stressed out. And I was scared about how I was going to get home,

* The whole affair did make me feel paranoid. People would come up to me – in motorway service stations, in pub toilets, in the street – and ask me if I was one of the writers of *Jerry Springer: The Opera*, and I never knew if they were going to congratulate me or attack me. I was even threatened with physical violence by a busker in an Edinburgh subway as a result of the opera. He raised his guitar like a weapon on behalf of aggrieved Christians everywhere, before backing down when I lost my temper with him and briefly became berserker fearless, shouting, 'Come on then, come on then, for fuck's sake, you fucking idiot.'

† This story makes its way into our tale from a weekend's writing retreat with Richard Herring in 1992, to the home of our radio producer, Sarah Smith, in the spooky Suffolk village of Hoxne, where none of the bar staff in the pub saw fit to tell me that you shouldn't drink barley wine in pints. I have never been so sick. I slept on the floor in an attic, the walls of which were covered in ancient LSD and magic mushrooms and Hawkwind-themed graffiti, and woke in a carpet of vomit. Just once, before I die, I'd like to do this sort of thing again.

in the dark. But I set off along the road. And after about two minutes, exactly what I was worried about happened. A big lorry came round, I thought it was going to hit me. I had to jump into this kind of agricultural drainage ditch. I, I came out all covered in water and mud and animal excrement and stuff. Carried on walking along the road. And then about four minutes later, about three hundred yards ahead of me on the right, I saw this kind of white figure, like a, like a ghost, right.*

Now. I'm not superstitious, I was drunk, and I was under a lot of stress, and paranoid. So I thought, 'I'm imagining this.' I ignored it, right. And I tried to walk past it. When I got about ten, fifteen feet away from this thing, I recognised it as being Jesus, right? But even so, I still thought it was my imagination, OK? Because we all know that Jesus should be black or Arabic or Jewish or whatever. I had given Him the face of Robert Powell – the nineteen-seventies television Jesus. So I thought it was my subconscious. Or Jesus was real and He had chosen to appear to me in a form that I would recognise. 'Cause He would know that I also used to watch *The Detectives*. Mm? He could have come as Jasper Carrott, which is the same initials, right, but Robert

* Looking at this now, I think it's another example of the Irish comedian Dave Allen, a TV staple during my childhood, making his way into my subconscious. The long shaggy-dog story, often with a supernatural element, during which they would dim the lights in the studio, was a staple of his stand-up, and here's me, ripping this approach off. Find some old Dave Allen on YouTube. It seems impossible that comedy so sophisticated and subtle and damned well enlightened was ever considered for broadcast. There was no tradition in stand-up that explains the emergence of Dave Allen. Was there a whole school of deadpan rationalists bubbling away in Ireland that we knew nothing about? Where did he come from? Sadly, *Dave Allen: The Biography* by Carolyn Soutar tells us nothing.

Powell is a more holy kind of figure, isn't he?*

So . . . But even so, I thought, 'This is my subconscious, I'm going nuts.' I tried to walk on past it, but as I got level with Jesus, He took my hand and He started to lead me along the lane. Even then, I thought, 'This is still my subconscious.' What do I want? (a) I want to get home safely, and (b) I have this anxiety about reconnecting with faith. And He's taking my hand, in my imagination that's what that is, right? It's not real.†

But then He started talking to me, Jesus. He said to me, 'Stew' – that kind of swung it – He said to me, 'Stew, I know that my representatives on Earth have come out against you and your co-workers and loved ones and accused you of blasphemy,' He said. 'But I forgive you,' He said. 'And I want you, if you can, to find it in your heart to forgive me.'‡

* Here I'd use the whole space of the stage, marking out the territory in which this encounter happened, and I'd try to play all the musing on Robert Powell and Jasper Carrott as if they were the ramblings of a deranged and distracted brain, rather than as if they were attempts to be funny.

† Again, despite not believing in God, I think part of getting this bit to work was about imagining, convincingly, the amount of comfort that physical contact with an apparently forgiving Jesus would give you, if you were seriously worried about being cast out from faith. To have a holy figure take corporeal form and hold your hand on a dark lane would be something we could all respond to. How wonderful it would be to have this kind of vision. Is it any wonder than sometimes people will such experiences into being?

‡ Here I suppose I am playing the religious right, our tormentors, at their own game. Holy figures, like Jesus, are vessels for carrying whatever message is poured into them. People with particular political ends attribute their own beliefs to these avatars and impose their own values on them. Here, instead of allowing the religious right to monopolise him, I am co-opting Jesus to my own ends, and my ends involve establishing that I am the new Jesus.

And I said to Him, 'What do you mean, Jesus?' And He said, 'Well, Stew,' He said, 'there was another man, wasn't there, two thousand years ago, who annoyed the religious establishment of his time. In fact, a lot of people didn't like some of the true things that he had to say. And . . . in fact, they crucified him for it, Stew, and . . . maybe, just maybe, you are the rightful inheritor of his crown.'*

Now can I just make clear at this point, right, I am not saying that I'm Jesus, OK? I'm not saying that I am Jesus. That's for you to think about at the . . . I'm not saying I'm Jesus, right, I'm not. But if I was Him – I'm not – but if I was Him, this – not – but if I was Him – I'm not – but if I was Him – I'm not Him, I'm not Him, right, I know you think I am but I'm not. You're going, 'Yeah, but if you were, you would say you weren't, wouldn't you? To trick us.' I'm not. I'm not Him, right? I'm not Jesus, I'm not Him, come on. That would be ridiculous. That's the . . . I'm the last person that He would come as. It definitely wouldn't be me. Oh, maybe He would . . . I'm not, right. I'm not Jesus, right.†

* Here is an unselfconscious echo of every hero myth ever written, from King Arthur to *Star Wars*, where the role of the champion is passed on to the unwilling youth. Again, it also reincorporates the 'I am not saying I am Jesus' riff, last seen after the mosque-fart-atrocity bit in last year's *Stand-Up Comedian* set, but with its origins in Lee and Herring double-act material. The key here was to play it with absolute sincerity. In last year's set, it was a knowing joke, from behind which I winked out at the audience. This time around I was asking them to consider the suggestion that in my mentally deranged state, I think I may have been handed the mantle of 'the new Jesus' by Jesus himself, in order to combat injustice. 'Take this cup away from me!'
† Again, like the Ang Lee routine in last year's show, this was another moment where I had to kind of forget what I was trying to

But if I was Him, this is the kind of place I would come and speak, isn't it? Yeah. Not in the vain, arrogant Millennium Centre. I would come here, to this humble place, and I would speak to people like you – to drunks and whores – I would come here. I would come here. I would come here. In Canton. To this simple, humble place with adequate but ultimately limited wheelchair access.* 'Cause I would know from the first time around they will come, clamouring, 'Heal me, Jesus, heal me.' There's only so much one

---

say, and approach it in a new way every night. Groping towards the right words to express the idea, in real time, I'd meet the audience halfway.

* Wherever I was I would play off the 'humble' venue I was in against the grand one round the corner. 'Humble', it must be said, is another very Richard Herring word, as is 'vain', as we established earlier. Richard writes comedy in the vocabulary of a sexually frustrated Methodist preacher, and his influence upon me is once again apparent. On this recording I use the Cardiff Millennium Centre, which is the most conceited and inhospitable venue in Britain, and the Chapter Arts centre, which is lovely, as the vain and humble venues, respectively. Pretty much anywhere will do to make the limited-wheelchair-access joke, as the audience's assumption is always that wheelchair access is limited, even when there's wheelchairs all around them.

Again, I had to play the wheelchair joke straight, so that it was about the suffering of the harassed healer, namely me or Jesus, and not making fun of the wheelchair users. If you played it straight, as if the presence of wheelchair users were a terrible inconvenience to a mystical healer, you could do it to a row of wheelchairs and not worry. If you played it for laughs, you couldn't. It was about my pain. It had to be inclusive, not exclusive. On a good day, this is the difference between Ricky Gervais and Jim Davidson, a difference Davidson fails to grasp and one which, to be fair, becomes increasingly irrelevant to Gervais's audience too as it grows larger and less finessed.

man can do. You can't have a quota system. So it's better to just speak in a place where they can't get in. With the best will in the world, with the best will in the world, with the best will in the world. We mean nothing by it.

So He was leading me along the road, Jesus. And within about a minute the same thing had happened again. Another big lorry came round, I was scared. But He seemed to do something to either slow it down, or we became immaterial. It passed through us, we weren't hurt. But that panicked me, and the alcohol kicked in, I started stumbling around. What He did, Jesus, was He grabbed my right arm and He hooked it over His shoulder, like that, and He started carrying me along, like you would a drunk mate, you know. Now initially I thought this was a bit of an imposition but then I realised He did have some previous experience of carrying a heavy burden in that way. And to be honest, under more difficult circumstances.* And He seemed to like the warmth, the human contact. And in that way, we finally got to my mum's front door.†

* So here's a thing. This image of Jesus bearing the drunken narrator seems, admittedly, disrespectful towards Christ's sufferings whilst carrying his own cross to Calvary, but, on the other hand, you're going to have to know your New Testament fairly well to get it. Hopefully, it flatters the biblical knowledge of some of the very people who might be offended by it, putting them in something of a quandary. Also, it seems important that Jesus is supporting me, helping me.
† Here I am beginning the process of humanising Jesus, and making him physical, ready for our pungent encounter in the toilet. 'He liked the warmth, the human contact.' One imagines he would, after centuries as a bloodless metaphor. Let's make him real and see what that would actually mean. Though it was not a decision I was aware of making during the writing process, I wonder how much of the effect of this decision to place a physically real Jesus in a world of drunkenness and vomiting was a subconscious attempt to ape

And I started trying to get the key in and fumbling around. And then I thought, 'This is a bit weird. Jesus is here. What's the correct etiquette? Am I supposed to ask Him in for a coffee? You know, and hope He doesn't read anything into that.' OK, I'm not saying that Jesus is gay. That's part of what caused the problems last year. But one in ten people are and you can't – especially in a port town – you can't make assumptions.* And while I was thinking

---

the idea of 'the Word made flesh'. Part of the charm of the gospels is to do with the story of a divine figure who chooses to engage with the physical world. And here he is doing it again.

I wrote a story at school, when I was fifteen, about finding a dead African baby in the park on Christmas Day, in which I described its body in terms of Christmas paraphernalia – crackers, streamers, turkey bones. No one knew whether to punish me for poor taste or give me a prize for having a social conscience. Twenty years later, I am doing the same thing as a stand-up, trying to give form to an abstract idea.

I suppose this is what all stand-up, what all comedy, what all satire does. You take an idea and say, 'What if this was actually real, what would it be like?' If Jesus was really the loving and wise Jesus of the New Testament, rather than the angry and judgemental Jesus of the Christian right, then just as he fraternised with prostitutes and tax gatherers so he would help me, the drunken blasphemer comedian, home.

* To a degree this is deliberately provocative. One of the planks in the Christian right's case against *Jerry Springer: The Opera* was that we had portrayed Jesus as gay. We hadn't. We had written a lengthy dream sequence in which the titular talk-show host is forced to confront his demons and his guilt in the form of an imaginary chat show set in hell, where the symbolic figures from Judaeo-Christian mythology all appear with problems of the sort one might see on an American talk show. An audience of demons taunts Jesus for supposedly being gay, and he counters, 'Actually, I am a bit gay,' over a dancing, dainty rhythm that ensured it always got a laugh. Richard Thomas wrote this line. I remember him singing this

about this, He disappeared. And I felt bad because I was, I was grateful that He'd helped me home. But I was relieved that I didn't have to deal with what to do. And I, and I felt like I'd betrayed Him, but He'd gone and I was relieved.*

------

new section through for the first time in his damp and cluttered studio under a Brixton railway arch, where he would urinate into pint glasses and then hide them under piles of rubbish, rather than make the lengthy journey to the dark toilet, some five metres away outside the door. It was an irresistibly funny bit, but we knew we would be challenged over it, so we needed to get our defence straight in our heads. First of all, it didn't really matter what it meant, as it was happening in a vivid fever dream, as a result of taunts by devils, as Jerry's life flashed before him in-between the moment he is shot and the moment he dies. Secondly, we decided that we wanted our Jesus to speak for all mankind and embody many varied fragments of all human sexuality.

It wasn't a line I felt I personally could have submitted to the opera, as it flirts with a kind of schoolboy homophobia, albeit ironically and in the mouths of demons, whom one assumes aren't operating to a contemporary moral agenda, and are in the dream of a dying talk-show host anyway. But Richard is 100 per cent gay, without a straight bone in his body, so it was up to him to use these words if he wanted to. I seem to remember that he has come out to his family, but if this is not the case, I do apologise for breaking the news so clumsily here.

The character of Stewart Lee on the doorstep here, unsure of whether to ask the vision of Jesus in, in case he assumes he is propositioning him, is an exaggerated form of myself, so worried about what is the politically correct course of action that I may end up making a massive social blunder. This Stewart Lee doesn't want Jesus to assume that he thinks he is gay, but if Jesus is gay, he also doesn't want Jesus to think he has a problem with that. The joke is on me here, but I distanced Jesus from the suggestion that he is gay via my own panicked assumptions about his sexuality.

* It's important that I feel I've betrayed Jesus by being hesitant about asking him in. I need to establish that there's a kind of bond

210

And I let myself into the house, and as soon as I got in I realised I was going to be sick. But I didn't want to go upstairs where my mum was asleep and wake her up. So I ran round to this little room my mum's got by the back door. Your mum's probably got a room like this, OK? It's about as big as the front of this stage, OK? And there's a little hand basin here, and there's a toilet here, and here there's a towel rail. And in the towel rail is a little hand towel. That hand towel isn't to be used for hands, OK? That hand towel is only to be used for wiping the cat's feet when the cat comes in wet from the garden, OK? It's the cat's-feet towel. 'Don't wipe your hands on that, Stew, it's the cat's-feet towel. Use your hair.'*

So I ran round to this little room. But before I could get a grip, I was immediately sick all over the floor, right, all

---

developing. This moment also deliberately echoes Peter's denial of Christ after his capture. The suffering servant knows we will betray him, but forgives us and loves us all the same.

* Despite the obscenities that follow in the next fifteen minutes, many people would talk to me after the show about this 'cat's-feet towel' idea, about how they had had cat's-feet towels in their childhood homes, or that they had one now. The cat's-feet towel becomes more important as this routine drags on, an island of domestic normality in the midst of a horrific nightmare.

I discovered the comedic power of the cat's-feet towel entirely by accident, while looking to give the story of my imaginary encounter with Jesus in my mum's toilet the ring of truth by loading it with vividly remembered local detail. We had a cat's-feet towel in the toilet, so I put it in the story. I didn't realise how strongly people would identify with it. I had a brief taste, by complete accident, of what it must be like to be Michael McIntyre at Wembley, on a massive screen, talking about a drawer full of insulating tape. Ironically, I am reliably informed that Michael McIntyre doesn't actually have a 'man drawer', and invented the concept in order to ridicule ordinary people, for whom he has nothing but haughty contempt.

over my mum's floor. So I bent down – I wasn't myself, remember, I was mad. And I tried to scoop up the sick. But doing that made me be sick again. And I was sick all down my clothes, until my clothes had become covered in, in sick. And I groped around and I ended up grabbing the cat's-feet towel. And I used that to try and wipe it up, but there was too much and the cat's-feet towel became over-whelmed, saturated with sick. If the cat had come in now, with wet feet, they would have had to stay wet. Or have sick put on them. Which would leave worse footprints.*

And looking at that cat's-feet towel, that made me be sick again. And I was sick into the, to the basin, until the hand basin was overflowing with sick. So I tried to scoop the sick out of the hand basin and fling it into the toilet. But doing that made me be sick again, and I was sick on top of that sick in there, until the toilet was blocked up with sick. And I stepped back and I shut my eyes and I thought, 'That's it now, surely. No more.'

But then I felt the sick rising in me again, and I thought, 'What am I supposed to do? The floor's covered in sick. My clothes are covered in sick. The cat's-feet towel is a write-off. Frankly. The hand basin's overflowing with sick. The toilet's overflowing with sick. What am I supposed to do?'

---

* This routine, with the addition of the new cat's-feet towel ele-ment, is a jazzed-up version of one of the first routines I wrote, from about 1991, when I was beginning to develop the irritating repetitive style with which I am closely associated today. It is based on an entirely true incident when I still lived with my mum as a teenager and came home from a heavy Christmas Eve and vomited everywhere, and blocked up the sink with sick. As explained in the previous chapter, an impulsive improvisation off the back of this bit, late at night in New Zealand in May 2005, provided the starting point for this whole show.

212

And I opened my eyes and I looked down, and on my left, on the floor, kneeling down, smiling, looking up at me, was Jesus. And He was pointing at His open mouth, as if what He wanted was for me to vomit into the open mouth of Christ. And I looked down and I thought, 'This can't be right.' But He was pointing and laughing and smiling, and encouraging me. And then I remembered He did have some history of sacrifice. So against, against my better judgement, at his apparent insistence, I did it – I vomited into the open mouth of Christ, until the mouth of Christ was overflowing with my sick.

Now, right. I've been doing stand-up for seventeen years, OK? And I can sense when there's tension in a room. And I know why it is and I un–, I understand it. Basically there's a performer–audience bond of trust built up. We have worked on that together over the last hour. And, and, and you think, 'Yes, there is, Stew, but you've broken that bond of trust. Because we weren't expecting to be made to visualise this image. There was no warning of this, it wasn't flagged up. There was no indication that you would do something like this, especially when you opened with all that light-hearted material about the bombings.'* And if you feel betrayed, I am . . . You have my sympathies, I'm sorry, right, there's . . . But I'm just trying to understand

---

* Here I am trying everything I can, with soft-voiced confidentiality, in order to give the audience permission to laugh. 'Permission to laugh' is a phrase I always remember the dramaturge Tom Morris, of Battersea Arts Centre, using when describing the comedy process, and I think it's an extremely helpful notion. We can appear to deny the audience permission to laugh at something apparently serious, thereby ensuring that they laugh, or we can try and find a way of giving them permission to laugh at something about which they may feel uneasy.

this. And there is a performer–audience relationship, and there are probably people here thinking, 'Yes, there is, Stew, and you have presumed upon that relationship. This is inappropriate, it's too much too soon. It's gone too far. It's presumptuous to do this. It's like fingering someone on a first date, you wouldn't do it. Even at arm's length, wearing a mitten, through the shattered window of a rural bus shelter, at the end of an otherwise pleasant evening, as an inappropriate gesture of thanks. You wouldn't do that, Stew, so why are you doing this? Why? Why?'*

And there are probably other people here going, 'Yeah, it is like a relationship, Stew, the performer–audience relationship. But tonight, with what you've done, you've made it feel like a marriage, and it feels like a marriage that's gone on for too long and is in its death throes.' And if you feel like that, if you feel like this is a marriage that's gone on too long, right, then maybe it's time for you to start seeing other comedians. Right? And I can't pretend that I'd be happy about that, right, I wouldn't be, OK? But if that would help to keep the spark of this alive, then you should do it. You should go and see them. Go and see them. And I will wait for you to come back to me because I love you.

And I will come here, come here when you're all laughing at something else, when you're laughing at Nicko and Joe's Bad Film Club, I will come here and I'll be behind

* When some horrible English sports fans came to see this show in New Zealand during a British Lions rugby tour, this was the only bit they laughed at. 'Now you're getting somewhere,' they said, when I used the word 'fingering', after they'd spent the previous hour sabotaging the show. It seems too coarse in retrospect, this bit, to sit in amongst the rest of the story, strangely. But it got a laugh in a dry patch, and if one must write about teenage sexual fumblings, at least let it have lyrical Proustian pretensions.

those railings up there.* And I'll be watching you giving them the laughs that you owe to me. And I'll be crying. But because it's you, because it's you and I love you, I won't be able to stop myself from becoming aroused. Behind the fence thing. And I'll be crouching down. And I'll be watching you all laughing – 'ha ha ha' – and I'll be crying, right, but I will also be masturbating. Right? And I will be enjoying that unique fusion of profound grief and violent sexual arousal. And that's the most profound feeling anyone can ever have. And if you have never had that feeling, you won't understand me. And if you don't understand me, how do you expect this to work out, right? So you have to understand that feeling. If you've never experienced that, then . . . If someone that you love has, has died, right, don't take flowers to the grave, take whatever apparatus you need to achieve a state of mind whereby you can pay them the highest tribute of all.†

* Nicko and Joe's Bad Film Club was a regular night at the venue where this transcript was recorded, the Chapter Arts Centre, Cardiff. During this bit, I would try to hide somewhere in the dark, in the back of the room, leaving the audience looking at an empty stage for as long as possible. Since '90s *Comedian* I always aim to try and spend as much time during the show offstage as possible. I interviewed Mark E. Smith of The Fall for the *Sunday Times* in 1996, who at that point was spending increasingly long periods of the band's shows offstage or hiding behind curtains and amplifiers while singing. Oddly, this absence of a focus point only seemed to make the performances more exciting, an effect I expect I noted. Smith joked that his ambition was to be able to vacate the stage permanently during his own shows. 'That'd be ideal,' he said, 'I'll just stand down the front watching with a pint.'

† I never articulated the course of action suggested here, and preferred to let the audience figure it out for themselves, absolving me of blame. I can honestly say I have no idea where this notion came

[*back on mic*] So I'd vomited into the open mouth of Christ. And I stepped back and I shut my eyes and I thought, 'That's it now surely, no more.' But then I felt the sick rising in me again, and I thought, 'What am I supposed to do now? The floor is covered in sick, my clothes are covered in sick, the cat's-feet towel is covered in sick, the sink's overflowing with sick, the toilet's overflowing, the open mouth of Christ is overflowing with sick. What . . .? What . . .?' And then I opened my eyes and I looked down, and He was there again, Jesus, on my right. But this time He had His back to me and He was doing a kind of handstand by the sink. And His raiment had slipped down, it looked like a kind of third-length, floral-print hospital gown. And He had His right hand on the floor to, to balance Him upside down, and with His left hand He was using the fingers to kind of splay open His anus. As if what He . . . As if what He wanted was for me to vomit into the gaping anus of Christ.

[*off-mic, shouting*] And don't imagine, Cardiff, that I come here and talk about this lightly, OK? I thought about it, I asked around – well, I know it's a bit much but I asked around, I said to – oh look, I asked Tony Law, he's a Canadian stand-up comedian, he's the most reasonable man I know. I said to him, 'Tony, do you honestly think I can go round the country in front of people and use the phrase, "I vomited into the gaping anus of Christ"?' And he said, 'Well, possibly, if it's in context. But', he said, 'you won't be able to use it as the title of a live DVD.' I said, 'I'm not going to do that, Tony, I'm not insane.'*

---

from, and I don't think I'd have the courage to try and make something like this work now.

* I would launch into this bit, again off-mic, after a big pause. It was based on an actual conversation with the sturdily surreal Canadian comedian Tony Law, and he did say, 'Possibly, if it's in context,

216

But imagine this situation, it is impossible. There is no right way out of it. I bent down, I said to Jesus, 'Are you sure this is what you want?' And He said to me, 'Look, you're going to be taken to court for blasphemy for doing nothing, I feel like I owe you one, knock yourself out.'*

So against my better judgement, 'cause He told me to, I did it. I vomited into the gaping anus of Christ till the gaping anus of Christ was overflowing with my sick. I did that. Are you happy now?†

---

but you won't be able to use it as the title of a live DVD.' But we were not discussing this piece of material. We were discussing a routine I had written about the idea of parents embarrassing their children, based on something my father said about a woman he saw coming up a gangplank onto a pleasure cruiser on the Thames in May 2000. It was a sentence which, almost brilliantly, managed to be simultaneously racist, sexist, fattist and blasphemous, and yet concealed within it an obvious lust for its subject that seemed, somehow, to render it almost charming, which was my father's gift. And yet it remains a sentence so offensive that even here, in a section of this book in which we are discussing at length the idea of vomiting on Jesus, I am not prepared to repeat it. And yet Carol Cleveland quipped that I was sick and needed help.

* This was usually a real watershed moment, where even punters that were until now suspicious would buy into the show. In my twisted cosmology, Jesus has offered himself up for humiliation in an attempt to redress the balance of the wrongs his followers have done unto me.

† This whole shtick of dropping the mic, wandering about in despair, falling to my knees, lying on the ground and then reconnecting with the mic has become a regular trick in all my recent sets. When I finally got to play bigger rooms, I'd end up in balconies and the back of the circle, standing on chairs, shouting. I recently saw a young comic called Ahir Shah do a miniaturised, shot-for-shot duplication of it in a ten-minute benefit slot. It's probably time to stop now.

[*back on-mic*] And then I stepped back, and I shut my eyes, and I thought, 'That's it now surely, no more.' But then I felt the sick rising in me again. And I thought, 'What am I supposed to do? The floor is covered in sick, my clothes are covered in sick, the cat's-feet towel is ruined, the sink's overflowing with sick, the toilet, the anus of Chr– . . .'

Then I remembered, lads, you know when you're doing a wee in the toilet, right? And there's a bit of poo on the back of the bowl. And you think, 'Ooh, I'll hose that off. That's my cleaning done for the week.'* So what I did was I got my penis out and as, as respectfully and tenderly and accurately as I could, I urinated into the gaping anus of Christ so that all the vomit there kind of foamed up and went on the floor, leaving just enough room for me to vomit one second and final time into the gaping anus of Christ, which I then did.

* This joke was one of Dave Thompson's, which I remembered from touring with him in the early nineties. I can't remember if I bought it off him, but I certainly asked his permission to use it. I felt at this point that I needed to slip into stand-up comedy mode, to change the mood and get a good solid laugh before going deeper up river with the climax of the routine, and Dave's joke popped into my head.

Dave was one of the best comics around when I started out, and once performed a one-man show in Edinburgh in a leotard in which he did the dance of an imaginary worm. Dave also wrote the most brilliant proper gags, but was best known as the original Tinky Winky on *Teletubbies*, a role he was then sacked from after the producers claimed he interpreted the purple-bodied felt creature 'incorrectly', though Dave has a more sinister story about his dismissal, involving a dog. Dave subsequently enjoyed more costume-character work, though his role as a horse in the 2004 live Harry Hill show *Hooves* was similarly compromised, as Dave was too weak to carry the floppy-collared loon™ on his back.

And then my mum came in. She looked at the sick on the floor. She looked at the sick all down my clothes, she looked at the cat's-feet towel, all covered in sick, she was irritated by that. She looked at the sink overflowing with sick, the toilet overflowing with sick, the gaping anus of Christ overflowing with my sick. And she said to me, 'Have you been sick? Into the gaping anus of Christ?' And I said, 'No, this was like this when I got here, the cat must have done it.' And she said, 'The cat's in the garden and his feet are wet. And I'd like to know what you propose to do about that, given the current state of the cat's-feet towel.'*

And then she said to me, 'It was you, wasn't it?' And I said, 'Yes.' And she said, 'Let me give you some advice.' And I listened because I love her and she tends to be right. She said, 'Given your current situation,' she said, 'and the state of the world as it is,' she said, 'under no circumstances can you ever consider talking about this incident onstage.'†And I said to her, 'Well, I might have to.' And she said, 'Well, I can't stop you, but', she said – that's what she always used to do when I was a kid, 'I can't stop you, but', it's like putting the ball in your court – she said, 'I can't stop you, but', she said, 'if you are going to talk about this, you have to know why you're doing it, what kind of point you're trying to make.'‡

* Again, this is the bastardised pay-off to the lengthy 'vomiting in my mum's toilet' routine I did in the early nineties, with added religious elements and cat's-feet-towel coda.
† But look! That's just what I am doing!
‡ It would be incredibly naff for an artist to explain the point of their work onstage. But by talking about it to my mother, in the form of reported speech which the audience are overhearing, I was trying to circumvent any wilful misinterpretation of the show by journalists, fundamentalist Christians, etc.

And I said to her, 'Well, three things, Mother. Firstly, to make the point that a symbol, be it an icon or a flag or whatever, is only as worthy of respect as the values of the people that appropriate it. Secondly, that if a symbol goes out into the world, into places where it's perhaps not understood or wanted or valued, you shouldn't be too upset if it then takes on a shape you don't recognise as your own. And thirdly, that if you attempt to apply limits to freedom of expression, either through legislation or intimidation or threats, what will then happen is that reasonable people, often against their own better judgement, will feel obliged to test those limits, er, by going into areas they don't feel entirely comfortable with.' I personally haven't enjoyed the last half hour at all, I do it only to safeguard your liberty. And ...

[*Applause.*]

Ah. That's never had a clap before, which probably means it is time to stop doing this show.*

---

* On this recording, I was clearly preaching to the converted. In the week that I performed this show for the last time in the UK, in February 2006 at the Hackney Empire in a double bill with Kevin McAleer's Chalk and Cheese, Danish police arrested three men plotting to kill one of the cartoonists alleged to have insulted the prophet Mohammed the previous September. Even as I stood onstage there, saying this conclusion, I realised that it now seemed glib. If you were writing a show about religious censorship, even six months later, you would have had to take on board that the odd Christian death threat and the financial collapse of a theatre project was less significant than the (partly manufactured) global panic about the Danish Mohammed cartoons. The bar of religious intolerance had been raised, and one would have been obliged to contextualise the *Jerry Springer: The Opera* issue in a wider, and more complex, arena.

Would I have dared play fast and loose with Islamic symbols

And then she said to me, 'That's very interesting, Stew, but I don't believe you. Why would you really be telling that story?' And I said to her, 'All I want, Mother, is just once in my life to be able to put my hand on my heart and say in all honesty that I've written a joke that Joe Pasquale won't be able to steal.'*

Thank you.

_____

in the same way I did with Christian ones? Well, not being from an Islamic culture myself I wouldn't have felt the sense of entitlement. And also, I wouldn't have known how to deploy them for the effect I wanted, not being entirely familiar with their individual resonances, and my audience, low as it is on Muslims, wouldn't have known how to interpret whatever I was saying with them anyway. But despite these reasonable reasons, the elephant in the room remains – is it a degree of ignorance of Islam or is it fear of Islamic extremists that prevents non-Muslim comics and satirists from engaging with it with the same commitment they have for the faiths of their own cultures?

I tried to address this concern in my 2009 TV show, *Stewart Lee's Comedy Vehicle*, and it was the only section of the series that BBC legal advisers asked me to drop. Maybe if the *Daily Mail* hadn't been on at them over Sachsgate at the time they'd have been more confident. I ended up doing a routine about not being able to do the routine, and then was interested to read the usual people insisting online that apparently I was lying, and I was allowed to do the routine about Islam that I wanted to, but that I was just too politically correct and too scared to do it.

* Zing! Take that!

4

2005–7

'90s Comedian was a hit. A mathematically inclined PR person subsequently informed me that in terms of its average star rating, statistically it was the best-reviewed show ever in the history of the Fringe. You can prove anything with facts. After the Fringe, I hit the road with the same set in the company of Steve Carlin, a mysteriously underexposed and puritanically rational Scot given to the driest of one-liners and the most enjoyably torturous extended riffs, and we split the driving around twice as many venues as on the *Stand-Up Comedian* tour, playing longer runs in the small rooms and one-nighters in bigger venues than before. I still rarely did anywhere larger than 300 seats, but the Soho Theatre run of *'90s Comedian* was double the length of the previous year's, and Arthur Smith, an inspirational performer and the stepfather of Alternative Comedy, called me 'the eminence grise' of stand-up. And yet it proved nearly impossible to find someone willing to film the show for a DVD release.

For several reasons, I really wanted to record *'90s Comedian*. Taping *Stand-Up Comedian* had forced me to ditch that set, draw a line under it and move on, which had been hugely useful creatively. It killed the possibility, which had stifled me in the nineties, of dragging the same dead stuff around the clubs for years. That set was now out there, and people who had seen it would be ready for more extreme material, both in terms of content and of style. In addition, I had a sense that '90s Comedian was significant because it reflected a very particular period of public anxiety about taste and decency. I also knew that there was a limit to how long I could go on performing it: religious paranoia was either going to pass, or worsen, and '90s Comedian was of its time.

However, my management, who had filmed and produced my first DVD for 2entertain, were unable to find anyone interested in releasing the '90s Comedian show commercially. I told them to offer the material to cable TV channels, like Paramount, for free.* But there were, appar-

---

* Recently, a former comedy executive from Paramount told me she didn't remember being offered the set for free. Now you have to take stories like this with a grain of salt; people want to appear like they have always been on your side. And even if, despite being asked to, my management hadn't offered my material free to Paramount – and of course there is no actual evidence to suggest that they hadn't – it would only have been sound business practice. It would make no sense, from a strictly commercial point of view, for them to value the commodity of my critically acclaimed act at zero. In the poker-playing school of artist representation they subscribe to, big management is biologically impelled to bluff its way towards a higher fee, even at the risk of blowing the whole deal. But this financially driven waiting game is sometimes the opposite of what an artist wants, namely to move forwards creatively. None of my favourite albums of the eighties – The Nightingales' *Pigs on Purpose*, The Fall's *Hex Enduction Hour*, Dick Gaughan's *Handful of Earth*, Eleventh Dream Day's *Prairie School Freakout* or The Dream Syndicate's *Days of Wine and Roses* – would have seen the light of day if the artists behind them had had my management, waiting to sell their stock at the crest of a wave that never came. I once overheard my manager telling someone that his acts didn't 'get out of bed for less than a grand'. Simon Munnery explained this meant he was spending a lot of time in bed.

ently, still no takers. Despite all the good press and growing audiences, I could not give this set away.

I mentioned my frustration at my management's failure to find a way of documenting *'90s Comedian* in interviews. A comedy fan from Cardiff, Chris Evans, contacted me directly and offered to step into the breach. Chris was an IT professional who also ran an online baby-clothes company called Go Faster Stripe. He knew three *Top Gear* studio cameramen on whom he could call for a favour, and a woman with video-editing software on her laptop. Chris offered to film *'90s Comedian* at his local arts centre on a micro-budget and sell it through his baby-clothes company's Paypal site. We agreed to split any profits, should there ever be any, once he had covered his overheads. The room and the crew fees were taken care of by ticket sales. Chris bought the editor a camera as a thank-you for her work. The only real expense was the fee for DVD certification by the BBFC, which came to just under a grand.

Chris quickly covered his costs, and the availability of the show on DVD, and also bootlegged onto the internet, has certainly helped me to build an audience over the last few years. Meanwhile, Go Faster Stripe has gone on to film sets by the sort of comedians other comedians and comedy connoisseurs love, but whom big DVD companies never think to capture, with the result that it now has the most important catalogue of British live comedy anywhere and really ought to get a grant from the BFI. There are three commercially available live DVDs of Peter Kay doing the same set in different rooms. Now, thanks to Chris, there is at least one of John Hegley or Simon Munnery or Tony Law or Robin Ince doing something.

In May 2005, my manager had told me that the then head of BBC2, Roland Keating, wanted to see me about doing a

TV series. It is very strange to be asked in to see a TV executive at their request. Usually you have to beg, like a dog. But maybe my manager had been begging on my behalf, like a dog, and had managed to get Roland Keating of BBC2 to disguise the meeting as having been his initiative, because he knew I had my pride and wasn't keen to ever do television for anyone ever again anyway, having had enough of being fucked about by Roland's predecessor in the nineties, the unfathomable Jane Root. Or maybe it was some kind of agreed compensation for the BBC broadcast of *Jerry Springer: The Opera*, a decision that ultimately cost the show whatever live commercial future it might have had.

I asked my manager why this meeting had been requested. He said Roland Keating of BBC2 was 'very excited about my work'. I asked him if Roland Keating of BBC2 had ever seen any of my work, as I found it difficult to believe a TV executive would be 'very excited about my work' if he had ever actually seen any of it. My manager diplomatically avoided confirming whether Roland Keating of BBC2 had seen any of my work, but just smiled his enigmatic Cheshire Cat smile and repeated that Roland Keating of BBC2 was very excited about my work.

It's possible, I suppose, that Roland Keating of BBC2 had seen my work and was very excited about it; and that my manager was being mysterious to allow me the possibility of believing that it was he, my manager, who had engineered the degree of excitement about my work, despite the very excited executive never having seen it; or it is possible, I suppose, that Roland Keating of BBC2 hadn't seen my work but was still very excited about it; or it was possible that my manager had done some deal to encourage Roland Keating of BBC2 to commission something off me. Who knows? TV is insane.

I told Roland Keating of BBC2 that I wanted to make a stand-up show like Dave Allen did in the seventies, slow and ponderous, with no fast cuts or exciting camera angles, thinking this would shake him off. But Roland Keating of BBC2 then told me I could have this series without even doing a pilot, and that I was to get on with writing it. After we left the meeting, it was heartening to see my manager genuinely surprised for once. The head of BBC2 had just told me, with witnesses, that I had my own TV series, no pilot required. It did seem too good to be true.

After I'd begun work on mapping out ideas for the show, it turned out the TV series was to be made by the production company owned by my manager, which came as a surprise to me. My manager told me that he assumed I understood that the show would be made by his production company and sold on to the BBC, but I had assumed it would be in house at the BBC. Maybe he had told me otherwise. I wanted it to be in-house BBC as my experience with my manager's production company was that although well-meaning, the actual work they produced was not to my taste, whereas my experiences of the civil-servant creatives toiling within the BBC itself had usually been good. But my manager said that when he had said 'we' were going in to see Roland Keating of BBC2, this meant I was going in as the artist and he was going in both as my manager but also as a representative of his own TV production company to see if 'we', i.e. me and his production company, could get a deal. It is possible he explained this. I got tinnitus while auditioning opera singers at the National Theatre in the autumn of 2002 and it's never quite gone away, meaning I often miss sounds in the upper frequencies, and my manager had a very high voice, like a vole or a little girl. Or perhaps these details had been in an email or a letter

I hadn't seen fit to read. Obviously there had been a terrible misunderstanding. I explained to my manager that I didn't want to do the show with his production company as I hated all their TV output, which always looked cheap and shoddy and tasteless, and he graciously allowed me to reposition the project as a BBC in-house one, which I had always assumed it would be, a kindness and an act of self-lessness which would have cost him thousands of pounds' worth of business had the series been commissioned.

At some stage around this point, the head of BBC2's offer of a series without needing to make a pilot was reduced to me being offered a pilot. I can't remember why, although it is true that I hadn't approached getting on with writing it with much enthusiasm as I never seriously thought the series would happen anyway. I wanted to concentrate on building up the live audience, a much more practical and achievable aim. Not unreasonably, my manager lost patience with me and told me I had to 'stop behaving like Jerry Sadowitz or someone and start making some money for the company', and that I couldn't just do what I wanted in life. Then the star producer Armando Iannucci was attached to oversee this pilot for the BBC, in house, and I began to take the possibility a bit more seriously.

One of my ideas for the series was to perform stand-up sets of different styles in different places. I decided to try and do a set of observational comedy, from the perspective of an insect, whilst dressed as an insect, in front of an appropriate audience. Then I was approached by an old friend, Bridget Nicholls, an eco-activist with pirate blood who was organising an entomology-based arts event called Pestival at the Barnes Wetlands Centre that May. Would I do the opening-night cabaret in some capacity? I decided to do my proposed insect act there, Armando began to make tentative arrangements to film it on the night, and I investigated costume-makers.*

* I think, looking at it now, that like many things in my shows, this insect idea also has its roots in a conversation with Simon Munnery. For one of the Cluub Zarathustra cabaret shows, Simon had come up with the idea of an insect comedian of some sort. There was a precedent for this in his work. During the Edinburgh Fringe in 1990, I had helped Simon experiment in an onstage collaboration with a worm by driving him to Mike's Tackle Shop in Musselburgh, where all kinds of worms were commercially available in large quantities.

As Simon's proposed act involved the worm being publicly slain, I overcame my ethical opposition to this by suggesting that rather than being dug up from the Scottish earth, the worm should be purchased from somewhere where it would otherwise have been sold to a fisherman, who would only have impaled it on a hook and fed it to a fish anyway. Normally, I don't think I could have countenanced assisting someone in slaughtering a worm in the name of entertainment, but I had recently read Hemingway's persuasive 1929 book on bullfighting, *Death in the Afternoon*.

In *Death in the Afternoon*, Hemingway convinces the reader that the artistry of the bullfight is so great that we can spare a few bulls and discount their pain. As a toddler I remember being taken to a bullfight in Spain by my mother and amusing the locals by cheering for the bull to kill the man, and I put a load of slides my father had taken of the event down the toilet in protest, but *Death in the Afternoon* swung me, albeit temporarily. And I was convinced that whatever the comedy genius Simon Munnery had in mind for the worm, it would at least be the match of the artistry of the capering Spanish butchers. And certainly, the tiny hangman's gibbet that he was constructing out of balsa wood in our flea-infested Edinburgh flat was a work of art in itself.

Simon was booked into the Fringe Club that night, a massive space in the student-union building. Back when the Fringe was run on dole cheques and goodwill, before the money men moved in, the Fringe Club offered free showers, free poster space and free nightly entertainment to masses of ungrateful people drunk on subsidised booze. Simon took the stage in the persona of The League Against Tedium, a top-hatted dictator character given to highly quotable and unforgettable aphorisms, usually about his superiority to all other living things, and a kind of right-wing mirror image of his earlier Alan Parker Urban Warrior incarnation. I don't remember it going especially well that night, but by the end of Simon's allotted time his failure was sealed.

In an attempt to display his superiority to worms, The League Against Tedium took the worm and tied it with cotton to the gibbet, which was set on a table front-lit by a powerful lamp that back-projected the shadow of the worm's wriggling body thirty feet high onto the rear wall of the venue. Then, to a cacophony of boos and jeers, and the sound of women bursting into tears, The League Against Tedium took a pair of scissors and ceremoniously snipped the worm in two, the half of its body that remained tied to the worm-gibbet jerking spasmodically in confusion and discomfort.

Hemingway convinced me that bullfighting was worth a few worms. But as he exited through the back entrance of the building, to escape a crowd baying for his blood, Simon Munnery had not convinced me that he was worth even one worm.

For the Cluub Zarathustra insect act, five years later, Simon suggested putting an insect in a tank and pretending it was a comedian, though at no point was killing it in public ever discussed. I thought the insect should be as big an insect as possible, like a stick insect or a praying mantis, and that it should have some kind of mini-microphone stand in the case. Simon wanted to get the comedian Jeff Green to voice the insect's act from offstage, whilst a camera relayed footage of the insect onto a big overhead screen. Jeff's act at the time was composed of good-natured laddish bits on everyday experience. I think Simon just wanted Jeff to do his actual act, and for that to be the stand-up act of an insect, whereas I wanted to write something like the act I ended up doing here in *41st Best*. But we both agreed that for some reason, Jeff Green's voice, a high and keening Scouse falsetto which was instantly likeable, would be the ideal voice for the tiny insect comedian.

Well, of course, like so many things, this never came to anything, but there are morphic resonances of it throughout British comedy ever since, of which my own attempt at observational insect stand-up is but one. My wife Bridget Christie, entirely unaware of the Jeff Green/Stick Insect idea, has recently been appearing around London in a home-made ant costume – not onstage, though – just for her own amusement. And when I was script-editing Harry Hill's shows for Channel 4 in the late nineties, the floppy-collared loon™ became fascinated by the comic possibilities of flies, filling miniature television studios, sealed inside Perspex tanks, with hundreds of them, specially bred from sacks of maggots which were delivered at the start of shooting.

I contacted Harry through his spokesman to ask him for his memories of the fly skits, and this was the reply I received:

> The fly thing is a while ago but I believe it to be my idea. The first one was *The Fly Cruise* and we also did *Play Your Cards Right*. I can't really remember. I think we did about five and that Al Murray did the buzzing noises of the flies. The flies were supplied by an animal wrangler who had to get the maggots at the right stage to hatch in time for the show. Although the mini sets were filmed under Perspex boxes inevitably a lot of the flies got out and then turned up on the set for the recording of the stand-up sections of the show which led to many retakes being needed.

Thanks, Harry!

It was the job of our director, the old-school BBC bow-tie-and-moustache man Robin Nash, to try and film convincing light-entertainment-style footage of the massed flies. Robin was mentioned earlier in this book, as it was he who insisted on splitting Queen's 'Bohemian Rhapsody' into two parts when he produced *Top of the Pops* because he thought it too long for television. Perhaps Nash was being punished by the ghost of Freddie Mercury, now an actual lord of the flies with power over insect life, by being made to film his unruly subjects.

For the fly sketches it was difficult for Robin, even with many years of experience filming Pan's People and Legs & Co., to get what we television professionals call 'singles', which are shots of performers in isolation from their fellow actors. The flies had proven resistant to direction, and many of them had died and were just lying in a heap. To this day I remember Robin standing in the gallery and

The pending Pestival performance aside, I'd already agreed not to do a new stand-up show for the summer of 2006, intending to leave the field fallow for a year, hoping to escape an inevitable critical backlash after two well-reviewed sets. And Roland Keating's promise of a small BBC fee would create a degree of what we now know as quantitative easing, so I threw myself into some theatre projects: a workshop of something about William Blake I was toying with for the National Theatre Studio, featuring Johnny Vegas and the folk-singer Eliza Carthy, and directing a revival of *Talk Radio* by Eric Bogosian, an American performance artist and comic I used to listen to on the Peel show as a teenager, with Phil Nicol for Underbelly in

---

tearing his hair out in rage as he bellowed to the camera operators on the studio floor, 'No, on his face! On the fly's face!!'

TV's Harry Hill takes up the tale:

I too remember Robin shouting 'No! On the fly's face!' And also, one of the first things I ever saw at the Edinburgh Fringe festival was Simon Munnery at the Fringe Club cutting a worm in half and I remember being quite shocked by it. I think he was booed off. That same night I saw one of my future managers heckling an Asian woman in a wheelchair by shouting 'Sad fuck!' It was the year of Newman and Baddiel. All the flies are dead now.

Warming to his insect theme, Harry continues:

I recently resurrected the fly thing and did insect *EastEnders* on *TV Burp*, my multi-award-winning ITV show. It was a proud moment – an all-insect-acted sketch on ITV prime time. Oh my! If you'd told me that I would be doing that thirty years ago when I originally thought of insect-acted sketches I would have collapsed in a big old heap of laughter.

Dear readers, despite it mentioning Hemingway and describing the execution of a worm, this footnote has been the most showbiz section of this book so far. I bet you liked it.

Edinburgh. But on Friday 7 April 2006, in a pub across the road from the National Theatre rehearsal studios, my manager told me the BBC had now withdrawn their offer of even a pilot.

A few weeks later, I went in to see my manager for the official line on the withdrawal of the BBC offer. I sat opposite him in his office, and he sat behind a computer, reading out a letter from the head of comedy, Lucy Lumsden, which explained that the work I had done on the proposed show no longer fitted with the BBC executives' 'original vision of the programme'. The cancellation blew a minor hole in my finances, knocked my faith in the trustworthiness of TV executives and, more pressingly, left me obliged to do my insect act at Pestival without anyone to foot the bill for the insect costume.*

That summer, in Edinburgh, I realised what the 2007 stand-up show could be about. I wanted to explore the bureaucratic process by which a firm offer of a TV series, with no pilot necessary, could eventually be withdrawn, without any real explanation. Even though the actual story was very specifically about television, there were universally applicable themes, such as the Kafkaesque way our progress in life is impeded or aided by official decisions made for apparently random reasons by pen-pushers we never even meet, that anyone could relate to. I wanted to call it 'The Decommissioning Process', and use my decommissioning letter as a starting point for the story. I saw my manager sitting on a bench in the Pleasance Courtyard

---

* In the end, I just did Pestival as me, talking about insects, but pretended I did it in the insect gear when I came to retell the story in the subsequent stand-up show, *41st Best Stand-Up Ever*. A transcript of this is presented here as Appendix VI.

with Paul Schlesinger, the head of BBC Radio Comedy. I asked my manager if it would be possible to see a copy of Lucy Lumsden's email cancelling my pilot. He said I couldn't, because I would probably do a show about it.

Notwithstanding the truth of his observation, I was shocked to find that I began to wonder if the email ever existed at all. By which I don't mean that I think the email did not exist. I think it probably did. What shocked me was that I was in a state of such low confidence in the entire infrastructure of the comedy business that it was possible for me to imagine my manager fabricating the contents of a non-existent email for some unknowable purpose. Again, I am not saying he did this. But I sat opposite him when he read it out, and never thought to jump over his desk and look at the computer screen, as that would have been the behaviour of a madman. I realised, in my ongoing state of general paranoia and distrust, I had reached a stage where I was prepared to believe the people who worked *for* me were reading out emails that didn't even exist. Even though the email and its contents probably were real, the fact that I entertained the possibility that they weren't meant that in my delusional mind, I had reached a position of total breakdown in trust.*

At the start of the nineties, being with my management

---

* There were other factors leading up to this. The advertising for the desperate live tour of the opera in 2006, and for the show's final London dates, had copy along the lines of 'Can you handle this shocking show?' and 'Come and see what all the outrage is about,' which we had agreed it wouldn't have; a documentary about the blasphemy laws entitled *New Puritans*, which I made for a company my manager co-owned, was retitled *Stewart Lee Says What's So Bad About Blasphemy?* before broadcast without anyone consulting me, leading to predictably negative comments in the press; and

had seemed like the alternative. They represented Jerry Sadowitz and Simon Munnery and Newman and Baddiel, who, whatever detractors might tell you, at the time were in the process of forging a new vocabulary for stand-up in Britain. And when the management took on Frank Skinner in 1991, they brought a unique working-class voice into an otherwise largely middle-class comedy community that paid lip service to the idea of social equity, but could sometimes be quite uncomfortable with the reality of what that might mean. And they operated out of one room just off Charing Cross Road and the Christmas parties were in the bar downstairs. The first year I was with them, the little manager gave me Nick Cave's *Kicking Against the Pricks* LP for Christmas, and the handful of acts, the two managers and a nice woman who'd been taken on to answer the phone, whom I later lived with, all got drunk together and then went home. Ten years later, the Christmas party was in a club in Fulham, we all got miniature tellies or some other shit, and there were dwarves, yes dwarves, dressed as Christmas elves in green tights and hats with bells on handing out canapés to fat executives and skimpily clad media women. I asked one of the dwarves if he liked being a Christmas elf. He said he thought of himself as a 'seasonal worker'. I never went to my own management's Christmas party ever again. When I saw Ted Chippington opening for The Fall in 1984 and decided to be an Alternative Comedian, at no point did I envisage that decision might

-----

promises to sound out legitimate record-label interest for an audio release of *Stand-Up Comedian*, which I thought would help build an audience if properly distributed to reviewers, came to nothing. Cumulatively, this sort of stuff makes you paranoid, especially if you know 65,000 people are actively trying to have your work banned.

one day implicate me in being handed a vol-au-vent by a Christmas dwarf, whose probably dismal fee I had partially subsidised. The unknowable email was the last straw, but I'm surprised I survived as long as I did.

So I wrote nice, and genuinely heartfelt, letters to all the people who had looked after me at my management over nearly two decades, recalling all the good times, and quit, for the vaguest reasons I could think of. And there were good times, despite the dwarves and the debt and the disillusionment. My management had pulled off some spectacular moves over the past seventeen years. They had hospitalised me when I was sick, and even housed me when I was homeless, and it was sometimes a heady experience to be in their orbit when their daring schemes bore fruit. One day in particular stands out, but it didn't involve business or bullshit or brinkmanship. In the summer of 1991, my manager had accompanied me to St Andrews, where I had a show with Frank Skinner, Jim Tavare and Richard Thomas's double act, Miles and Milner. His father had been a famous scientist, and as we walked along the beach in the sun, he picked up various specimens and explained the biological complexities of the little shellfish stranded on the sand. But that was a long time ago now.

On my arrival home from Edinburgh, I tore up any documentation relating to *Jerry Springer: The Opera*, which was represented as a 'property' by my management, who also produced it, and which I was entitled to 'further exploit'. (Such ugly language!) In the event of it ever turning a profit, I did not want to be tempted to engage in a costly legal battle to clarify my position regarding any rights I might have over the work. Instead, I prepared to sit out the six-month period during which it was legally advisable for me to remain unrepresented. I expected to be sued, or at least shouted at, or threatened with legal action and a gagging order like other former deserters, but nothing happened. Harry Hill took me out for a farewell drink, where he and many of the acts I'd known for years who were still represented by the company sat around as another prop in their collective act of faith fell away. Somebody was complaining about how the management had fucked up booking one of his regular corporate gigs for him. The fee he had lost was more than I would hope to earn in a year.*

On the train home from Edinburgh, I had been called on my mobile by a radio producer called Alison Vernon Smith, who ran an independent company from a desk in an alcove in her Brighton bungalow. She had been negotiating for some years to get Radio 4 to stump up for the two of us to fly to New Mexico and make two half-hour documentaries about the sacred clowns of the pueblos, which had been an ambition of mine since I first read about them

* Six months later I was in Nottingham, doing a benefit to raise funds for Daryl Martin, an enterprising local promoter whom all comedians feel duty-bound to come together and help whenever possible. I went out for a curry afterwards with Daniel Kitson and Sean Lock. Kitson managed to escape the Death Star Light Ent tractor beam of the Perrier Award he inadvertently won in 2001 by leaving his management, doing all his own admin through his own company and systematically carving out the cleverest and coolest audience in comedy, without ever doing interviews or television appearances of any kind. I asked him if he would consider being my manager, as my future plans consisted of just trying to copy his business practices anyway. He declined. Sean Lock, listening in mounting disbelief as he nibbled his naan, became furious with both of us, describing us as 'two idiots wasting their time'. But I think he was irked anyway because I kept going on about his vagina-shaped-shit routine from 1990 all night, and asking him when he was going to do it again.

237

in Howard Jacobson's book *Seriously Funny* in 1997. Finally, everything was in place, and we were due to go to Taos later that month, me speaking and Alison recording on a little portable unit. But with audible unhappiness, Alison explained that we would now not be able to go. The plug was to be pulled by her superiors as my management were insisting I flew business class, a cost equal to half the tiny budget of the programme.

There was a showbiz legend that my manager used to ring a bell and make everyone in his office stand up and applaud whenever he made a TV or radio producer cry on the phone. Of course, it was not true. But it was with some relief that I was able to tell this particular distressed producer, one of many over the years, that the resignation letters were already in the post. We'd both fly economy, for God's sake, and I'd get to do the job of a lifetime. My nineties comedy rock-and-roll management were standing between me and the shaman clowns. Was some unseen hand organising events for maximum dramatic effect? If this were a novel, this would be exactly the sort of contrived symbolic incident a good editor would delete. But it was real. In the end, seeing the sacred clowns of the Tewa people at work was to renew my faith in the point of comedy itself, just when it was in danger of being buried by the brutal business practices surrounding it. Making the radio documentary, and getting my thoughts on the Pueblo clowns in order for a *Guardian* article, filleted below, helped me enormously as I looked around for reasons to go on.

As planned, Alison and I attended the St Geronimo feast-day celebrations at Taos Pueblo, New Mexico, one of the few events where outsiders get to see the sacred clowns perform. For a long time I had fondly imagined that the clowns of the Pueblo Indians, who take over the village for the afternoon on the second day of the festival, might be a key to understanding, on some essential level, what comedy is and what it is for. In 2000, I had stayed on the Hopi reservation in Arizona and seen the pueblos and plazas where their clowns would have performed, while researching a novel set in the region. Writing the book was sidelined for two years by a fascination with the Pueblo clowns, part holy men, part fools.

The Hopi clown's function was to manufacture inappropriate behaviour. The clowns would spend months studying the social tensions of their pueblo before, on special feast days, exploding them with carefully considered transgressive acts – simulated sexual assaults, absurd interruptions to sacred ceremonials, parodies of their oppressors' Christian services, incoherent reinterpretations of the life of Christ, and obscene scatological acts. The American army officer John G. Bourke's 1881 pamphlet *The Urine Dance of the Zuni Indians of New Mexico* was one of many texts that led to the invading powers' active suppression of the pagan comedians of the pueblos, driving the clowns literally underground, into kivas, the sacred ceremonial chambers used by the Pueblo clowns and other secret societies of the community. In those close-knit communities, perched on the high mesas, the Pueblo clowns pushed at the limits of socially acceptable behaviour and showed the people, for better or worse, what lay beyond. Could comedy act as both a social barometer and a social pressure valve? Was there a purpose in it?

The drama-student recreation of the medieval fools' day I'd seen five years previously near Béziers in Languedoc was a construct, but the performance Alison and I were about to see was the real thing, and research suggested the

Pueblo clowns seemed to have a more pronounced philosophical dimension. Just after lunch, ten figures appeared, silhouetted against the blue sky on the roof of a stack of brown adobe buildings. They were naked but for loincloths, their bodies painted in rings of concentric black and white stripes, their hair decorated with jagged stalks of corn. They screamed and bellowed. Children ran away, afraid. After a while, the clowns made their way down into the plaza, where they spent the next three hours running between the stalls and houses, intimidating and entertaining, overturning every social norm at hand and reshaping the rules of Pueblo life. Babies were snatched from their parents and thrown into the river for clown baptisms. Food was stolen from stallholders and redistributed. We were shouted at, shoved and shocked. Our drinks were flung on the floor.

We followed the clowns into the chief's house, where an absurd tourist-type Indian dance was performed at the dinner table for the benefit of his white guests. Back outside, white men were forced to face off in mock cowboy gunfights, and white teenage girls were forcibly press-ganged into ungainly Britney Spears dance routines. Beautiful Pueblo women were mocked and made to wear different-sized shoes, so they struggled and stumbled as they walked. Handsome young men were clad in dresses and forced to skip. Elderly women were gracefully wooed or crudely propositioned. And when confronted with someone in a wheelchair or a mentally handicapped onlooker, the clowns would fall before them on their knees in worship.

Despite our BBC credentials, Native American commentators were reluctant to explain the theory behind any of this practice in detail, the folk memory of the white settlers' suppression of Pueblo clown ceremonials perhaps still strong, but gentle pressure revealed the suggestion of a social, maybe even moral, purpose at work. By reversing the norms and breaking the taboos, the clowns show us what we have to lose, and what we might also stand to gain, if we step outside the restrictions of social convention and polite everyday discourse. This core idea holds whether it is played out up close in the plaza of a New Mexican pueblo or miles away by the tiny dots of television stars on the stage of a vast arena.

That autumn I was getting married. Things were a bit difficult financially as I was supposed to be writing for the BBC series that now wouldn't happen and I hadn't set up any live work. So I did some of those TV panel games for the money. You get about £600 for *Have I Got News for You* after commission. I'd been offered these kinds of shows before but I didn't really thrive on them, as you have to be snappy and tight, rather than slack and monotonous, and I realised they weren't really for me. The weekend after *HIGNFY*, which gets millions of viewers, I was in Aberdeen, on the way to our foolishly chosen mid-winter honeymoon destination, Shetland. Drunk men recognised me from the telly and shouted 'Quiz show cunt' and such like at me in the taxi rank. It's a lot of aggro for £600.

In January, I pulled together an experimental theatre piece, *What Would Judas Do?*, for a month's run at the Bush Theatre on Shepherd's Bush Green in London, again having 'scratched' it at Battersea. It was produced in a double bill with *Product*, by Mark Ravenhill, the terrible child of British theatre, who is really a nice *Doctor Who* fan. I got paid Equity minimum, £375 a week. To have developed the same piece in Edinburgh in the nineties would have cost me thousands of unrecoupable pounds. Radio 4 drama dithered around trying to decide whether to broadcast the show, but time was passing, so I taped it and Go Faster

Stripe put it out as a triple CD for sale on the internet. By the time it had sold two hundred copies it had paid more than Radio 4 would have done, and I had not had to compromise it in any way.

Edinburgh was looming. I had a new promoter, a flamboyant and disarmingly straightforward Soho face who had brought various American legends of stand-up to Britain in the nineties and claimed once to have dined with the surrealist occultist Ithell Colquhoun. But most importantly, he didn't have a TV production company on the side, meaning the live books had to balance in my favour as there was no Jim Crow system in place for me to work off any losses picking cotton on the boss's plantation. And Underbelly wanted me to play their big tent, The Udderbelly. The show I'd thought of last year, *The Decommissioning Process*, had withered on the vine, and I was now committed to an idea called *March of the Mallards*. A preview was booked in under this title in the Glasgow Comedy Festival in March 2007, which Tommy Sheppard of The Stand very kindly allowed me to cancel when it became clear to me, days before the proposed debut of the piece, that it wasn't really going to work. I was hoping to hinge a show about scientific truth and religious lies on all the tonal and factual fudges of the hit documentary film *March of the Penguins*, but couldn't make it fit, and instead was left with reams and reams of facts and a deluge of liberally biased opinion which I was to try and make funny by delivering in a sarcastic voice. I had no wish to tread on the toes of the comedian Robin Ince, who has made an art form of exactly this chaotic approach, and so decided that discretion was the better part of valour.*

---

* The ten minutes of useful penguin material that I did have appeared in early versions of *41st Best*, as I explained what the show

Print dates were closing in for the 2007 Edinburgh brochure and I still didn't have an idea, or a name, for the new stand-up show. Then, a few days after the *March of the Mallards* cancellation, I found myself featured in a spurious Channel 4 clip-show rundown of the supposed hundred best stand-up comedians of all time, placed at an

---

would have been about, and then made its final bow in a much improved form in my 2009 BBC2 TV series *Stewart Lee's Comedy Vehicle*. I also tried to make use of my *March of the Mallards* material later that same year at Nicko and Joe's Bad Film Club, at the Brighton Picture House. Bad Film Club is a night when a comedian chooses a film they hate, explains why they hate it, and then screens it, with hopefully amusing interruptions. I had already enjoyed doing the nasty anti-CND propaganda film *Who Dares Wins* for Bad Film Club at the Barbican, in which Lewis Collins's bullet-headed SAS hero goes undercover to have sex with a feminist, endures a political benefit gig performed by moonlighting members of Fairport Convention trying to sound like a New Wave band, and then shoots his duped and sullied peace-whore to death in an embassy siege, before returning to his clammy wife and terrifying Midwich cuckoo children. I tried to get the wine critic Oz Clarke to attend the screening, to discuss his brief cameo as an ineffectual and racist customs official, but the grape-smeared epicure would not return my emails.

In Brighton I chose to ridicule and discredit the American moral-majority puff piece *March of the Penguins*. But the British cinema edit of *March of the Penguins* that was screened on the night differed from the American edit on the DVD release that I had prepared my notes from, in that the most extreme examples of scientifically unsustainable anthropomorphism and born-again Christian subtext had been quietly excised, leaving many of the audience wondering why I was so down on this charming, if rather sentimental, look at cuddly penguin life. What had I got against penguins exactly? Why would someone waste their time travelling to Brighton to attack the heroic and flightless seabirds for their apparently innocuous behaviour?

astonishing number 41.* Now, I know these shows are bullshit, and they jiggle the order so that sweary comedians get to go after the watershed, and the production company have got commissioners breathing down their necks saying, 'You simply must fix the figures to include [insert name of current flavour of the month here]', and that Daniel Kitson was only included because if they didn't they would have no credibility with clued-up comedy fans whatsoever, and that it's patently absurd that I was placed higher than Chic Murray or Bob Newhart or Andy Kaufman or Dave Allen or George Carlin or Tommy Cooper or Sean Lock or Johnny Vegas or Dave Gorman, and that Simon Munnery and Kevin McAleer and Greg Fleet and Boothby Graffoe and various other of my totemic figures were not even placed, and that if it had been done two years earlier the little wave of good press that had got me placed at all wouldn't have happened yet . . . but I thought, 'Hey, I can use this.'†

* What dreadful things these programmes are. I often read on internet message boards that I am 'best known as a regular on clip shows'. I have only done one, the *100 Greatest Stand-Ups*, because they told me I was going to be on it, and I thought I'd best try and say something modest. The only other times I have been a talking head on TV is on documentaries about Spider-Man, comic books, Ted Chippington and The Fall, all of which I love. I have never taken money to try and fabricate a memory about some aspect of mass culture in which I had, at the time, no interest. People who think I am a regular on clip shows are confusing me with the comedian Robin Ince, who is like a higher-voiced and slimmer version of me, and who, like Stuart Maconie, is prepared to pretend to remember anything if the fee is high enough. Peter Kay used to be particularly superb on these ultra-short-term nostalgia clip shows, often being able to remember in detail aspects of everyday life, such as the Space Hopper craze, which pre-date his actual birth.
† In early stages of the subsequent stand-up show, I would

A show called *Stewart Lee – 41st Best Stand-Up Ever* would seem to have its cake and eat it, mocking the poll but at the same time using it as a marketing tool. And I could hang all the things that had been interesting me in the previous year – the TV decommission, the Pestival performance, the fact that I couldn't get a mainstream commercial release for a DVD – on the disparity between my supposed high critical standing and the actual reality of my often precarious professional position.

The more I thought about it, the more little incidents from my life seemed to fit this structure. But I was looking for a through-line, a theme that would do the job the way the Joe Pasquale bit topped and tailed the '90s *Comedian* show. And then I remembered a difficult Christmas Eve of a few years previously.

I was at my mother's, and she had arranged for us to visit her friends round the corner. The evening started badly as I could see my mother was embarrassed that my

---

improvise a fifteen-minute bit about how any poll of comedy voted for by the public was invalid because they always chose Del Boy falling through the bar in *Only Fools and Horses* as the funniest TV moment ever. For a few months it worked really well, but after a while I forgot why it was funny, and I was never really able to get it back. There were no jokes, no lines as such, and it was all in the performance, which required me to put myself in whatever perilous positions were available – hanging upside down ranting on raised stages over precariously deep orchestra pits, or smashing my head repeatedly on the floor of stages surrounded by raised rostrum seating. In the end, I dropped it from the already overlong show. I got a good pass at the piece in the pilot of *Stewart Lee's Comedy Vehicle* in November 2007, but by the time I came to film it for the TV series, in January 2009, it was floundering again. People seemed to like it in the TV show as eventually broadcast, but I can see it's a mechanical and learned performance.

feet smelt, and assuming it was the stink of my old trainers, she told me that at her friends' house it was customary to remove your shoes on entry. I did this, and then realised that no one else had, and that the friends were looking at me like I was odd. In the car on the way there my mother had clearly improvised this supposed 'shoes off' custom to prevent me taking the smell of what she thought was my shoes into the house. However, the smell was not just my shoes, it was also my feet, which are gnarly and covered in a yellow fungus, so despite her quick thinking, the stink followed us into the house.

Later during the smell-ruined night, I was required to explain what I did for a living to the bewildered company, all of whom, it appeared to me, thought I was a deranged liar pretending to be a successful comedian, otherwise they'd have heard of me, surely. Various well-meaning old age pensioners kept suggesting I should do the cruises. My mother had seen Tom O'Connor, the seventies TV game-show host and former club comic, on a cruise, and had been especially impressed by a joke he had done about a sardine, which she tried to repeat, but fumbled, by getting the set-up before the punchline. Being a comedian is actually harder than it looks and is best left to the professionals. Anyway, the implication of all this discussion about cruise-ship comics was, to me, in my admittedly paranoid state, that if I was any good, I would be doing the cruises too.*

In the end, I sort of lost my temper and was forced to

---

* For those of you too young to remember Tom O'Connor, of the berry-brown face and frosty hair, here's a piece by Nick Duerden, in the *Independent*, from 27 August 2006:

Though he started his career on *Opportunity Knocks* as,

ostensibly, a comic, Liverpool-born Tom O'Connor was hardly a seminal stand-up. Instead, in the kind of jumper a sitcom grandmother buys for a sitcom grandson at Christmas, he possessed a comfortable television persona that, by the mid-1980s, had seen him anointed as the king of the cheesy gameshow.

'All told, I did 11 of them, and every one a winner,' he says in his room at London's Grosvenor House Hotel where, tonight, he will preside over a corporate awards ceremony. '*Name That Tune, Cross Wits, I've Got a Secret, The Zodiak Game.* Many more. Why so many?' He winks. 'Producers knew that I could make a middling gameshow great. How? I had the knack.'

In 1988, though, this former teacher and devout, married Catholic was reported to have fallen in love with an 18-year-old prostitute. The allegations were splashed all over the papers, and the gameshow host issued writs against three of them, before ultimately dropping each one.

'You certainly find out who your friends are when something like that happens,' he said at the time. Within a year, he'd lost all but one of his shows, *Cross Wits*.

When I bring this up, the 67-year-old winces and abruptly segues into a joke about a one-armed Irish swimmer, which he says always gets them laughing.

Life away from TV was initially difficult for O'Connor, largely because he had grown rather fond 'of the fame, the money, the fancy cars. I was an arrogant so-and-so, I thought I was invincible.' He was relegated to the cruise-ship circuit, presiding over the same gameshows but now adapted for OAP seafarers. These days, he is the king of the corporate event. Tonight, it's the motoring industry; last week, a pizza and pasta company. For someone who once dominated our TV screens, surely it's a bit of a comedown?

'At £4,500 a night, four, five times a week?' he says. 'Hardly. I'm doing very nicely indeed, thanks. There's respect out there for me, and whatever anybody tells you, there is life after TV. I'm living proof.'

Later, he performs 20 minutes of stand-up before a room full of drunken motoring types, some of whom talk all over his nostalgia-driven monologue. The one about the one-armed Irish swimmer still goes down a storm, though.

act like an intellectual and cultural snob in order to justify my position. 'Look, all those old-school cruise guys, they might be making loads of money, but they talk to us lot in astonished terms about our ability to actually write material about stuff, when they just do old gags. They're not going to get reviewed in the *Observer* or asked to play arts festivals. It's a completely different thing.' 'Well, I think I'd rather have the money,' said one of the old folk, clearly remembering queuing for that first banana after World War II, and then another added, in a tone which I, perhaps mistakenly, assumed to be provocative, 'Oh, so you're some kind of artist are you?'

This was the key to the show. Reviewing *'90s Comedian* in *The Times*, Dominic Maxwell wrote, 'Lee could do more to bring out the personal sense of hurt that came with his hounding as a blasphemer. Without it, the bad-taste Jesus anecdote is too long to sustain the ideas – of freedom of expression, of the mutability of religious icons – that it

---

What Duerden doesn't say is that O'Connor's seventies stand-up was much better than the usual working-men's-club fare of the time, with an uncharacteristically sensitive streak, a neat line in social observation and a real flair for authentic-sounding dialogue. I hate it, obviously, because I am a pretentious elitist, but what Duerden describes as a 'nostalgia-driven monologue' had, in its day, exactly the same flavour and tone as current work by northern observational comics like Peter Kay or Jason Manford, both of whom enjoy critical acclaim in broadsheet newspapers. Now that there is a school of criticism for comedy, and an audience for it beyond the working men's clubs and shit ITV shows of the seventies, it's reasonable to assume that if Tom O'Connor were starting out today he could easily be a stadium-filling, TV panel-show regular selling thousands of DVDs at HMV and Tesco. And if he was embroiled in a scandal he could always just do a one-man show about it and try and get David Baddiel to co-write a film about sex addiction with him.

supports.' The personal is absent from my work. The me you see onstage is largely a construct, based on me at my worst, my most annoying, my most petty and my most patronising. But the things I was hoping to drive at in *41st Best Stand-Up Ever* needed a personal grounding if they were to mean anything to anyone. That's what Daniel Kitson does so well, and why he remains the best stand-up I've ever seen. He's funny, but alongside that Kitson can show you heaven in a wild flower, and eternity in a slice of parkin, which is some kind of foul Yorkshire cake the blind, bald, woman-hating racist eats at Christmas with his sweaty family. The *41st Best Stand-Up* show needed anchoring. At the moment, it was just a discussion about my supposed place in the rarefied world of stand-up comedy. But with a personal story attached to it, the *41st Best* show could become something anyone could relate to, a story about how we still feel we need the approval of those we love, whatever we do for a living, irrespective of whatever accolades we might have bestowed upon us, irrespective of whatever we might supposedly have achieved.

Besides which, the shock-horror tactics of *'90s Comedian* already felt dead in the water. There was suddenly a macho element to the presentation and consumption of transgressive material. 'Are you man enough to handle my act?' Jim Jeffries, who in the flesh is a charming and unassuming former opera singer, was pictured on his poster as an avenging angel involved in rising flames, and was being promoted as 'the most offensive comedian you will ever see'. And there had been Americans in Edinburgh whose professional publicists were employed to tell us they had AIDS, or hepatitis, and that they were on drugs, and had been prostitutes, and advocated the compulsory abortion of all living things. And that they hated you, and the world, and everything you stand for. Some even appeared, alongside Australian and British guests, under the banner heading of The Unbookables – though, ironically, they had been booked – and people flocked to see them to have their sensibilities trampled in front of their astonished faces. These unbookables were, it seemed, eminently bookable. I liked lots of them, and would have booked them if I ran a club, but when I was invited onto an Edinburgh panel by *The Aristocrats*' director Paul Provenza to discuss taste and comedy, I hadn't felt any especial kinship with any of the unbookable outlaws he was talking about, despite having spent half an hour onstage talking about vomiting into the anus of Christ. Instead, I thought about Boothby Graffoe and his guitar and his funny song about a mouse, and how he still made you feel glad to be alive without his act being the least bit shit. And I wondered if there was some way of taking all the tactics of my previous work and using them to say something that was unambiguously positive.

And in the April before the 2007 Edinburgh run, we had a little boy. And when he laughed at us, that was worth more than all the Perspex Chortle awards in the world.

5

41st Best Stand-Up Ever

A transcript of the show recorded on
7 April 2008 at The Stand, Glasgow

PRE-SHOW MUSIC: *RIDDIMBUGZ* BY DAVID ROTHENBERG*

* The pre-show tracks for *41st Best* were a recording of the American musician David Rothenberg improvising on the saxophone to a tank full of chirping insects called Riddimbugz, followed by lengthy blasts of Evan Parker playing saxophone to field recordings of birds and bugs made in Cornwall and the Isles of Scilly by Ashley Wales. Rothenberg's recording is not commercially available, as far as I know, but I tracked it down via the art radio station Resonance FM, which broadcast the Pestival Insect Festival cabaret evening at which we both appeared, and where Rothenberg and his unwitting insect slaves performed this piece. The Evan Parker tracks appear on *Evan Parker with Birds*, on the Treader label.

The Rothenberg piece is quite ambient, but the Parker tracks were mysterious and arresting. I played these to punters on the way into the show in Edinburgh in August 2007, when I found myself in an acoustically problematic circus big top, The Udderbelly. Here, crowds of meandering weekenders, who just wanted to see 'some of that comedy', wandered into my dreary and pretentious show by mistake, resulting in inappropriately packed Friday and Saturday sets and predictably sluggish response times for the weird stuff. The insect-based improvised music was just the beginning of their nightmare.

I take no pleasure in the fact that during the show's Fringe run, the alluring title of the piece, and its prime location in Bristo Square, drew to it many people who just wanted a fun night out and would probably prefer to have seen something else rather than

VOICE OFF: Ladies and gentlemen, will you please welcome the 41st best stand-up ever, Stewart Lee!

Thank you very much, thank you for coming. Thanks for coming to this show, which is called *Stewart Lee – 41st Best Stand-Up Ever*. It wasn't originally going to be called that. I started writing it in about May last year. I didn't know what it was going to be. And then, as luck would have it, about that time I appeared in one of those programmes – you know those terrible Channel 4 programmes, they're about nineteen hours long and they go out on Friday or Saturday nights, and they're a countdown of the hundred

---

me, such as paint drying, for example. Daniel Kitson won't even play weekends in Edinburgh, for fear of short-changing these legitimately aggrieved fun-seekers. Next time I did a stand-up show at the Edinburgh Fringe I went to The Stand, a small room stuffed with dedicated aficionados of comedy, and left a far smaller number of people bored and annoyed.

As a younger man, looking at the fed-up faces of a minority of an audience amused me, in my conceited insolence, but now, as a parent of a young child, for whom organising any night out is a logistical nightmare, the thought of grown-ups having gone to the time and trouble of leaving the house and then being subjected to something that wearies and irritates them fills me with nothing but shame. I regret wasting their evening and babysitting costs. I try and make it clear that the shows are not for everyone, and indeed the poster and publicity material for *41st Best* included one Chortle website punter's review – 'The worst comedian I have ever seen' – in an effort to deter the casual comedy consumer.

Of course, it was always possible that someone who came in hoping for something that they didn't get actually preferred what turned out to be on offer. These were the key marginals I was interested in winning. In theory there were enough threads to grasp in *41st Best* to continue building the new audience, as well as satiating those who had particular expectations of me.

best things of a thing, ever. And each one of the things is separated from the next thing by a bought memory from Stuart Maconie. He is an amazing figure, Stuart Maconie. He is able, if the price is right, to recall almost any aspect of the entire spread of all human existence. He's an incredible figure, Stuart Maconie. He's rather like an omniscient alien super-being, a giant baby that lives in space, bald, wearing only a toga, orbiting the earth, able to view the entire span of all human culture and existence, and yet tragically, by the creed of his alien race, Stuart Maconie is forbidden from ever intervening directly in human affairs.*

If you didn't get that reference, this show isn't really aimed at you. You may enjoy it anyway, the words and shapes, but it isn't aimed at you. This is not for you. You are welcome to stay. But this is not for you.†

* This is, as everyone knows, a reference to The Watcher, the Marvel Comics character created by Stan Lee and Jack Kirby in 1963 whose physical appearance – that of a giant and wise baby – and his role as an omniscient but non-interventionist observer make him very similar to the TV pundit and DJ of worthwhile pop music Stuart Maconie. And also similar, perhaps, to the idea of the non-interventionist God that New York comic-book writers, drawn from the post-war Jewish diaspora, must have felt had abandoned their people, looking on, unable or unwilling to act. Only a minority of the crowd would ever spot the reference, so I would then stop and talk to these people about it, and explain to them that they were my target audience, and that the show was not really aimed at the rest of the room. The same Chortle punter who described me as 'the worst comedian I have ever seen' said my act was aimed exclusively at 'atheist, comic book reading, Morrissey fan nerds'. This is, of course, entirely accurate, and I am delighted that my market-driven attempts to win the loyalty of this key consumer base came across.
† Someone emailed me after the Edinburgh run of *41st Best* in the big top quoting an exchange in Bristo Square after the show, where

So I was on this programme, right, the hundred best stand-ups of all time. And I came in at number 41, and I was very, I was very surprised to be placed, I was very pleased to be placed, um, er, you know, I'm not exactly a household name. I'm the only person on that list of the hundred best stand-ups of all time who regularly plays in this venue, for example. And is glad of the work, is glad of the work.*

Um. I was surprised to be placed. I've had a sort of an odd relationship with the press. In fact, when this show was running in London in December, I got a review describing me as looking like a squashed Albert Finney. Nine years previous to that, the same paper, the London *Evening Standard*, described me as looking like a crumpled Morrissey. And it's good, you can see a kind of trend developing there of comparing me unfavourably to various stocky, greying celebrities in increasingly terrible states of physical distress. And a squashed Albert Finney is arguably worse than a crumpled Morrissey. As a crumpled Morrissey, there's the possibility the Morrissey could be straightened out, put to work. But, er, a squashed Albert Finney is of no value. Except perhaps as a coaster

---

a disgruntled punter had come up to me and said, 'I didn't enjoy that very much, to be honest,' and apparently I'd said, 'I'm sorry, but I don't know what you expect me to do about that now.' I don't remember this. Although I regret wasting people's time, the work is what it is, and I can't go back in time and change it now. I am like The Watcher myself in that respect.

* No matter how big or prestigious the venue I was playing, this line would always get a laugh. Most people think we are all doing much better than we really are. But you can be a megastar in the Edinburgh Fringe and find your mother's friend still doesn't believe you when you say you are doing well, otherwise she would have read about you in the paper.

made of meat. Um. Or a white pudding, as I believe you Scots would call them.*

So it was weird, I was surprised to be placed, number

---

* It is a shameless hack move to open a set with a line like, 'Hey! I know what you are thinking – it's the bastard love child of Mark Knopfler and Iris Murdoch,' or whatever combination of recognisable faces one resembles, and something I suspect vulnerable young people are encouraged to do on these stand-up comedy courses that they have now. But here I disguise this same hack move as a discussion of some admittedly genuine reviews. In the past I have been described as looking like Ray Liotta, Leonardo DiCaprio, Edwyn Collins, kd lang, Morrissey, Albert Finney and a heraldic lion or lamb on a medieval tapestry (by Richard Herring); and I have irritated members of the public, who will not take no for an answer, by denying that I am Mark Lamarr, Roland Gift, Ben Watt from Everything but the Girl, Terry Christian, Todd Carty, the bloke who committed suicide that Todd Carty replaced in *EastEnders*, and the lead singer of UB40. Basically, they half-recognise me because of my carefully cultivated F-list celebrity status, and their brains misfile me into the nearest possible fit.

My mother pointed out that I looked like Terry Christian in the early eighties, before he was even famous, when he was interviewed as a teenager by Gus MacDonald on an ITV discussion show about young people's attitudes. 'That boy looks like you, but less scruffy and miserable,' she said, and the comparison went on to haunt me. I had a twenty-minute conversation with a polite man in a Thai restaurant in Stoke Newington in 1999, during which I gradually realised that when he was asking about my cancelled television series and absence from our screens he actually thought I was Terry Christian, and it got to the stage where it would have been embarrassing for both of us for me to explain that I wasn't. Instead, I continued to pretend to be Terry Christian, improvising successfully around my limited knowledge of Christian's current projects, until the man paid and left. Perhaps I should have carried on being Terry Christian from that point. We have aged in the same way, same receding hair, same sagging jowls, though I am fatter than him. Perhaps I could

255

41, I thought, 'It's not bad', you know, number 41, it's quite good. And in fact soon after that list was announced, Bernard Manning, who was in the top forty, he died and I thought that meant I would move up a position. But it wasn't the case, even with, er, a letter-writing campaign to the family; they were distressed, if anything. 'Why, why are you doing this? Please stop.'*

So you know, it's great. I'm not joking, I was pleased, I was pleased and surprised, but you might have a similar experience to me. You might be supposed to be good at something, but it doesn't necessarily count for anything with your family 'cause they know who you really are. And my mother, for example, is still as ashamed and embarrassed as she ever was of me being a stand-up comedian. It's not something that she's interested in, stand-up comedy. My mum's main area of interest is quilts.† Making

---

have faked a Manchester accent, killed Terry Christian, usurped him and lived his life, like Martin Guerre or the bloke in *Mad Men*.

Last year, I found myself sitting next to the Fine Young Cannibals' Roland Gift, who is of mixed race, outside a crêpe stall in Edinburgh. Like some kind of delusional fantasist, I said, 'I expect you find this hard to believe, but I have been mistaken for you in the past.' He said, 'I think you look more like Ali Campbell from UB40.'

In order to save waste, I recycled a variation on this mistaken-identity theme in my 2009/10 show, *If You Prefer a Milder Comedian Please Ask for One*, adding Hattie Jacques and a thirties newspaper cartoon of Tarzan's face to the lookalike list.

* I'm sure the tone and delivery of this 'Why, why are you doing this? Please stop' is copied from somewhere, but I can't place it. It sounds like something the comedian and man Richard Herring would have said, or at least would have had said to him on numerous occasions, in his everyday life.

† My mother is unpredictable and mysterious, like God or the

quilts and talking about making quilts. And a new kind of quilt she's been making lately, I don't know if you've heard of this, it's called a quillow. And that is a quilt which rolls up into a pillow. Although it comes with its own unique set of problems, 'cause if you think about it, for a relaxing night, you need both . . . you need both a quilt and a pillow. So with the quillow, you either are cold with a comfortable neck, or are warm with backache. And the only solution, of course, is to use two quillows – in many ways, defeats the unique selling property of the quillow – or alternatively, to revert to the traditional quilt–pillow combo.*

But my mum's not impressed by me being a stand-up, it's not something she's† . . . For my mum, me being the

------

sea. She talks to me for hours about things I am not interested in, such as golf, and then quietly and fascinatingly becomes a master quilt-maker, fashioning award-winning quilts inlaid with beautiful designs, without really ever seeing fit to mention it.

* I am being facetious of course. The quillow is superb.

† It's hardly surprising that I would assume my mother is not interested in me being a comedian. She struggled to bring me up as a single parent, blagged me into the local Church of England junior school, where I studied alongside the middle-class elite of Solihull and got an inroad to a life of educational privilege, took on extra evening jobs and took in student lodgers to make up the shortfall in my fees after I got a charity bung and then a part-scholarship to the local independent boys' school, and then watched me get a place at Oxford University, an opportunity of the kind she never had, only to blow it outta my ass by becoming a stand-up comedian.

I'm not even sure my mother really believed I was making any kind of living as a comic until the 2009 TV series, as I was never really written about in the normal newspapers, except as a scourge of society and proponent of mass choral swearing. But she came to see me twice on the 2009 tour, having not seen me since 1990. The first time, I think she mistook my whole onstage approach for me being actually unable to do comedy properly, and seemed to pity

41st best stand-up of all time – which I am, remember, they can't take that away now – that's about as impressive to my mum as if I were to be voted the world's 41st tallest dwarf. Taller, admittedly, than many other dwarves, but still essentially a dwarf, and as such prohibited by law from applying for any job with a minimum height requirement, such as policeman, basketball player or owner-operator of an enchanted beanstalk.*

I don't know if you can hear that at home but there's a

---

me afterwards, but after the second show, in the company of some enthusiastic former workmates, my mother seemed to have really enjoyed the event. I was surprised how relieved this made me feel. I suppose I didn't want her to feel I had wasted my life and, by association, her efforts to give me a good start.

Earlier this year, I found out that my mother had been keeping a scrapbook of press cuttings about me all along, so this whole routine, about my mum's supposed indifference to my work, is based on a false premise. She's just a quiet and modest woman, and probably worries that anything she said about my work would be the wrong thing, me being a temperamental artist and that. And in 1992, my mother recently reminded me, she even wrote to the *Daily Mail* radio critic, the dishonourable Quentin Letts, to reprimand him for failing to credit the writer, me, of a show he had reviewed favourably. At the time I was faintly embarrassed by my mother's behaviour, but now I am very proud of her. More people's mothers should write to Quentin Letts, and *Daily Mail* journalists generally, and tell them off. Perhaps Richard Littlejohn wouldn't have said that the murder of all those prostitutes in Ipswich was of no consequence if some nice mums had written him a few stiff letters earlier in his career of evil.

* The comedian Simon Munnery, who was once an expert swordsman, has since stolen this idea. He says – onstage, mind – that the title of *Celebrity Mastermind*, which I won, entirely legitimately, on the BBC show in January 2010, is of no value, as the *Mastermind* part of the title is degraded by the appending of the word 'Celebrity'. 'Celebrity Mastermind', he says, 'is a bit like being Tallest Dwarf.'

strong uptake for that joke in this area, and the laughter ebbed away as we went towards the bar. Now, there might be a lot of you in who've not seen me before. If you've not seen me before, right, a lot of what I do, er, it's not jokes as such, it can just be funny kind of ideas or little, er, weird turns of phrase like that, yeah? So, 'owner-operator of an enchanted beanstalk', yeah? And that's a giant, isn't it, a giant. Yeah? It's a giant. Little turns of phrase. So all I'm saying, all I'm saying if you've not seen me before, yeah, is the jokes are there, they're there, but some of you, you might have to raise your game. We'll be all right, we'll be all right, we'll be all right. 'Cause there's harder stuff than that in this show, there's a bit that's borderline incomprehensible, about insects, even to me, right, so, um, and I wrote it and I don't know what it is, right.

So my mum's not impressed by me being a stand-up. My mum has already seen the best stand-up she's ever going to see, she is adamant about the fact that it isn't me. My mum's favourite stand up is the nineteen-seventies-stroke-eighties TV comedy-quiz-show host of *Name That Tune* fame, Tom O'Connor.

A couple of people, down here, remember Tom O'Connor, but on the whole the demographic of this room is such that no one knows who Tom O'Connor is really, no one remembers him. And that's a shame, 'cause I'm now going to talk about Tom O'Connor for about twenty-five . . . twenty-five, thirty minutes.* Tom O'Connor, he

* I realise that I often do this – point out that the majority of the audience aren't interested in what I am talking about, and tell them that I'm about to discuss it for half an hour or so anyway. Again, it's a counter-intuitive move, but one that tells them they may not be getting what they want, so they may as well try and like what they are given.

259

was a Liverpudlian comic in the seventies and he . . . and then he ended up doing game shows. And my mum saw Tom O'Connor doing stand-up on a cruise that she took ten years ago when she retired, and this had always been a dream of hers, yeah, to go, to go on a cruise, not to see Tom O'Connor doing stand-up on a cruise. Seeing Tom O'Connor do stand-up on a cruise, it's not even a dream of Tom O'Connor's. In fact, in many ways it's his worst nightmare. And one that Tom O'Connor has now been trapped in for ten years. Like some kind of silver-haired Scouse groundhog.*

In fact, ladies and gentlemen, Tom O'Connor has now been performing stand-up exclusively at sea for so long that he has developed scurvy. Yeah? That's a sea-based illness, isn't it? My wife wrote that joke, it's not one of mine. No, she did, my wife wrote it, it's not the kind of joke I would write, it's too . . . It's got a good kind of rhythm, hasn't it, conventional sort of rhythm to it, it's good but it's not the kind of thing I would do. Um, but I put it in because it's better than most of what I would do.†

* I regret being cruel to Tom O'Connor here. He is, after all, a fellow comic, and therefore by default I have more in common with him than with any actor, musician or member of the public. But the problem is, it was Tom O'Connor that my mum saw on a cruise, and I cannot tell a lie. On this occasion.
† It occurs to me as I reach the third transcript in this book that all my best jokes have been written by, inspired by, duplicated independently from, bought off or suggested by other people – Dave Thompson, Simon Munnery, Ian Macpherson, Michael Redmond, Louise Coates, Kevin Eldon, Richard Herring and my wife, Bridget Christie. I begin to sympathise with people who think I am a charlatan. In fact, the good jokes in my set are starting to stick out so obviously by this stage in my career that it even feels necessary for me to attribute them to their writers, live onstage during the show,

Now, my mum saw Tom O'Connor doing stand-up on a cruise, and whenever the subject of stand-up comes up, she never stops talking to me about Tom O'Connor. She goes, 'Oh, he was amazing, Stew, Tom O'Connor, take your feet off that quilt, it's not finished. He come out, Stew – he's a comic, like you – he come out, Stew, on the cruise, Tom O'Connor, and he said to this chap in the front row, "What do you do for a living?" And the man said that he worked for Esso or Shell, one of them firms, you know. And Tom O'Connor, Stew, he was, oh, he was quick, he was quick-witted. He said to him, off the top of his head, he said to him, "Are you a sardine?" It was hilarious, Stew. [*long pause*] I have remembered it wrong, yes.*

———

as they are so clearly not of a piece with my own interminable and self-regarding material.

* There are few things funnier than the frustration engendered by my mother, or indeed any civilian non-professional comic, failing to tell a joke properly by getting all the details in the wrong order. I love it. It's like someone's given Georges Braque a 'Why did the chicken cross the road?' set-up and he's handed in a painting of a road that looks like a chicken with crosses for eyes. My favourite example of this was a Liverpudlian cab driver trying to tell me a joke set on a building site, during which he became totally bogged down in the idea of 'the camaraderie of the building site' and kept stressing it at every point, mistakenly imagining it was somehow an important element of the joke, the entirety of which I have since forgotten, except that it involved 'the camaraderie of the building site, you know, the camaraderie, of the lads, on the building site . . . the camaraderie of the building site, the camaraderie, it was because of the camaraderie like, the camaraderie of the building site'. I am pretty sure I hijacked his weird and strangely hypnotic rhetoric to achieve maximum tedium in the telling of the sardine joke here.

Since doing this set, I've found a new mode of being onstage, which is to take on the persona of an old lady – not strictly based

'Yeah, he come out, Stew, Tom O'Connor – don't touch those bits of felt 'cause they're cut into the shape of lions, for a jungle scene to go on it, it won't just be . . . – he come out, Stew, on the . . . Tom O'Connor, yes, he's like a comic, and he said to this chap, "What do you do for a living?" And the man said, Stew, he said, "I'm in oil." Tom O'Connor, he was . . . He was quick, Stew. He was quick as a fl– . . . he's like lightning, coming out of a dish. And he said to him, "Are you a sardine?" No, he wasn't a sardine, Stew, he was er . . . he was a man. Why? Well, if he'd been a sardine, it wouldn't have been a joke would it? It would have been a statement of fact.*

---

on my gran in any real sense, but channelling elements of childhood memories of many dotty aunties and neighbours – who is trying to tell a story in a mild Midlands accent about something she does not really understand. This has been the key to me being allowed to ramble incoherently around various subjects for minutes on end, and resulted in the 'Rap Singers' routine on the first episode of *Stewart Lee's Comedy Vehicle*, during which section of the show, viewing figures record, 300,000 people switched off or died of boredom.

* The repeated image of Tom O'Connor being quick, like various animals and objects, is indebted to Julian Barratt of The Mighty Boosh, whose 2000 Edinburgh show with Noel Fielding, *Arctic Boosh*, I directed and essentially script-edited. The free-form narrative approach I struggled to impose on *Arctic Boosh* later became the basis of the ungrateful duo's multimillion-pound touring shows and many hit television outings, but during my tenure with them they accused me of being 'like Hitler, stamping all over us in your jackboots . . . trying to make us write a fucking play or something', and sacked me, like the jazzed-up wankers they are.

But there was one sentence in *Arctic Boosh*, typical of the boys' approach, wherein Julian described himself, with the most brilliant throwaway timing, as 'coming at' someone like a particular thing, and this thing would be changed every night in the pursuit of

'Yeah, you don't understand it. He come out, Stew – listen – Tom O'Connor, yes, from *Crosswits*. Don't touch that. It's a quillow actually. It's both a . . . And he's come out, he's a comic, he's like you, and he said to this chap, "What do you do for a living?" The man said, "I'm in oil." And Tom O'Connor, Stew, he – oh, well – I think he saw the window of opportunity. And hurled hisself through it bodily. And he says to him, "Are you a sardine?" Yeah, you're right, Stew, it doesn't make sense, strictly speaking. Yes, you're right. If you said to a sardine, "What do you do for a living?", no, it wouldn't say, "I'm in oil," you're right. No, it's not its job, it's not its job. Well, it's swimming around, yeah. It's not waged, no, it's voluntary. Yeah, you're right, Stew, the only circumstances under which a sardine would reply "I'm in

---

spontaneity, and in order to remove definite cues so as to make the show impossible to tech in any meaningful way, and also making anyone kindly trying to structure it, for no fee, out of the goodness of their heart, feel like some kind of loser or fascist.

Most comedy happens in 4/4, or at least in a recognisable rhythm. The punchlines fall on the beat. But The Boosh are like Sunny Murray, the free-jazz drummer who reinvented time for Albert Ayler and Cecil Taylor in the sixties. There's a pulse in their heads, but only they can hear it, and the timing of the funny lines is falling all around it, like dried stalks of spaghetti being dropped onto a china plate. You're laughing on the off-beats, and the on-beats are empty, glaring holes. It is brilliant, and disproves the rigour of accepted comic theory. But as with all art, you can only really do it wrong if you've first mastered doing it right.

Once, in the late twentieth century, when characteristically annoyed with their refusal to conform to my ideas of what comedy should be, I said to the two surly young Booshes, probably racked by my own bitterness and envy, 'The problem is, you two think you're Miles Davis and John Coltrane, but actually you need to realise you are Flanagan and Allen.' But it turns out that Noel and Julian were The Mighty Boosh all along. And I was wrong.

263

oil" is if you said to it, "What substance do you expect to be preserved in for retail purposes in the event of your death?"*

'He come out, Stew, Tom O'Connor – listen, don't touch those pins, they're holding the lions on – and he's a comic. He *is* the same as you. And he said to this chap . . . The man said, "I'm in oil." And he flew at him, like a wolf, Stew, and he said, he said to him, "Are you a s– . . .?" Yes, you're right, Stew, they don't always come in oil. They can come in tomato sauce, yes. No, he could have made that work, Stew. He could've . . . Tom O'Connor could've done, Stew, 'cause he's quick like Zephyrus the wind, and he'd . . . and Mercury, and he would have said to him . . . If he'd said

* The 'I'm in oil'/'Are you a sardine?' comeback could have been achieved nightly by O'Connor simply relaying back the supposed quote 'I'm in oil' through his mic, irrespective of the actual reply from the floor to his own question, presumably 'What do you do for a living, sir?' But it had enchanted my mother. It is a constant source of frustration to comics that you, the public, are often inordinately thrilled by things that we do which are quite easy, and baffled or bored by the stuff we are proud of, or else assume that our finest moments are errors or accidents. But it was ever thus.

Until fairly recently, most newspapers were so contemptuous of stand-up that they'd send a bloke who usually wrote about fishing or cake to review a month of it on the Edinburgh Fringe, despite the fact that he had never seen any live comedy before. In week one of the Edinburgh Fringe, the poor fool, leagues out of his depth, would file copy like: 'The man came on. It was funny.' By week two he's progressed to: 'He made fun of a bald man in the front row and said to a young heckler, "I remember when I had my first pint." His mastery of improvisation was astonishing.' Then by week three he's learned the rules and is so jaded he only wakes up out of his coma if he sees Kim Noble masturbating a cat to death or Daniel Kitson visibly weeping at the childhood memory of some home-made biscuit onstage in a broom cupboard at three o'clock in the morning.

to the man, "What do you do for a living?" and the man had worked for Heinz and he'd said, "I'm in tomato sauce," Tom O'Connor could still have said, "Are you a sardine?" And there would have been a pause while the audience thought, "Hmm . . . well, they normally come in oil, surely. Ah, but they can come in tomato sauce! I should never have doubted Tom."

'He come out, Stew – listen – Tom O'Connor, he's the same . . . – don't touch that, it's the pattern. He said, "I'm in oil," he said, "Are you a sardine?" Yes, Stew, it was the funniest thing I've ever seen. Yes, it was better than anything you've ever done. And you know why? 'Cause it was clean. He come out, Stew, Tom O'Connor, and he said to this chap, "What do you do for a living?" And the man, he wasn't a plant. He said, "I'm in oil." And Tom O'Connor, Stew, he said, "Are you a sardine? Are you a sardine? Are you a sardine? Are you a sardine? Are you a sardine? Are you a sardine?"'*

Of course, what my mother doesn't know is that since

---

* All this stuff was different every night. Again, like Fred Frith said at the ICA when distracted by the camera flash, the key to this, the Ang-Lee's-angry bit in *Stand-Up Comedian* and lots of the back end of '90s Comedian was in the process of forgetting what was supposed to be funny about the story, even in the act of telling it, so that I could be genuinely surprised or delighted or confused by events and phrases as they unfolded out of my unknowing mouth. On a good night, I could repeat 'Are you a sardine?' at the end for minutes and take the crowd through waves of boredom, into hysteria, and back into boredom again. It was a rare source of some pride to me that I usually managed to sell this to many of the doubters who were now coming to see me off the back of three years' good press and my official 41st-best rating.

The composer John Cage said, 'If something is boring after two minutes, try it for four. If still boring, then eight. Then sixteen.

a nervous breakdown that Tom O'Connor suffered in the mid-eighties, as a result of having been outed by the tabloid press for allegedly having had an affair with a teenaged prostitute, Tom O'Connor has answered any dialogue he becomes involved in with the phrase, 'Are you a sardine?' And like a stopped clock, Glasgow, inevitably this means that Tom O'Connor will be right at least twice, and simple, grinding, tedious repetition will take on the illusion of genius. And yes, there is a subtext there, there is a subtext.* And, yeah? Oh right. The last time that Tom O'Connor was right to reply 'Are you a sardine?', the last time, was about ten years ago, and my mum saw him on a cruise. He came out, and he said to this man, 'What do you do for a living?' And the man said, 'I'm in oil.' And he said, 'Are you a sardine?' I don't know if you remember that from earlier, from earlier in the show, way back, way back at the beginning? Yeah? Yeah, you remember that.†

And the other time, the only other time that Tom O'Connor was right to reply 'Are you a sardine?' was in 1987. Now, to try and patch things up after the sex scandal in the tabloids, Tom O'Connor took his wife, Mrs Tom

———

Then thirty-two. Eventually one discovers that it is not boring at all.' I am glad I found this quote, as the next time someone says, 'This is boring,' I can now say, 'No. It isn't. It is part of the tradition of the post-war avant-garde.'

* This is a signal to listeners that I know that the criticism of 'tedious grinding repetition', which is a phrase I actually took from a review of the fabulous Andy 'The Red Clown' Zaltzman, could be applied to me, and that many people think my supposed talent is an illusion propagated by journalists and pseuds.

† Having gone on too long about the same thing already, I knowingly insult the audience further and bait the bored ones by reminding them just how long exactly this section has been going on without any end in sight.

O'Connor, on a bargain-break weekend. And they went to Lisbon in Portugal, yeah? And while they were there, they were in a plaza, a piazza, a public square of some sort, and Tom O'Connor was approached by a small, oily fish. And the small, oily fish said to Tom O'Connor [*falsetto Portuguese*], 'I am a traditional street festival snack of choice every year here in Lisbon on January the 19th, the feast day of St Cuthbert. But, Tom, I am also a traditional summer delicacy throughout all of rural Portugal as well. What am I?' Yeah! That's how they speak, that's how they speak.*

In the end, I got sick of my mum going on about Tom O'Connor all the time. I said to her, 'Look, Mum, when you've made a new quillow, I don't say to you, "I saw a much better quillow than that on a ship," and then make a joke about a quillow, do I?' And she went, 'No, Stew, 'cause you wouldn't even be able to think of a joke about a quillow. Tom O'Connor could, Stew, he's quick. He come out, Stew, on the cruise . . .' I said, 'Shut up, shut up about Tom O'Connor now.' I said to her, 'I'll let you into a secret, Mother, a trade secret, right. I don't want to break your heart, but in the trade of stand-up comedy Tom O'Connor is regarded as a ludicrous, absurd, sad figure, and here's why,' I said to her, right. ''Cause when he's onstage, Tom O'Connor, his wife, Mrs Tom O'Connor, sits in the foyer behind a little kiosk they take round with them that Tom

* Here, I would normally climb up on a chair and try and take on the persona, voice, accent and physical movements that I imagined a Portuguese fish would have, which was an unexpected gambit from a comedian usually described as 'deadpan' and 'inert'. This was another good example of, ideally, not needing to finish a joke off. I enjoyed playing the Portuguese fish and would like to experiment with the portrayal of more racially specific sea creatures in the future in an attempt to expand my range.

O'Connor's made out of all plywood and hay and mud. And to try and grub up a few more pennies, like a pig in the dirt, Mrs Tom O'Connor sells – and this is true – she sells golf umbrellas with a drawing of Tom O'Connor's face on them. And that is sad.' And my mum said, 'It isn't sad, Stew, it's good. And anyway, you haven't even got a golf umbrella with your face on it.' And she's right, she's right.*

---

* It was the comedian and potter Johnny Vegas who told me that Tom O'Connor was pushing golf umbrellas with his face on them. Apparently, Tom's wife would sell them from a little portable booth they set up in the foyer after his shows. This may not be true. But for a comedian, the key to successful merchandising is knowing your audience and their interests. Robin Ince should sell Robin Ince bookmarks to his clever audience of readers. Paul Foot should sell nice tea towels with one of his witty sayings on them to his delightful fans. And Paddy McGuinness should sell mittens, tied together by string, with the words 'left' and 'right' written on the appropriate hands.

In the nineties, the comedian Simon Munnery, who once drove a pimped Robin Reliant all the way to Edinburgh to use in a show in a room the car was too big to drive into, used to sell women's knickers with a photo of his own face, making an expression of bold, angry defiance, printed on the crotch. As I say, you have to know your market. Before she became one of the famous TV stars of the twenty-first century, the comedienne Catherine Tate once fled her Camden flat during a fire in the small hours and ran into the arms of a waiting and delighted fireman, whilst wearing only a pair of these Simon Munnery souvenir knickers. This moment remains the closest Simon has come to mainstream acceptance.

Simon and I were discussing merchandising opportunities recently, when the face-knickers came up. Simon was in his twenties when he made and distributed these arrogant pants, and back then they seemed rather charming. Now that Simon is a forty-something married man with children, he agreed that it would be inappropriate for him to sell women's knickers with a photograph of his own face on the crotch. In the words of the late, great comedian Jason Freeman, 'context is not a myth'.

Twenty years, twenty years in the business. 41st best stand-up ever apparently. Yeah, I'd go to the golf-umbrella comedian-marketing manufacturing company. 'Can I have my face put on a golf umbrella?' 'No. You're just not getting the figures, son.' Twenty years. Nothing to show for it. And we've just had a little baby. And that's not cheap.*

So all I'm saying, 41st best stand-up ever, it doesn't necessarily count for anything. What does it mean in real terms, being the 41st best stand-up ever? It means nothing at home. And I thought, 'Where was this list?' It was on Channel 4, on television, Channel 4, the worst television station in Britain. Who I've just realised probably won't be buying this for transmission.

Even as I said that, I realised, 'Ah, there's a potential market just . . .' But they are though, aren't they? It's awful, Channel 4, awful. It used to be good, didn't it, in the old days, but not any more, it's rubbish. Last year they had this twenty-fifth anniversary, when Channel 4, it used to screen all the brilliant programmes it used to make twenty, twenty-five years ago. Channel 4, it's like a syphilitic old man leafing through a photograph album of all the society beauties he used to romance, all of them now dead. Because of him, because of what he did. Channel 4.†

I don't like television generally. I've got nothing against

---

* This was a heartfelt bit about the disparity between my critical acclaim and my ability to shift merch units, a problem that remains to this day despite having had a TV series, and one which Faber and Faber themselves will soon learn about, despite their claims to be 'not about the bread, man'.

† In Edinburgh, the Udderbelly venue that I was in was sponsored by E4, a subdivision of Channel 4. But I still said it because I don't do what the Man says I should, even when the Man is trying to help me in a mutually beneficial relationship. Fuck that shit!

the medium of television, right? It's great, it's just colours, lights, shapes and sounds, God knows we all love them, don't we? Over here, the people over here like them, over there, they like them one at a time. All together, it's a bit much, isn't it? A bit much. Have to ration them out ... The problem with television, I think, is it's increasingly incapable of dealing with anything thoughtful or serious, yeah? And a good example of this was this time last year, the *Celebrity Big Brother* racism scandal. You remember that? There was an Indian woman in the house and, er, everyone picked on her. Now, it was awful but I was kind of fascinated by it 'cause it showed us how television can't cope with a serious thing. And I sort of love the *Celebrity Big Brother* racism scandal for that. I loved it for three main reasons.*

Firstly, I loved the *Celebrity Big Brother* racism scandal 'cause it meant that because of the bad racism, the show's official sponsors, the Carphone Warehouse, were contractually obliged to issue the following genuine press statement. This is a genuine press statement from the Carphone Warehouse: 'Racism is entirely at odds with the values of the Carphone Warehouse.' Entirely at odds. I don't know about

* In 2007, Channel 4's flagship atrocity, *Celebrity Big Brother*, was caught up in a scandal when other contestants were supposedly racist to the Indian actress Shilpa Shetty. The glamour model Danielle Lloyd called her 'a dog' and said she should 'fuck off home'. Erudite pundits have pointed out that the real clash was about class, and that Lloyd and Jade Goody, who back then was alive and loathed rather than posthumously beatified, would inevitably have been rubbed up the wrong way by the gentle Shilpa's perceived airs and graces. This was no doubt envisaged by the cynical Channel 4 scum who put *Celebrity Big Brother* together, but I have chosen to ignore the class clash and concentrate on the supposed racism in order to contrive this routine.

you, Glasgow, but I was hugely relieved to read that press statement, because prior to reading that press statement, I had suspected that the [*falsetto Irish*] Carphone Warehouse was in fact a front for a white supremacist organisation.* And I have in my hand here a piece of paper bearing the true values of the [*falsetto Irish*] Carphone Warehouse, the true values of the [*falsetto Irish*] Carphone Warehouse.

1 Sell phones.
2 Sell more phones.
3 Deny the Holocaust.
4 Sell more phones.
5 Deny the Holocaust again, this time by texting your mates.
6 Lobby for the return of the gollywog and the *Black and White Minstrel Show*.
7 Sell phones, sell phones to cars, sell as many phones as . . . quickly, sell phones, sell the phones, sell . . .!

The values of the Carphone Warehouse. The sheer transparent naked hypocrisy of even imagining for a moment that such things exist as the values of the Carphone Warehouse. Do you follow the values of Jesus or Buddha or Marx? No. I follow the values of the Carphone Warehouse, committed as they have been these past twenty years to fighting racism through the unusual medium of discount phone retail, a sure method which for so long eluded the ANC or the Rock Against Racism movement. The values of the Carphone Warehouse.

* It amused me, privately, to say the words 'Carphone Warehouse' in an exaggerated attempt at the voice of Ed Byrne, who advertises the Carphone Warehouse, and is far better a comic than it is necessary for him to be.

At what point do you think it was that the [*falsetto Irish*] Carphone Warehouse decided that *Big Brother* was no longer compatible with their values? Was it about three series ago when Channel 4 broadcast live footage of a clearly inebriated twenty-year-old woman inserting the neck of a wine bottle into her vagina? Did the Carphone Warehouse go, 'Yes, at last, random objects inserted into the vagina of a drunk and the Carphone Warehouse are a brand-profile awareness marketing marriage made in heaven. And what a missed opportunity for product placement.' The values of the Carphone Warehouse, of which there are none.

And the second great thing about the *Celebrity Big Brother* racism scandal was this. There's a programme on that you may have seen called *Big Brother's Big Mouth* or *Big Brother's Little Brother*, something like that. Anyway, it's not on Channel 4 normally, it's on E4. And E4, if anything, is worse than Channel 4, isn't it? 'Cause Channel 4 is like a flood of sewage that comes unbidden into your home, er, whereas E4 is like you've constructed a sluice to let it in. Ah, another potential market has disappeared. Just the Paramount Channel left then. They've been good to us in the past.

Um, so . . . *Big Brother's Big Mouth* or whatever, it's on E4. And they have experts on – sociologists, psychologists, psychiatrists – and they provide expert insight into and expert analysis of the phenomena of some twats in a place. And this programme's hosted by Russell Brand. And what it meant when the bad racism happened, it meant that Russell Brand was contractually obliged to look meaning-fully into the camera, making a serious face, and condemn racism in the strongest terms possible, whilst dressed as a cartoon pirate, before going back to his ongoing life's work of thinking up cutesy, diminutive Mr Men names for his own penis. Mr Winky. Mr Dinky. Mr Dingle-donky-dinky-winky-wooky-woo-wa-ner. And the way that Russell Brand thinks up cutesy, diminutive Mr Men names for his own penis makes him sound like a child molester who is trying to convince himself to allow himself to molest himself.

And when Martin Luther King saw racism in nineteen-sixties America, Martin Luther King called it out in the strongest, most visionary, eloquent terms possible. Martin Luther King said, 'I have a dream that my four little children will one day live in a nation where they will not be judged by the colour of their skin but by the content of their character,' Martin Luther King. And when Russell Brand saw racism in his place of work, *Big Brother*, Russell Brand said, 'Oooh, there's been some bad racism and stuff going down today and no mistake, my liege. It's made Mr Winky go right small, it has. Oh yes it has, oh yeah. And my ball-bag, my old ball-bag, has only gone up my bum. Here's H from Steps.'*

And the third great thing about the *Celebrity Big Brother*

---

* Russell Brand didn't actually say this. He said, 'Racism, it's such a wank thing, innit? It's such a pain in the arse that someone would go around being racist. And individually, I think, if people were made culpable for their actions, and were made to look at themselves they'd think, "Oh God, I shouldn't say that." And yet the way they are behaving collectively is obviously abhorrent,' which isn't too bad at all, on the spur of the moment. That said, no matter how good Brand's handling of the situation, he was still hosting *Big Brother's Little Brother*, a programme which clearly contributes to the creeping death of civilisation as we know it, and alters, for the worse, the lives of all those who watch it or participate in it.

Legally, when this set was released on DVD, I covered my arse by having a DVD extra where Johnny Vegas challenged me at length about this bit. (Much the same function is performed in this book by the above quote and Appendix V.)

racism scandal was this. There was a glamour model in the house, you may remember, Danielle Lloyd, a former Miss UK. And she said the worst racist things, arguably. And as a result of this, for the next three or four months, Danielle Lloyd lost a lot of lucrative glamour-modelling work. Now, what this means presumably is that the editors of *Nuts* magazine and *Zoo* magazine and *Loaded* magazine and *FHM* magazine must have sat around and tried to decide whether their readers would feel comfortable masturbating over images of a racist. And they decided that they would not, yeah, which I feel is to underestimate the tenacity of the readers of *Nuts* magazine and *Zoo* magazine and *Loaded* magazine, who I think would have given it a good old go. I think they would have tried to find the inner strength to push through whatever ethical barrier the racism of the naked woman had presented them with. Um, who knows, who knows? The sheer wrongness of it may even have created an extra sexual frisson. We can't tell, can we, we can't be sure. We can never really know without carrying out a controlled experiment. And there's no money for that now, not with, not with the Olympics coming up, it's all . . . Those kind of things are all cut. So, um . . .

So there's some kind of theoretical objections to television, and that's all well and good, well done to me. But, er . . . But if I'm honest with you, the real problem I've got with television is it's now coming up to twelve years since they've commissioned anything that I've written. Um . . . But it nearly wasn't the case, um . . . I'm going to sit down for this bit, 'cause it's a little story about TV and it gives it the flavour of a . . . sitting down makes it feel like a sort of Ronnie Corbett monologue, which is good.* So, it nearly

* The show is far too narrative-heavy at this point. There's way too

wasn't the c– . . . I've been doing this about twenty years, like I said, and I'm on a kind of seven-year cycle of being fashionable, right, and it's good that it's so regular 'cause I can plan expensive medical crises around them.*

The last kind of critical peak for good reviews and stuff was about the start of 2006, and we're just on the downside of the curve from that now. Um . . . But anyway, as a result of being trendy about two years ago, I got asked in to see the head of BBC2, which is really weird because normally we have to petition them to be seen. But he asked me in and he said to me, 'We're all very excited about your work, whatever it is. You can do anything you like for the channel. What would you like to do?' And I thought . . . So I chanced my arm. I said, 'I'd like to do six half-hours of stand-up, fairly straightforward, like the old Dave Allen shows.' He said, 'You can. You don't need to do a try-out, get on with it, it won't be a problem.' So I left this meeting – I didn't even know what it was for – and when I left, my whole life had been completely transformed, professionally, financially, I suppose, everything.†

So I started writing this series, right. And I had this idea

---

much plot exposition and not enough jokes. But I found that sitting down on a stool at this point, as if admitting failure, let me off the hook, and let the audience relax. It sort of lowered their expectations, somehow, and allowed me to take on the role of someone just telling an anecdote at a bar. And if it was at all funny, then that was just a bonus. Perhaps Ronnie Corbett realised this, all those years ago, and that is why he sat down to tell his funny stories? If only Ronnie Corbett could speak, he would have so much to tell us.

* These phases were, to date: 1990 – *City Limits* New Act of the Year; 1995–6 – BBC2's *Fist of Fun*; 2003–6 – *Jerry Springer: The Opera/ Stand-Up Comedian/'90s Comedian*.

† This is entirely true, as explained in the introduction to this show.

that each week, I'd do a bit where I did a bit of stand-up to a weird group of people in an odd place, right, and I'd film it. So first of all I wrote a set that would work for really little kids, right. And it was about how when I was a kid, my mum said, 'Eat your greens,' and I didn't, and I got smaller and smaller, and then I got carried off by a bird, right. Yeah. Now, it's not aimed at you, but they like it, don't they, they like it, the people, yeah . . . It's for children really, but you know . . . Imagine me, being carried off by a bird, it'd be hilarious . . . 'Help!' . . . So, er . . . Especially if it was a funny bird, like a budgie or something . . .

So, I started doing this at kids' parties and stuff with a view to filming it at some point. And kids are really funny, right, 'cause they don't heckle. But what they do do is they put their hands up like that and then you have to decide whether to accept the heckle. It's a good system, you know.*

So I was doing this kids party on a Sunday afternoon, I was talking about becoming really small and whatever. And this little girl about seven put her hand up. And I went, 'What?' And she said, 'If you were so small then, why are you so fat again now?' And that's funny, isn't it? So, um . . . No, it is, you know. So I said to her, 'Well, I may be fat, but at least I've got some pubic hair.'† [*shouting*] 'Cause the

---

* I did this at the Comedy for Kids Sunday afternoon gigs run by James Campbell, where you have to tweak your material to work for children, some of whom do their own kiddie-comedy before the adult headliner. Detractors say it's all a bit middle-class and trendy, but I found the experience of trying to think from a child's point of view very rewarding.
† I didn't say this at Comedy for Kids. This bit is reworked from an old routine about putting down an intrusive and overcurious child in the showers of a public swimming pool which I hadn't done for about fifteen years. Of course, the tension and the humour in the

routine relied on the possibility of there being some wrongdoing afoot, before a 'pull back and reveal' at the end of the bit revealed that rather than being a paedophile, I was just an overliteral and linguistically zealous parent instructing children in the scientific names of genitalia, which they insisted on calling by their playground slang titles.

The last time I performed it was at a comedy and folk club in Manchester (those were the days) in about 1992, opening for a folk singer called Sally Barker, subsequently of The Poozies. The club's host called himself Agraman the Human Anagram, as there was a fashion for names of that nature in the eighties alternative scene (perhaps the eloquently furious veteran Ian Cognito would have got the recognition he deserved under a different name). The Human Anagram's act did not, of course, include any elements of wordplay. Before the show the Human Anagram explained to me that he didn't like swearing, and I explained he didn't have to worry as I didn't swear. Then, during this fake-paedo bit, the Human Anagram came on and physically removed me from the stage, at the behest of a woman sitting next to him hissing, 'Get him off. Get him off.' By removing me from the stage before I had finished the bit, the Human Anagram made the whole situation worse as the admittedly uneasy audience were denied the opportunity to see that their assumptions were unfounded, and presumably just thought a man about to advocate some kind of sexual assault had been stopped from doing so.

Often, jokes, stories and words only make sense if they are allowed to be viewed in their completed form. You would have thought that, of all people, a Human Anagram would appreciate this. Before the show, Sally Barker had been quite nice to me, but she never spoke to me again, and has never responded to the thousands of letters and drawings of her I have sent over the years since. And the poor and confused Human Anagram was visibly bewildered and upset by me, saying that he had told me about not swearing. I understand, from the comedian Richard Herring's amusing parody of them on his Warming Up blog, that the comedian Peter Kay's books consist largely of him settling scores with people whom he imagines to have wronged him in the past. I have no wish to be parodied in a similar fashion by the merciless sword of justice of

old skills kick back in, Glasgow, twenty years, twenty years, night after night after night. I didn't want to say it but it's like Pavlov's dog. Pavlov's dog! Any seven-year-olds that cross me will be crushed into the ground 'cause they don't have twenty years of road-hardened skills!*

---

the lawgiver Richard Herring, and hereby forgive the Human Anagram for his erroneous assumption, and thank him for the work he has given me since. And I hereby forgive Sally Barker too, who has a new album out, apparently, called *Maid in England*.

* In a way, I am glad that I never became a Comedy Store or Jongleurs regular, although the money and the camaraderie of the building site would have been nice. In 1991, after my fourth or fifth open spot at The Store, in the old Leicester Square space, the then booker, a Scottish choreographer called Kim Kinney, said he would give me paid gigs, but I reminded him too much of the act he disliked the most in the world, Simon Munnery. As you can see from my ongoing Oedipal references to him throughout this book, I had already decided that Simon was, contrary to Kim Kinney's view, the best comedian in the world at the time, so I more or less gave up on The Comedy Store at that point. There's still a publicity photo of me from the period, looking like an arrogant, self-obsessed child, on the steps on the way into the new venue.

That said, never doing The Store, or Jongleurs, meant I never really developed those road-hardened skills that you see proper comedians deploy with devastating accuracy to 2 a.m. stag-night crowds, and I was allowed instead to develop a gentler, more coercive and admittedly less reliable approach. I hate having to put people down in an audience, and hate it when they force me to do so by going on and on with their unfunny shit. Also, as a lot of my act is about failing, it is difficult to continue to tell stories in which you are the low-status victim when you have been forced to take the upper hand and be high-status to sort out a persistent heckler. Part of my deliberate repositioning of myself when I returned to stand-up full-time in 2004 was about trying to find venues where, and an audience for whom, my failure to have developed the crowd-control skills of a Comedy Store veteran wouldn't matter.

278

And the other thing I wanted to do, right, wasn't just that. I wanted to do like a kind of parody of observational comedy. Now, The Stand audience, you see lots of comedy, you'll know what observational comedy is. Observational comedy is when the comedian pretends to have the same life as you, right, rather than being a philandering coke addict. This is what observational comedy's like, isn't it, it's like this.*

[*sniffs*] 'Wa-hey! Who's, er, who's married? Who's married, who's got a girlfriend? Who's ever seen a woman, you seen a photo of one, you know what they are, you've seen them around, yeah? Yeah? Not men, with the hair. Are there any in? Any women in? Any women? Girls, answer me this. Why do you take so long to get ready, what's going on? What's going on? What's going on? What's going on?

* The best and most economic parody of observational comedy comes, as usual, from the comedian Simon Munnery, who simply says to the audience: 'Anyone ever noticed anything, ever?' A more elaborate one was an early nineties act by the sometime local-radio DJ and full-time loony Tom Binns called *Some Kind of Comedian*, where he stood in a metal dustbin and said stuff like, 'Think of a thing. Think of a thing, right. Are you thinking of it? Now, think of that thing on drugs.'

This observational-comedy section was one of the rare occasions onstage in which I try to act, as I take on the amped-up persona of a formerly fêted mid-nineties hit Edinburgh Fringe solo-show comic, now working the length and breadth of the country with the same twenty minutes every night to support his mortgage, kids, maintenance payments and coke habit, with flashes of genius filtering through a firewall of saleable content. I have no one specific in mind here. In the mid-nineties, many circuit comics imagined they were Britpop rock stars, and then came down from the contact high and realised they were still variety turns. We're all turns. There's no shame in it! Turn, turn, turn again!

Why do you take so long to get ready? What's going on? What's . . . Who's got kids? That's finished, that bit. Who's got kids? It's finished! It's finished! It's fini– . . . Who's got kids? I've got a little boy. Have you got a little boy? How old is he, fourteen? Mine's three. It's the same, it's the same. It's the same! Some of the things he says, though, they're mad, it's hilarious, it's mad. It's like he can only understand the world from the perspective of a child.'

Anyway. I've got a terrible feeling there's some people at the back there going, 'Now he's cooking, now he's cooking.' Why do they take so long to get ready, the women, if only we could ask them, but they'd go mad. So, I thought, what's the best way to do a parody of observational comedy? And the best way to do a parody of observational comedy, I thought, was to do it from the point of view of an insect, about being an insect, whilst dressed as an insect, right. So, I'm an insect comedian, right, it'd be like this. I'm an insect, yeah?*

[*sniffs*] 'Right, who's er, who's killed a grasshopper? Come on, we've all done it, haven't we? Friday night, we've all done it. There's a bloke down there laughing, he's on film now, he's on film, and he's done it. And um . . . We've all done it, Friday night, killed a grasshopper, you get 'em, don't you, in your mandibles, yeah, and er – not what you were thinking, mandibles, yeah, what are you think-ing, what are you thinking – you get 'em and you spit your enzymes onto 'em, don't you, yeah, your enzymes, yeah, you spit your enzymes on 'em, on the grasshoppers, to

* As explained in the previous chapter, this was a genuine idea I had for my proposed BBC TV show, but as I began to make plans to try it out, performing onstage as an insect at various comedy ven-ues, I felt executive confidence in the programme gradually ebbing away.

dissolve 'em, yeah, into a liquid, yeah, you dissolve 'em into a liquid, yeah, so you can feed 'em to your grub. Who's got a little grub, who's got a little grub? I've got a little grub, honestly, some of the things he says, they're mad, it's hilarious, it's like he can only understand the world from a larval perspective.'

So. I wanted to do that insect comedy but I didn't know where to film it, right, for this programme that I was given. And then it turned out, as luck would have it, that in May last year there was a three-day event happening at Barnes reservoir, the wildlife reserve in south-west London, and there were entomologists, insect scientists, coming from all over the world for a three-day celebration of insects, and this event was called Pestival, right.* Pestival. That's not my joke, that's an entomologist's joke. Don't judge me. And on the opening night I found out they were having an insect-themed cabaret to welcome all the entomologists, and they'd already booked Robyn Hitchcock the singer-songwriter, 'cause he's got loads of songs about bees and ants and things.† And they'd booked this saxophonist David Rothenberg, who was going to improvise live to a tank of crickets and stuff, right. So I – no, he was, it was good, actually, so – so I rang up the organiser Bridget Nicholls and I said to her, 'Can I come to Pestival and do

* As explained in the introduction to the show, Pestival was a real event which now goes from strength to strength. 2006 was the inaugural year.
† Pestival approached me, rather than me approaching them. I changed it for the story to work. I often seem to share backstage space with the psychedelic troubadour Robyn Hitchcock at benefits for every lost cause going. I remember once we tried to Stop George Bush. In the end, George Bush stopped anyway, irrespective of our best efforts.

half an hour of stand-up about being an insect whilst dressed as an insect to the world's three hundred leading insect scientists?' And she said, 'Yes, that would be exactly appropriate. But', she said, 'we can't pay you. Do you love insects?' I said, 'Yeah, I love insects. I luv them.' And then she said, 'Also, there's a party of entomologists in from Prague and we're excited to have them 'cause they made a breakthrough study last year into the life cycle of the peach potato aphid, so it would be really great', she said, 'if most of your, er, gags, quips could be about aphids.' And I said, 'That's fine, I've got loads. I've got loads, 'cause I started out doing stand-up in the eighties, you remember stand-up in the eighties? It was all aphid stuff, wasn't it, aphids and, er, Thatcher, the milk snatcher, remember, snatching all the milk?'*

So I, er, so I rang up this guy Martin Soan and I paid him 500 quid to make the insect costume.† I thought I'll

* I was booked by Bridget Nicholls to appear as an insect at Pestival, but the idea that she insisted I do stuff about the peach potato aphid is a fabrication.

† I didn't ring up Martin Soan. I rang up a guy who had made a dolphin costume for Jo Neary or something. But back in the Cluub Zarathustra days, I would have rung Martin Soan. Martin was one of the naked balloon dancers in Malcolm Hardee's *Greatest Show on Legs*, and we heard about him earlier in the book when he noted some crossover between his material and that of Joe Pasquale on the Royal Variety Performance. Martin is really your man for crazy home-made props.

For Cluub Zarathustra, our Dadaist cabaret of the mid-nineties, Martin built us, amongst other things, a CUNT Ray, an anti-audience defence weapon conceived by Simon Munnery. The CUNT Ray was a massive black tube, about four feet wide, with black gauze on one end with the word 'CUNT' written backwards in a fine transparent mesh over it. Concealed inside this comedy cannon was a powerful

get that back from the programme eventually, and the producer said he could secretly film it for this TV series. And then about two days later, my then manager Don Rodeo, he got an email from the BBC withdrawing the offer of the whole series, out of nowhere.* Now, I mean, I was disappointed obviously but it was a strange disappointment, 'cause the whole thing had always seemed too good to be true.

You don't get what you always want, it just doesn't happen, getting what you want, but what had happened . . . It's like going up to a little child and going, 'Hello, what thing would you like to have most in the world? What's your favourite thing? What?' 'A toy red fire engine.' 'Is it? Well, I've got one for you. There you are, that's for you. And that light flashes and the ladder goes up . . . No, it is, it's for you, you can have it, really. Take it, there it is. [shouts] Oh dear,

---

flash gun of the type used on industrial-strength fashion shoots. The CUNT Ray was suspended at the back of the stage to be activated at persistent hecklers individually or at unsatisfying audiences en masse. After the powerful flash blast from the CUNT Ray, as soon as the audience shut their eyes the word 'CUNT' would appear flashing beneath their eyelids, burned semi-permanently into their retinas.

* I had begun to make enquiries into having the costume made, and Armando Iannucci had begun making arrangements to film my performance at Pestival, when this cancellation was announced on Friday 7 April 2006. There was still over a month until Pestival, enough of a window for me to cancel the costume and save myself the money which I could not now claim back, so I did. But I changed the story here, saying I had already had the costume made, in the interest of high drama. On *Jerry Springer: The Opera*, our chief investor, a sixties Mod hairdresser who was now a big TV exec in America, kept repeating the mantra 'Where's the jeopardy?', which we secretly found amusing, but actually it's always a question worth asking of any script.

it's been smashed in front of your stupid, crying face.'*

Don't ever dream.

But there were some practical problems with the sudden withdrawal of this work. First of all, um, I'm self-employed, I hadn't really earned much out of *Jerry Springer: The Opera* because it kept being banned, and I hadn't set up any other work because I assumed I was doing this TV series, we had a little baby due at the time, and, er, the other problem was it meant that I was now contractually obliged to go to Pestival at Barnes reservoir and do half an hour of stand-up about being an insect whilst dressed in a now unjustifiably expensive insect costume to three hundred of the world's leading entomologists for no fucking reason at all.†

And all I'm saying, Glasgow, is does that seem to you like something that should happen to the 41st best stand-up of all time? [*shouting*] Twenty years, twenty years, twenty y– . . . I should not at this stage in my career, I should not have to go to a reservoir to do half an hour of stand-up about aphids for no . . . I should at least be paid for that. And after twenty years, the places I perform, their principal purpose should not be the storage of water. They should be theatres or whatever this is, a cesspit with lights. I shouldn't even be in Glasgow at all, I should . . . I do a month in Edinburgh every summer, you should just travel, just travel . . . It's so near it's the same city basically . . .‡

It's a joke, isn't it, 41st best . . . I don't even have to . . . I can come, what, five feet from the front row, I don't even

* On a good night, the brutal enactment of smashing the child's toy could silence the room.

† Here I'd leave a big pause and then head off into the crowd, unplugged, for a fake nervous breakdown, Johnny Vegas style.

‡ This would be different every night, but it was very easy for me to find things to feel aggrieved about.

284

need to look round to know that there's people that can't even be bothered to turn thirty degrees. 'We'll just . . . He'll come back probably . . . I don't know what this bit is anyway. Is it innovation or a mistake? I'll just look at nothing, I'll look at nothing. Or at that . . .' 'Can I have a backdrop?' 'Yeah, what would you like?' 'Can it be of my face?' 'Yeah, we'll just distort it a bit.' 'What?'*

I should get respect, I should get . . . At the very least from children. There shouldn't be seven-year-old kids shouting out at me that I'm fat. I am fat, but not by the standards of a comedian. Roy 'Chubby' Brown is fat, that's in his name. And Fatty Arbuckle, and *Fatty* Arbuckle, yeah? And Large. They were fat. If you saw, if you saw me here on the tour for the last show, I have put on weight since then, I admit. And coming back here, I thought, 'I like The Stand, it's really nice, I'll try and lose some weight so I look nice for them.' But, you know, I'm glad I didn't actually, 'cause there's people going, 'Oh I won't even look at him. I'll look at a distorted, bad acid image of his own face rather than actually look at him.'†

(*goes back onstage*) I've been going to Weight Watchers

* Here I am referring to the arty photo manipulation of my face put up as a backdrop for the DVD shoot.
† If I'd had the guts, I'd have cut the following bit about Weight Watchers, and this clanking segue into it from the offstage rant. It's the only part of the show that isn't necessary for its forward narrative thrust. Tellingly, it's the only section, apart from the deleted Del Boy bit, that I was able to reuse for the BBC2 series *Stewart Lee's Comedy Vehicle*, in 2009. By which I mean that it was free-floating and inessential to the *41st Best* show as a hermetic whole. But it gets us into the realm of discussing political correctness, which gets us into the harsh routine about Richard Littlejohn, the uncompromising tone of which proves why, when I then come to conclude the show, I can't do the cruise ships.

anyway. I have been going to Weight Watchers. But I'm forty. I was forty two days ago. And it's hard to go to Weight Watchers as a middle-aged man, it's embarrassing. Everyone else there is women, so you feel embarrassed. And you have to be brave as a middle-aged man to keep going back to Weight Watchers, brave, braver in many ways than a fireman or someone fighting in a war. And I'm the only person currently failing to lose weight at Weight Watchers as a result of Islam. Some laughs here, mainly an anxiety in the room. Don't know what you're scared of. Haven't you got a bloke, an airport baggage handler, who can pretend to have kicked someone? It's an empire built on sand, that man's career.*

Don't worry, I'm going to talk about Islam, don't worry. There's people walking out, they're so afraid. Ben Elton says we can't talk about Islam because we'll be killed.† Well, I don't care. Don't worry, right, don't worry about where this bit's going, 'cause this, don't worry, 'cause this

* This was a comment, off the top of my head, relating to John Smeaton, an airport baggage handler who kicked a terrorist with one of his two Scottish feet at Glasgow airport during a failed attempt to blow up the place. He subsequently became a minor celebrity, though there were doubts about the full extent of his heroism. I don't have a genuine opinion on the matter. I just said it in the heat of the moment to be annoying.

† The month prior to filming this, in March 2008, the eighties comedian Ben Elton had told the Christian magazine *Third Way* that the BBC were too scared to broadcast jokes about Islam because he had had a line about 'taking the mountain to Mohammed' cut. I wrote a piece for the same paper at the time defending the BBC's position, and saying that Ben Elton had missed the point. But then the only piece of material cut from my subsequent 2009 series by the BBC was one that the compliance unit were worried broke an Islamic cultural taboo. Sorry, Ben Elton.

bit, if you're nervous, this bit was reviewed in the London *Evening Standard* as being 'tediously politically correct'. So, don't worry about where it's going. In fact, if you were confused so far, you can now add boredom to that.*

Now. I go to Weight Watchers where . . . I go to Weight Watchers, ladies and gentlemen, I go where I live. And I go to Stamford Hill library, Stoke Newington, in north-east London. And, um, there's only two men in my Weight Watchers group, me and an old Polish man in his late seventies. And everyone else is women, women of all races and creeds and colours and cultures and shapes and sizes. It's like a United Nations day out to a funfair hall of mirrors. Which they have actually, they have those. And um, I was in the queue waiting to get weighed, you queue up to get weighed, right, and three in front of me there's a young Muslim woman about twenty-five years old, and she was wearing the hijab, this is the headscarf they wear 'cause there's an Islamic taboo about men seeing hair. And she turned round to me and she said, 'I do apologise but I'm about to get weighed, would you be so kind as to go out in

* I was so bored of the way that being politically incorrect in comedy was being seen as an end in itself that I was actually very glad to be described by a reviewer as 'tediously politically correct', and decided henceforth to adopt the criticism that I was 'politically correct' as a positive thing, as something to aim for. (One way of defeating critics is to embrace their criticisms as positive things. I had 'surly, arrogant and laboured' made into a badge.) Over the preceding year, I had become more and more interested in all the right-wingers' exaggerated urban myths of political correctness, and this culminated in me losing my temper, quite unprofessionally, in a discussion on the subject on David Baddiel's Radio 4 show *Heresy* in May 2007, when the majority of the audience voted for the suggestion that 'Political correctness had gone mad', and Harry Enfield agreed with them.

the corridor?' Now, at the time, I mean obviously in ret-rospect, um, it was 'cause she was going to take the head-scarf off and I couldn't see her hair, but I didn't make the connection then and I thought she just didn't want me to see how much weight she'd put on. So I said, 'No, I'm not going out, and I don't know what you're worried about, love, you're not even that fat.' And then she said, 'No, it's the . . .'

And then I realised, right, and I started to apologise, but in-between me and her was a Hassidic Jewish woman about fifty years old, and she sort of budged in and she looked at the young Muslim woman and then she looked at me and then she sort of went [*sigh of exasperation*] like that. [*sigh of exasperation*] As if to go, 'First the suicide bombings and now this.' But the irony was that the Hassidic Jewish, they have a thing where they shave their hair off and the women wear wigs over it. So she's in a wig, the young Muslim woman's in this headscarf. Me, I'm an atheist, right, a fat atheist we've established, but I didn't see why my attempts to lose weight should be compromised in any way by the hair anxieties of a God I don't necessarily believe exists, right. But it looked like there was going to be a three-way argument. Everyone was looking at each other. And then I thought, 'I can't stay here to debate this,' I thought. 'I can't stay here. 'Cause if we ever are going to decide how exactly, if at all, God wants hair to be concealed, that's not going to happen at Stamford Hill Weight Watchers. It's Stamford Hill Weight Watchers, not Stamford Hill Weight Watchers and Religious Hair Taboo Discussion Circle.' Although I would go to that.*

* Everything here happened exactly as described, except that I didn't say, 'No, I'm not going out, and I don't know what you're

And I tell you what, it's really nice being back in a kind of cosmopolitan city like Glasgow, where you can say the phrase, er, 'Stamford Hill Weight Watchers and Religious Hair Taboo Discussion Circle' and you people realise that that is a joke, there's no such thing. Because what I've found is, in the north of England, right, in Carlisle or Derby or somewhere, when I say 'Stamford Hill Weight Watchers and Religious Hair Taboo Discussion Circle', there's no laugh, 'cause all the north of England people are going, 'Well, they would have that in that London – the kind of stupid thing that they would have there.' And what I say to people in the north of England is not every town has to have a cake named after it, yeah. And it's not strictly true, they haven't all got cakes named after them, right, but enough of them have, if you say that to a north of England person, they go, 'Oh, Bakewell, Eccles . . .' and then they get confused. So . . . 'Yorkshire pudding, is that . . .?'*

So, anyway, I went out in the corridor. And the young Muslim woman had already asked the old Polish man to go out in the corridor, and he was out in the corridor, and he looked at me and he made this kind of angry face, right.†

---

worried about, love, you're not even that fat,' to the Muslim woman. I just looked confused. When I did this routine on *Stewart Lee's Comedy Vehicle* for BBC2, they made me change the location of the Weight Watchers to Finsbury Park, to avoid the possibility that I had libelled anyone.

* I found that this routine worked better in cities. Perhaps in more rural areas of the UK, people genuinely believe their pretentious urban counterparts might actually be attending, in the interests of multiculturalism, a 'Weight Watchers and Religious Hair Taboo Discussion Circle'.

† The Polish man's face wasn't really angry. He just looked more like he was wryly amused but wasn't sure if he even ought to communicate this with me. I made him into a worse figure than he was

And I looked away, 'cause I was worried he was going to say something like 'fucking Muslims' or something, yeah, and I looked away. 'Cause I didn't want to have to agree with something racist out of politeness. 'Cause I can do that whenever I go home at Christmas. I say quilts, but they're flags really. Banners.

So . . . And then I was out in the corridor, and I was annoyed initially 'cause I thought, 'I've gone out, I've left

---

to make this story work. When I did this routine on Radio 4's *Political Animal*, I asked them to check it at length with lawyers before wasting everyone's time and getting me to record it and then having to cut it all out, as I had just had to cut a load of stuff that I wrote for Kevin Eldon's Radio 4 series *Poet's Tree* on the grounds of blasphemy, which wasn't even a crime any more by that stage. (I would like to do more BBC radio comedy, but the bullshit factor of the process massively outweighs the pleasure of doing it.) The lawyers of *Political Animal*'s production company said the routine was fine, I could even set it in Stamford Hill, and I recorded it for the show in front of a live audience. Then, after recording, it was decided by Radio 4 that the Polish man might sue. Was the man Polish? I wasn't sure. Would it be possible to cut the word 'Polish' in the edit? No, because it was important that the story was set in a multicultural area and that the man was also non-indigenous, to play up to the cross-cultural tensions, and to not make him the usual straw man of the supposedly racist white working-class male. Could the man's nationality be changed to some other Eastern European country? Yes, but as I didn't know if the man was really Polish, as I just identified him as having an Eastern European accent and assumed he was Polish, there was every chance, if we changed him to Hungarian or Czech, that we would be changing him from something he wasn't into something he was and thereby worsening the problem. Despite this, it was decided that this was the best course of action and I went in and overdubbed a new Eastern European nationality onto the now not Polish man. Honestly, it's political correctness gone mad. Or, as Simon Donald from *Viz* put it so brilliantly, 'It's political correctness gone mad gone mad'.

the Weight Watchers now, and I'm going to lose my nerve and I'm not going to go back in, and I'm going to get fatter and fatter.' But then I thought, 'You know what, it doesn't matter, right, it's ten, fifteen minutes out of my day, I can rejoin the queue.' And if I was a young Muslim in Britain today, maybe I'd feel quite put upon and maybe these kind of cultural signifiers would take on an extra importance – it doesn't matter. Then I thought, 'You know what, it doesn't matter, it's ten, fifteen minutes out of my day, I can rejoin the queue.' And if I was in a queue for something and there was someone behind me who was, like, blind or on crutches or mentally handicapped or something, I would let them go ahead of me. And then I thought, 'That's a bit weird, isn't it, 'cause I've just equated having a religious belief with being mentally handicapped.' Which obviously isn't appropriate. Even though it is correct.

And then I got annoyed, right, and I thought . . . I got annoyed, I thought, 'I'm going to go back in, I'm going to go to her, "You, a Muslim, may be a contributing factor in my ongoing weight gain. Driving me out, you know . . . And if you must wear your hijab to Weight Watchers, then what I suggest is that you take it off at home and weigh it separately before you come out, and then deduct its weight from your Weight Watchers total, giving you your correct weight, using maths, which I understand your people claim to have invented."' Yeah? But I didn't say that, right, I just went back in and er, you know, and I had, um . . . gained some weight.*

* Although I intended this bit to be absurd and silly, and I don't think any right-thinking fat person would be that bothered about having to leave Weight Watchers for a moment while a Muslim was weighed – I certainly didn't mind – the joke does have a serious resonance. As I write, Ed Balls is trying to standardise sex education

Now, one hesitates in the current climate to make a joke onstage about the Muslims, right, not for fear of religious reprisals, right – when's that ever hurt anyone?* – but because of a slightly more slippery anxiety, which is, like, basically, when you do, like, stand-up in a small room, it's like, 'We're all friends, hooray, and we can make a joke.' But you don't really know, you don't really know how a joke's received, and it could be that it's laughed at enthusiastically in a way that you don't understand, particularly out there, you don't know who's watching on television. I mean, if it's on telly on Paramount, probably someone horrible, an idiot, um . . . The kind of person who's awake at five in the morning, who knows what, it could be anyone laughing at this, you don't know, awful people. And um . . . So . . . um . . .†

———

across the school system to minimise teenage pregnancy, STDs and the bullying of homosexuals, but is, predictably, encountering religious resistance from faith schools, some of which believe their theistic scruples set them above the duty to help implicate generally applicable, across the board, ethical values in sex education. What is the politically correct response to this?

* This line was getting laughs for two reasons: (1) because I was known by some of the room to have had work closed down by religious people; and (2) because it is an understatement and people are being threatened all the time by the religious.

† As the missing presumed dead comedian Jason Freeman said as the punchline to a joke I've already quoted but long forgotten the set-up for, 'context is not a myth'. It's worth saying again. In the early nineties, Frank Skinner was able to break various taboos of gender- and sexuality-based political correctness, back when stand-up really was still in the shadows of a polytechnic-lecturer liberal orthodoxy, by using his easy charm and casually confidential air to make everyone in the room feel they were amongst friends, and that anything that was said was really just a joke.

So you don't know. And the problem is 84 per cent of people apparently, of the public, think that political correctness has gone mad.* Now, um, I don't know if it has. People still get killed, don't they, for being the wrong colour or the wrong sexuality or whatever. And what is political correctness? It's an often clumsy negotiation towards a kind of formally inclusive language. And there's all sorts of problems with it but it's better than what we had before, but 84 per cent of people think political correctness has gone mad. And you don't want one of those people coming up to you after the gig and going, 'Well done, mate, er, well done, actually, for having a go at the fucking Muslims. Well done, mate. You know, you can't do anything in this country any more mate, it's political correctness gone mad. Do you know, you can't even write racial abuse in excrement on someone's car without the politically correct brigade jumping down your throat.' And you don't want those people coming up to you after gigs, 'cause that's Al Murray the Pub Landlord's audience, missing the point and laughing through bared teeth like the dogs they are.†

* This statistic is based on my aforementioned unprofessional appearance on David Baddiel's *Heresy* in May 2007, when 84 per cent of the clever Radio 4 studio audience thought that political correctness had gone mad.
† I hope I didn't upset Al Murray personally by saying this, if he was ever made aware of the joke, as his nineties shows as the Pub Landlord were amongst the greatest stand-up I have ever seen. Back then, the Pub Landlord was a bulletproof satire of the soft right, with a prominent back story that informed his prejudice, played out to packed Fringe festival attics of adoring liberals. I am sure Al had legitimate artistic worries about the point of preaching to the converted, whilst also wondering how to broaden his appeal to achieve the premier-league position he craved (Al was subsequently to cook a high-profile fish pie on a celebrity chef show, which

'Cause I'm forty, like I said, I was forty last week, and I can remember before political correctness, that's why I think it's better. I remember . . . It's better now.* I remember when I was twelve, there was one Asian kid in our class, and every day when he read the register out, for a year, the teacher, instead of using his name, called him 'the black spot', every day for a year.† The street I grew up in, just

---

helped secure his Pub Landlord character a wider audience of ITV viewers). But the places the character appeared and the attitudes of the punters who flocked to see him in the noughties have inevitably changed the way the material is received. Some might say it's patronising to assume that not all the audience get Al's joke, but I wanted to be able to talk about race, for example, onstage without any risk of racists thinking that, covertly, I was trying to agree with them.

Even in my carefully filtered crowds, to which I attempt to apply the most thorough social-screening procedures, there could be trouble. When I did this bit in Hastings, where a sixteen-year-old Qatari student was randomly murdered by a white gang in 2008, some guys started shouting out 'rag-heads, rag-heads', and it was hard to plot a course back to the core of the routine as I saw it when the vibe of the room had been thus altered. They apologised, embarrassed, at the end, and I think they were just overexcited. In the words of the alleged murderers of Stephen Lawrence, justifying their racist language when interviewed by Martin Bashir: 'It was just banter, Martin, harmless banter.'

* The following routine, about examples of pre-political-correctness racism, is more or less what I said on David Baddiel's *Heresy* show. I just got a tape of the rant, transcribed it, cleaned up the factual inaccuracies a bit and spared the blushes of people I'd mentioned by name, and slotted it into *41st Best*. It was a rare example of something you say on the spur of the moment being worth repeating.

† I have seen people online saying I made this up. I didn't. And this sort of thing was common at the time. When the old-school comedian Mike Reid hosted the ITV kids' game show *Runaround*, I

south of Birmingham, there was I remember, 1972, a black family that wanted to move in and all the white families put pressure on the guy not to sell the house. And eight years previous to that, David Cameron never mentions it, but the Conservative Party won a by-election in Birmingham and they sent out little kids with leaflets that said, 'If you want a nigger for a neighbour, vote Liberal or Labour.' And if political correctness has achieved one thing, it's to make the Conservative Party cloak its inherent racism behind more creative language.* But . . .†

---

remember him routinely referring to black children, to their faces, as 'little chocolate drops', in an avuncular fashion, meaning nothing by it really. And I don't think my teacher meant any malice at all by saying 'the black spot' either. He liked the boy. I think he was being friendly in his pre-PC way. But I noticed one of my old schoolmates from the same class just popped up on the leaked BNP membership list, the twat. These two facts are, of course, related.

* For the TV series, *Stewart Lee's Comedy Vehicle*, I was obliged to tweak this line, legally, to '. . . it's to make racists in the Conservative Party cloak their beliefs behind more creative language'. Again, I've seen people online saying this slogan was never used, and as it was before my birth how could I remember it if it was. It was used, in 1964 by the Tory candidate Peter Griffiths, and I remember it still being used by grumpy Brummies where I grew up in the early seventies while they were out shopping for bananas to throw at black Aston Villa players. The granddaughter of Patrick Gordon Walker, the Labour MP who lost his seat to Griffiths as a result of his racist campaign, contacted me having seen the show live to say how much she liked the bit.

The reason young people assumed these bits were made up was because, I think, nobody under thirty would believe that they ever could have happened, living as they do in a society that has, at least cosmetically, benefited from political correctness.

† The 'but' here is appended directly onto the end of the phrase 'cloak its inherent racism behind more creative language' as a

But on the whole, when people say political correctness has gone mad, I think, 'Well, what do you mean?' Unless it's my nan, right. When my nan says to me, 'Oh, Stew, that political correctness has gone mad,' I go, 'Why is that, Nan?' She goes, 'Well, I was in the hairdresser's yesterday, Stew. And they said to me, "Would you like a cup of tea, Mrs Harris?" I said, "Yes please." They said, "Well, you can have one but you have to drink it in the waiting area, 'cause we can't have hot liquids at the work station." It's political correctness gone mad, Stew. It's old Red Robbo, Stew, he's saying that we can't have tea any more in case it annoys a Pakistani.'*

---

standard stand-up comedy trick known in the trade as Ó Briain's Truncated Appendage, as it was at its most obvious in the nineties work of the Irish funnyman Dara Ó Briain. If you are unsure as to whether an audience will laugh at something, because it is too risqué or contentious, you begin the next sentence immediately, as if you hadn't intended the line to get a laugh anyway. This relieves the audience of the obligation to laugh, and they then sometimes laugh anyway, as they don't mind giving you something you aren't waiting around begging for. It is possible to begin the next sentence with a half-formed word or non-specific vowel sound and then to wait for the delayed laugh, as in me saying 'but' in this instance. Or you can do what Dara did for a decade, which is just to make a funny, upwardly inflected noise, a sort of crescendoed mix of 'ah' and 'um', which, if snappy enough, will also provoke the laugh. Dara doesn't do this any more, and his clever live shows, which sneak subversive political comment and beautifully expressed social observation past hate-filled *Mock the Week* viewers who would presumably be happy with any old shit, are largely free of the Truncated Appendages he helped standardise. But if you find clips of the nineties and noughties Irish TV hits *Don't Feed the Gondolas* or *The Panel*, you will find Dara using the 'aaaaahh-uuuuuum' gambit in frequent full effect.
* Red Robbo is the seventies trade-union leader Derek Robinson,

Basically, there's a whole generation of people who've confused political correctness with health and safety legislation.* 'It's gone mad. They're saying I can't have an electric fire in the bath any more, Stew, in case queers see it. In the old days you could get your head and you could submerge it in a vat of boiling acid. And now they're going, "Oh, don't do that, what if Jews see it? Might annoy Jews . . ." You could get your whole family and you could jump in a threshing machine and dance around. All your arms would fly off and it was fine. And now they're going, "Oh . . ." They've banned Christmas. They've banned Christmas now.'†

---

a demonised figure in my family when I was a child who was routinely tutted at on television, as members of my extended family were employees of the Longbridge car plant, where Robinson frequently brought the workers out. To anyone of a certain age, 'Red Robbo' is subliminally associated with the now discredited idea of the seventies left, but find some YouTube footage of him and you'll see a self-taught Marxist locking horns with public-school-educated bosses on an equal footing, and find yourself longing for the days of a definable left and right, rather than the mid-mass mush of today.

* I'm absolutely sick of people blaming the restrictions created by health and safety culture, itself exacerbated in turn by a trend towards increased litigation, on the political and ideological doctrine of political correctness. They aren't the same thing, and are not symptomatic of each other. My nan wasn't especially concerned about political correctness, and none of this is based on anything she ever said. Instead, I made this Nan character a composite of every piece of anti-PC bullshit I had ever heard over the years, and the exaggerated voice I'd do for her left me free to improvise a stream-of-consciousness splurge of different made-up examples of political correctness gone mad every night.

† Did anybody ever really ban Christmas? Edward Stourton, in his brilliant book *Living in a PC World*, sees this as the ultimate anti-PC urban myth.

On the whole, when people say . . . I mean, there's a columnist for the *Daily Mail*, Richard Littlejohn, and he's got two catchphrases. One is 'political correctness has gone mad'. And the other is 'You couldn't make it up'. You couldn't make it up, which is ironic, given that the vast proportion of what he writes has no . . .* And about a year ago, Littlejohn did a whole page on political correctness gone mad. And it's gone to court now, this thing, but it's when there was a serial murderer killing sex workers in East Anglia, and the police and the broadsheets at the time routinely referred to – some of them were teenagers – and the papers would call them 'women that worked as prostitutes', rather than just 'prostitutes', and Littlejohn did a whole page on how this was political correctness gone mad, and you should call them 'prostitutes' and not 'women that worked as prostitutes', and anyway, it wasn't like any of them were ever going to find a cure for cancer. But it wasn't political correctness gone mad, it was the papers and the police thinking, 'Some of these people are really young, you know, and they have surviving family and friends and . . . and what can we do to cushion this ugly word "prosti-tute"? We'll blanket it in a, a qualifying phrase,' you know. It was a nice thing to do.†

But for Littlejohn it wasn't that, it was political cor-rectness gone mad and they were prostitutes and should

* Again, nice to leave the preachy line hanging and let the punters finish it themselves, so I look less of a would-be demagogue.
† In one edition of his column, for which he receives upwards of £700,000 a year, Littlejohn did a little skit on the phrase 'women who work as prostitutes', while in another on the same case he wrote, 'in the scheme of things the deaths of these five women is no great loss. They weren't going to discover a cure for cancer or embark on missionary work in Darfur.'

be called prostitutes. And one wonders how far Richard Littlejohn would go in his quest for the accurate naming of dead women. Would he go perhaps to a cemetery under cover of night, armed with a, a little chisel and a little torch? A chisel and a torch. And he's there at the grave that says, 'Here lies Elaine Thompson aged 19,' and he's there amending it. [*noise of chiselling*] 'Prostitute. [*chiselling*] Not a woman who works as a prostitute. [*chiselling*] A prostitute. [*chiselling*] P.S. [*chiselling*] I hate women, obviously. [*chiselling*] And I'm glad when they die. [*chiselling*] Yours, [*chiselling*] Richard Littlejohn. [*chiselling*] Cunt. [*chiselling*] Not someone who works as a cunt.'*

So the last time I was at home, my mum said to me,

---

* The chiselling here, where I tapped the mic stand with the mic, went on at some length, sometimes uninterrupted for minutes at a time, with me varying the rhythm and intensity of the tapping. This doesn't work on the page, and ideally, my ambition is to get to the point where none of my stand-up works on the page. I don't think stand-up should really work on the page, so the very existence of this book is an indication of my ultimate failure as a comedian. The text of a stand-up set should be so dependent on performance and tone that it can't really work on the page, otherwise it's just funny writing. You don't have to have spent too long thinking about stand-up to realise that even though critics and TV commissioners always talk about our art form in terms of its content, it is the rhythm, pitch, tone and pace of what we do – the non-verbal cues – that are arguably more important, if less easy to identify and define. (Ricky Gervais and Stephen Merchant brilliant side-stepped the inability of commissioners to interpret naturalistically nuanced scripts by submitting a film of *The Office*, not a script.) A good joke is rhythmical and physical. You're either slapped by the surprise of the punchline in a zingy one-liner, or tickled slowly into submission by the endless undulations of a shaggy-dog story.

I'm fascinated by issues of pitch and tone and pace and rhythm in stand-up, and had always wanted to do something that eliminated words and replaced them with abstract sounds, to see if you could tune an audience into noises alone and give them a rhythm, tone, pitch and pace which were funny. I wrote a long poem about this notion for a book of writing by comedians edited by the late Malcolm Hardee (see Appendix VII). This Richard Littlejohn bit, featuring as it did an incident involving chiselling with metal upon rock as a name is carved out, was the perfect meeting of form and content.

I can honestly say I was rarely happier in any show I've ever done than when I was just standing here for minutes on end, tapping the microphone on the microphone stand, scraping it round the housings and the bolts, waiting and waiting, changing the rhythm, trying to find the off-beats, letting the moment settle, and then starting again. Asked how long you could show a couple kissing in a bed, Alfred Hitchcock said, 'As long as you like as long as there's a bomb under it.' To quote the Mod hairdresser opera investor, that's the jeopardy. This routine, the audience knows, is a joke, so somewhere, after all the scraping and clinking, they assume there's going to be a punchline, and so the tension was, pretty much always, held.

I think this section, Littlejohn's chiselling at the grave, was the furthest I ever managed to get away from stand-up, whilst still remaining recognisably a stand-up, and I'd love to do something like it again, but the story suggested a sound, and I'd not feel comfortable reverse-engineering the same effect a second time, by finding a sound and then looking for a story that fit. I wish I could work my way back, in live shows, to this level of abstraction, but doing the TV series in 2009 necessitated, to some degree, a consolidation of my most accessible approaches, rather than a leap further into the dark, and for the time being, I've lost the thread and my nerve.

At the end of the chiselling, after a use of the word 'cunt' that I am sure even Frank Skinner would accept as necessary, there'd be a big laugh and then a long dead silence which I could flip over as soon as I started the next bit, to make it clear we were on the home straight, where everything ties together.

'Why can't you work the cruises like Tom O'Connor?'*
And then the phone rang and it was Bridget Nicholls from
Pestival, and she said to me, 'I hope you don't mind me
ringing up, but I'm just checking that you're still all right
for Pestival at the weekend.'† And I said, 'I'm glad you've
called, Bridget, 'cause I've no intention whatsoever of
coming at all.' And she said, 'Why? Why?' And I said, 'Well,
I was going to film it for this thing but they've cancelled it,
so it's a waste of time for me. I haven't written any aphid
stuff, it's . . . it doesn't sound very . . . it sounds stupid
anyway, and I'm not coming.' And she said, 'But I thought
you said you loved insects.' I said, 'I don't love insects. At
best, I'm ambivalent about them.‡ And there are many
that I actively dislike. Yeah? Those ladybirds, those new
French ladybirds, they stain fabrics, yeah?'§ And she said,

* You could sense the people's relief as I returned to this familiar
motif. Their inherent sense of structure in the show, the reason you
can't just gut it for five- or ten- or twenty-minute telly spots, tells
them it's nearly all over. When I had to give chapter titles to the
show for its DVD release, I called the closing section of the show
'Eight Callbacks'. A callback, seen in its most evolved form in the
stand-up routines of TV's floppy-collared loon™ Harry Hill, is
when the mere reincorporation of an idea from earlier in the set
can seem funny in and of itself, if its re-emergence happens at a
surprising or satisfying enough point. For the final section of *41st
Best* I aimed to create a domino effect of callbacks, weaving in as
many of the earlier strands of material as possible, like the design of
some enormous quilt cover. I worked out that there are eight iden-
tifiable callbacks here, but I could be wrong, and I can't remember
now exactly what I thought they were.
† This phone call never happened in reality.
‡ I have used the word 'ambivalent' many times since in this context onstage, and it has become a repetitive cliché of my work.
§ I would change this bit to a different insect every night in the
interests of fighting off my own boredom.

'Well, what am I going to tell the potato peach aphid study group, they're excited?' I said, 'I don't care. I don't care what you tell them, 'cause I'm not coming to your stupid thing.' And then, from the other end of the phone, I heard this sound:

[*whispering to female audience member*] Will you just cry into here?

[*Female audience member crying.*]

Oh dear. Well. I said, 'Can you just cry into here?' I've done seventy other dates of this tour where a person knows the difference between giggling and crying. And this is the one that's being filmed. Here in Glasgow, the city where all emotions are considered to be the same. 'I went out tonight, I had a feeling.' 'Were you happy or sad?' 'I don't care, a feeling is enough for me.' Imagine it was someone going [*crying*].*

Anyway, so it was that, three days later, I found myself onstage at Pestival, dressed as an insect, in a now financially unjustifiably expensive insect costume, trying to think of something funny about aphids to say to three hundred of the world's leading entomologists. And I, er . . .†

Now I realised I'd missed the point. Pestival was a really

---

* Trying to get a woman in the audience to supply the crying was an opportunity to do something fun to leaven the narrative-heavy course of this section of the show. And usually something unexpected would happen.

† This paragraph ends with a classic example of Ó Briain's Truncated Appendage, as you can see, while I give the crowd a second to take in the full enormity of my impossible situation. I actually performed at Pestival in my normal clothes, and not those of an insect. A transcript of the event as recorded, mushed in with the best bits of my notes, is available here in Appendix VI. It includes a Robert the Bruce joke reworked from a routine I wrote in about 1992, which I think may also have appeared, in some form, in a TV

good thing, actually, and I should just have done it with good grace, but it was too late and I was out there. I was looking at all these three hundred entomologists, I had nothing to say, a minute passed, nothing. Another minute, dry throat, nothing to say. And then I thought to myself, 'What would Tom O'Connor do?'*

So I said to a bloke in the front row, 'What do you do for a living?' He said, 'I'm an entomologist.' I said, 'Are you a sardine?' He said, 'No, no.' I said to a woman next to him, 'What do you do for a living?' She said, 'I'm an entomologist.' I said, 'Are you a sar . . .?' 'No.' And then I said to a bloke in the middle, 'What do you do for a living?' He said, 'I'm an entomologist. We're all entomologists. This is a conference of entomologists.' And I realised that Tom O'Connor had made it look easy. Yeah?

And I asked around other comics, had anyone I know seen him in his seventies heyday, before all the game shows. And it turned out Johnny Vegas told me he'd seen Tom O'Connor in a Catholic men's club in Liverpool in 1978, and that he was brilliant, and he should have been the new Billy Connolly, and he had all these fantastic routines about growing up and working-class life and kids and families and weddings and funerals, and it always went down brilliantly.† But remember, Glasgow, this was in Liverpool,

show I did with Richard Herring. The entomologists liked my set but they didn't exactly go nuts.

* The smarter punters know what Tom O'Connor would do. They've already worked it out, and are enjoying the inevitability of what is coming up.

† It turned out I had remembered this wrongly. Johnny's relatives had seen Tom O'Connor in the clubs, but Johnny only became familiar with O'Connor's oeuvre after he found loads of Tom O'Connor audio tapes abandoned in the dirt whilst playing on a

where cloying mawkish nostalgia is regarded as the highest form of entertainment.* And . . . Rather than fighting.†

And . . . And then I thought about what my mum had said, you know. And she was right: I had nothing to show for my career. But Tom O'Connor knows that when he dies, somewhere in a lock-up garage in Liverpool there's literally hundreds of thousands of golf umbrellas with a picture of his face on them. And when this world finally floods, and our civilisation is buried under thousands of feet of water, alien archaeologists will find those Tom O'Connor's face umbrellas, and they will assume that Tom O'Connor was a significant figure, perhaps a god. Maybe responsible for rainfall, whom we failed to appease.‡ Yeah? Rather than just a man, a man who spent his twilight years travelling the high seas, endlessly repeating the phrase 'Are you a sardine?' in the hope that it might at last be appropriate.§

———

spot of waste ground in St Helen's where burglars dumped stuff they couldn't sell. I assume this happened when Johnny was a child, but knowing him, it is possible that it was a recent occurrence.

* I am sure I copped the essence of this idea from the scene in Irving Welsh's novel *Filth*, in which Detective Sergeant Bruce taunts some Liverpudlians about all the tragedies that befall their city, whilst on holiday in Amsterdam, saying that Liverpudlians love misery.

† This is a dig at Glasgow, but doubtless equally stereotypical comments were available in my vast store of slander for other towns.

‡ I was so pleased when people laughed at this idea, which they rarely did. I kept it in for me, really.

§ I think there are elements of Coleridge's 'The Ancient Mariner' in this idea, a poem which I first learned about by association, as a child listening to my *Monty Python Live at Drury Lane* record, specifically the sketch in which John Cleese is a tormented theatre ice-cream seller, cursed to wander the world with an albatross in his ice-cream tray, which no one is interested in buying. 'I haven't

And I realised I'd underestimated my mother, and obviously whenever she goes on at me about Tom O'Connor she's not trying to wind me up, she's just trying to find some common ground.* And about a year ago, I was in a branch of WHSmiths and I looked up and at eye-level I saw a magazine I'd never noticed before, called *British Quilt-Making Monthly*, and there was a photograph of one of my mum's quilts on the front, and it turned out she's the 41st best quilt-maker. In Worcester.†

---

got any ice creams. I've only got this fucking albatross.' 'Well, what flavour is it?' 'I don't know. It's fucking sea-bird flavour.' I loved this sketch as a child and thought the whole idea of it was brilliant, but it was only when studying Coleridge at Oxford University that I realised its roots lay in his Ancient Mariner story, wherein a cursed seaman is forced to wander the world with the body of a dead albatross, explaining his decision to slay it. Very often, timid TV and radio comedy execs slash supposedly highbrow references from scripts on the grounds that people won't get them. But if the piece is properly written, it shouldn't matter whether people 'get them' or not. I loved John Cleese's albatross seller, on its own terms, and the fact that, years later, I discovered its debt to Coleridge just made it seem funnier.

* Now that I was a parent, knowing how sad I would feel if my son grew up to twist my actions into the basis of a joke, it seemed very important to me not to misrepresent my mother at the close of the show. I was now also able to empathise with her efforts to meet her child halfway, by going on and on about Tom O'Connor's sardine joke, however inappropriately. I am sure I will find myself struggling similarly with my own son, forty years down the line. This section also enables a gradual softening of tone as I work towards the uncharacteristically sentimental conclusion.

† I didn't see this magazine in Smiths. I saw it at my mum's house. She wasn't voted 41st best quilt-maker ever – that is just an exaggeration placed here to up the callback quota – but her quilt was on the cover. I hadn't really taken in what a significant quilter she was. She hides her light under a quillow.

So I rang her up, I felt a bit guilty, I said, 'I've written this new show and the main through-line of it is how you always go on at me about Tom O'Connor's sardine joke, is that all right?' And she said, 'That's fine, Stew, that's fine. He was hilarious though, Stew, Tom O'Connor. 'Cause he come out, Stew, on the cruise, and he said to this chap, "What do you do for a living?" And the man said, "I'm in oil."' And then she went, 'Oh, hang on a minute, Stew, come to think of it, I don't think it was Tom O'Connor that said that.' I said, 'What are you talking about? I've written this whole thing!' And she went, 'No.' She said, 'Tom O'Connor was on the cruise but there was another comic and he made the sardine joke, and his name was John Smith.' So it wasn't even Tom O'Connor that was better than me. It was someone that no one has ever heard of. 41st best, meaningless . . . meaningless . . .*

But there was one laugh that I got about eleven months ago that did seem to count for something, and um . . . It was when our little boy was about a month old, and I actually made him laugh for the first time. And the way that I did it was, I put this orange woollen giraffe on my head, like that, yeah?† Yeah, it's good, innit? Er . . . It's the direc-

---

* Hilariously, this is entirely true. After years of telling me about Tom O'Connor's sardine joke, it was only when I rang my mother, having largely completed this show, to check she didn't mind being mentioned that she remembered it wasn't Tom O'Connor who had made the sardine joke in the first place but another comedian, apparently called John Smith, who has proven impossible to trace due to his pre-Google name. Tom O'Connor was off the hook, and I was over the moon. Conceptually, my mother's failure of memory had given the show the perfect end. Thanks, Mum.
† A friend gave us this giraffe when our son was born. We were given a disproportionate amount of lovely soft toys, for which I doubt I ever got round to thanking anyone, and it seemed as if

tion I'm going in. It's not controversial, is it, it's just what it is, you know. And the way that you make a one-month-old child laugh by putting an orange woollen giraffe on your head is very simple. You put it on your head and then you stand still, silent and expressionless for as long as possible, as if doing this were the most normal thing in the world, right. Er, like this, I'll show you.

[*Long pause.*]

MUSIC. EXCERPT FROM THE SOUNDTRACK OF HAL HART-
LEY'S *SIMPLE MEN* BY NED RIFLE.

[*Deep sigh.*]
[*Long pause.*]*

THE END.

———

people hoped that I, that we might finally find some peace. Certainly, having a child makes all the professional struggles detailed in this book seem somehow irrelevant, and I wanted to end the show as if laying these to rest by standing, still and silent, with a giraffe balanced on my head, over a long pause, daring the audience to sneer at this sincere, if sentimental, gesture. And, God bless them, they usually accepted it in the spirit it was meant.

* Then the techs faded up a snatch of the soundtrack from Hal Hartley's *Simple Men* and faded down the lights, while I and the giraffe bowed and waved to the crowd, and closed the whole thing on a heart-stopping hanging cadence that usually brought gasps of admiration for its theatrical audacity, and even the occasional stifled sob. Apart from in Derby, where the guy forgot everything I'd asked him to do and just left me standing there, brightly lit, for ages and ages, while I waited to see if he would ever cue the music and the sound, until I eventually just had to walk off to silence, the cumulative emotional effects of the previous ninety minutes lost for ever, the audience confused and lost, the moment entirely wasted, the whole show ruined.

Ah well. That's showbiz.

Thanks very much, thanks for having us, cheers, good night, thank you . . .

EXIT MUSIC: 'STIFLED MAN CASINO' BY AIRPORT 5.

Afterword

In the summer of 2007, before I did *41st Best* in Edinburgh, my new manager suggested I went to see Roland Keating of BBC2 about my long-forgotten and cancelled pilot. I couldn't see what the point was, as nothing had changed, and I only wanted to do the same show, which, as the email I was read by my old manager made clear, the BBC were not interested in. But I went to see him anyway.

It was a strange meeting. I could never really work out why the original pilot had been withdrawn, and lots of areas of discussion were hurried through, but by the end of the short session, the pilot was back on the slate again. I didn't think for a moment it would happen, this being the crazy world of TV, where yes means no and up is down. But eventually a week of filming, followed by a live recording of some stand-up material, was scheduled for December 2007.

I was on the *41st Best* tour in Birmingham, in February 2008, with my Australian inspiration Greg Fleet, who had ludicrously agreed to open for me – probably on the run from the Melbourne vagrant who wanted his clothes back – when I heard that a series had been commissioned. We had just had breakfast in the world-famous Mr Egg cafe in Chinatown (advertised with the slogan 'Eat like a King for under a pound'), opposite the old Powerhaus, where I had seen Ted Chippington in 1984, when the mobile rang and my manager told me of the BBC's decision. It was while I was looking in the window of the Nostalgia and Comics shop opposite that I broke the news to Greg.

Greg couldn't understand why I wasn't more excited, and seemed annoyed that I had remained relatively placid. I suppose everyone thinks a deal like that would be the answer to all their worries, but I'd had this series commissioned and decommissioned once before. I think I was numb with the apprehension that it could all just fade away again, afraid of what it might mean to be recognised in the street and shouted at out of vans again, and worried about alienating the sustainable and supportive audience I was cultivating.

But that night we were on in Salford Quays, and we went to a Chinese restaurant before the show to celebrate. I felt I ought to. I felt it was what people would expect me to do. I ordered a bottle of champagne, but Greg spent most of the meal outside on his mobile, smoking and gesticulating, and so I finished it alone.

Eight years previously, I'd been sitting in the audience of the Rawhide Club in Liverpool, looking at a drunk man trying to formulate a coherent opinion about the shortcomings of British immigration policy, when, in an effort to seize control of my own destiny, I decided I had to stop being a stand-up comedian. Now, I was drinking champagne on my own in an empty Chinese restaurant in the antiseptic retail park of Salford docks, while my friend, who seemed disappointed in me, stood in the street shouting at someone far away. Tonight I was playing the 400-seater room at the Lowry, having successfully, over five years, built up a crowd in tiny rooms. We were performing to nice people who knew, at least partly, what to expect from the evening. I no longer lost money on live work. There were three DVDs available of stand-up sets of which I was not the least bit ashamed. And, it slowly dawned on me, it looked as if I was about to do the television series I thought I'd been offered four years ago, but on my own terms.

If my younger self could see me now, he would have said, 'If that Australian bloke's not going to eat that special fried rice, can I have it?'

Is it too much of a cliché to end the book with the phrase: 'And that's how I escaped my certain fate'?

No?

In that case . . .

And that's how I escaped my certain fate.

Appendices

I: Music Theatre

Music Theatre, the genre which gave us Andrew Lloyd Webber and the tribute show, combines the worst aspects of music with the worst aspects of theatre to create a mutant hybrid that is the worst form of live art that exists. There are few aspects of human artistic endeavour that are of less moral or aesthetic worth than Music Theatre.

As you may have guessed, I hate Music Theatre. What you may not have guessed is that for the last three years, without even realising it at first, I worked in the medium itself. In the spring of 2001 the composer Richard Thomas asked me to help direct, and write some extra words for, an opera he was writing about the American talk show host Jerry Springer. We worked the show up for eighteen months with friends and acquaintances who gave their time largely for free in small rooms at Battersea Arts Centre and The Edinburgh Fringe Festival and eventually the finished product, *Jerry Springer: The Opera*, was staged at the National Theatre and then London's West End, where it won four Olivier awards.

Somewhere along the line, a hit musical had been created. This was a strange and delightful surprise for everyone involved, and especially for me, as before I started work on *Jerry Springer: The Opera* I had never seen a musical. I had always assumed Music Theatre wasn't something

I'd enjoy. Out of professional curiosity I went to see some, and found Music Theatre to be even worse than I could ever have imagined. It is important for me to point out here that my views in no way reflect those of any of my co-workers or employers in *Jerry Springer: The Opera*, all of whom I have nothing but immense respect for.

Admittedly, my initial exposure to the genre of Music Theatre wasn't ideal. The first musical I ever saw was not *Carousel*, or *West Side Story*, or *Guys and Dolls*, but *We Will Rock You, The Queen Musical By Ben Elton and Queen*. It's as good a metaphor as any for the problems inherent in the genre. *We Will Rock You, The Queen Musical By Ben Elton and Queen* is set in a dystopian future where all rock music is banned. Some BBC comedy show wardrobe department style punks who live underground in an old tube station covered with generic rebel graffiti are inspired by the music of Queen to overthrow the state. In real life, Queen's relationship with politics is less clear cut.

Miami Steve Van Zandt was compelled to form Artists Against Apartheid after Queen broke an international cultural embargo and played South Africa under apartheid in the early 80's, and who will ever forget Brian May playing the National Anthem off the Queen's roof in jubilee year? When Hendrix massacred The Stars And Stripes it threatened the status quo. What Brian May did to God Save The Queen merely confirmed it. At one point in *We Will Rock You, The Queen Musical By Ben Elton and Queen* a list of people who, like Freddie Mercury, 'died for rock and roll', invokes Nirvana's Kurt Cobain. Ironically, Kurt Cobain's own suicide note offers Queen's relentless professionalism as an example of one of the things he didn't want to become, as one of the reasons he is taking his own life. The teenage American hardcore punk in me wept fan tears of anger.

316

But the real problem with *We Will Rock You, The Queen Musical By Ben Elton and Queen*, is not these moral-philosophical quibbles. It was just the sheer lack of ambition. Put 1000's of people in a room, get them to sing along to a bunch of songs they already know, string them over the loosest story line possible, give them glow sticks to wave and send them home happy. All you can take away from *We Will Rock You, The Queen Musical By Ben Elton and Queen* is huge admiration for the way the cast do their best to make it work, confirmation that music theatre performers, whether they love a show or hate it, remain the super-efficient, highly trained warrior-ninjas of the stage. Most British people go to the theatre only three times in their lives. It is sad to think that for many people, *We Will Rock You, The Queen Musical By Ben Elton and Queen* will be one of those three times, and that it is a wasted opportunity to show them what great theatre can be.

We Will Rock You, The Queen Musical By Ben Elton and Queen remains the worst musical I have ever seen, and obviously the show can only have been conceived in a spirit of extreme cynicism. But its problems define the genre's physical limitations. There is a perceived crisis in Music Theatre. Where are the new ideas?, ask opinion pieces in the industry papers. The answer is, they are out there, but not in Music Theatre, and under current circumstances, never will be. Music Theatre is fatally compromised.

Some art exists to ask questions, and to play with expectations. Some people want art to take them to a place they would never have imagined going to in the company of people they would never have imagined meeting. Bob Dylan, Samuel Beckett and Reeves and Mortimer all do this. Other people want art to reconfirm the things they already know, and send them away feeling better about

317

themselves. This is the job of Coldplay, Music Theatre and those kind of Comedy Store/Jongleurs stand-up comedians who invite the audience to think, 'Yes, that's exactly what happens whenever I try and open a sachet of tomato sauce too, brilliant!' These polar opposite intentions can be equally difficult to achieve, and I'd wager that there's an element of genius involved in simply thinking of the idea of *SingalongaSoundOfMusic* equal to the moment of epiphany enjoyed by Beckett when he realised it would be a good idea to strap Billie Whitelaw into a harness and light only her mouth while she rambled all but incoherently for twenty minutes in *Not I*. But one of these end points is clearly vastly more valid than the other.

The tragedy of Music Theatre is that it cannot afford to occupy the superior position. West End ticket prices, caused by the vast overheads such shows incur, are high. Broadway prices are even higher. Seats are filled up with coach parties whose bookers can't risk alienating their clients, and people for whom seeing the show is the one big night out of their year, possibly even of their lives. Economically, tribute shows to Abba, Queen and Rod Stewart are safe. Demographically they're hitting the exact strata of society and generation of music fans that has the money to sustain them. The Madness musical, *Our House*, discovered a viable musical coherence in the working class milieu of Madness songs and played some interesting games with narrative structure. But Madness fans aren't yet old enough or wealthy enough to give such a show a long run. And they fight in the bar at half time which scares off the American tourists who make up 50% of the audience of any big London theatre show.

Music Theatre can't afford to be the space that punters enter in order to be challenged, changed or confused.

When I was genuinely baffled by the appeal of a recent West End production, a Music Theatre professional, whose abilities I respect, explained to me why I hadn't got it. 'You check your brain in at the door,' he explained, 'and just go along with it all.' It seems sad that even industry insiders justify the genre as an opportunity to suspend your judgement, rather than engage it.

I saw *The Producers*, which opens in London this Autumn, on Broadway last year. On some level, part of its impact was due to embracing Music Theatre's limitations. It is the story of two producers who try to actively lose money by staging what they imagine will be the worst musical ever, a song and dance show based on the life of Hitler. *The Producers* is very funny. It seems to be a surreal, panic response to Nazism and the Holocaust. You either cry, or make a comedy musical about it. But it also addresses, sublimely, the basic insincerity of Music Theatre, its reliance on camp humour and kitsch values, and shows how ineffectual they are for dealing with significant issues. When the audience have hysterics at *The Producers*, they are in a way acknowledging the banality of the medium they themselves are complicit in endorsing. Great art exists in the spaces between the certainties. Economically, culturally and artistically, Music Theatre can't afford spaces, only certainties.

Esquire magazine,
October 2004

II: English Hecklers in New Zealand

Here's a piece written on the evening after a terrible gig – not for publication, but for my own benefit – in a righteous, misanthropic and entirely unattractive spirit of arrogant and precious self-justification. It is an example of why no one should blog. Nonetheless, I've included it because it captures the feelings of a comic who has just died, and reveals lots about my confused state of mind, professionally, at the time.

I have had a great run so far at the New Zealand comedy festival in Auckland. The Classic on Queen Street is one of my favourite five spaces to perform worldwide. It's a converted porn cinema, there's table service but it's genuinely unobtrusive, and it has the kind of faded glamour you can't manufacture. Pretty much all the shows here have enabled me to do what I hope to do – take people on funny journeys into spaces they wouldn't have expected to arrive at in a stand-up comedy set. When there have been heckles or interruptions they've been playful, witty, supportive – things you could have fun with – or just genuinely confused people who want to understand, asking questions, with whom you could also engage in a positive way. When there was heckling it normally had the feel of a lively debate, or a flirtation. Nobody was humiliated or hurt, onstage or off.

I like to watch the crowd come in. I play a CD of a long Evan Parker sax solo while they do. I figure if people can't put up with that then they will probably not be able to put up with me. About one in ten times someone will come up to the sound desk and ask to have the fucking horrible music turned off. The people that do this are always subsequently the people in the audience without the patience to enjoy my set. Tonight an English man in a red football shirt took a table with a party of ten to fifteen other men and started shouting from his seat for the music to be turned off. I identified him as the alpha male of that group and realised the evening would probably stand or fall on his approval. The kind of people that go to comedy in a big party usually need their laughter to be approved of by one particular member, and the sort of person who is that member of such a group will usually feel that I am threatening to their status as the clown/leader of that group and will try to undermine me. Since I came back to stand-up I have largely been playing to people on my wavelength, and I was never a Comedy Store or Jongleurs act, so I rarely encounter this mentality.

Sure enough, within a few minutes I realised the show was sabotaged. The man began jumping into crucial little spaces between feedlines and punchlines with his own attempts at pay-offs that were not as funny as mine, and usually reactionary in nature, but which nevertheless slowed the momentum of the show. I said to him, from the stage, calmly and politely, that I had identified him as the alpha male of his group even before the show started, and realised that as clown/leader of his pack I knew he would subsequently be obliged to undermine me. Even this bald statement would not silence him. He and his pack were here for the Lions tour. The Lions are a British rugby team.

Things in the set that I considered to be in playful bad taste were so enthusiastically gobbled up by the British sports fans that I felt their meaning and intent changed, and I felt ashamed to say them.

Towards the end I use the word 'fingering' in a set-up towards something else. At the arrival of the word 'fingering' came the shout, 'Now you're getting somewhere.' I explained that this section was my least favourite of the show, and the fact that it seemed to have struck a chord with the rugby fans showed we really were on different wavelengths.

Usually I can silence hecklers with relentless logic, but what I was doing was so far away from what the sport fans expected from comedy that they didn't even realise that, to all intents and purposes, they had been defeated, and so their barrage of witless inanity continued. Of course afterwards, they all want to buy you drinks, and genuinely seem to feel their interruptions have done you some kind of favour. One said his favourite comic was Eddie Izzard, which I accommodated, but when they expected me to engage in an enthusiastic debate about how brilliant Peter Kay was I felt I was out of my depth and left. They didn't even know what they had done. They thought they had helped me to be more like a proper comedian. They thought they had improved the show.

It's funny and sad that my only disastrous show here in Auckland should be as a result of the kind of British people I never usually encounter in Britain actually coming to my show, but when I went back to the flat later I began to feel depressed. The British rugby fans were trying to defeat the world of new experiences, rather than embrace it for what it is, or enjoy its difference. This is why British holiday resorts in Spain are full of British-style pubs and Fish and

Chip shops. This is why there aren't any Spanish locals on Spanish beaches making a killing selling delicious Spanish-style food.

Privately, the debate continues amongst comedians, 'What is Daniel Kitson doing?' Why, many wonder, does he do The Stand when he could do the big room at Assembly? Why does he insist on shaking off half the following he has established every couple of years by doing a sensitive story show? Why doesn't he have a nice haircut – surely he could afford it now? But Kitson once told me that after his Perrier nomination, he was doing a run at the Soho theatre. Sitting in a toilet cubicle one night he overheard some of his audience standing at the urinals talking, didn't like how they sounded, didn't like them, and realised he would have to begin a process of refining his fan base.

Scott, who runs the Classic and promotes me here, said I was wrong about the heckler being the alpha male of the sport fan group. He said the alpha male would have money, cars, women and be silent. The heckler was a kind of delta male, the jester to the king alpha male. He would spend his life in the orbit of power, trailing it, circling it, but never achieving it. This is of course true. But it didn't give me any pleasure. It just made me even more sad to think that a perfectly serviceable show had been sabotaged as just yet another act in the drama of some inadequate's quiet, or in this case not so quiet, desperation. What a wretched night.

Personal Diary Piece,
May 2005

III: Derek Bailey/Ruins/*Aristocrats*

At the Royal Festival Hall in 1997, Derek Bailey played a
double header with the Japanese duo Ruins. I seem to
recall a moment where the septuagenarian genius, lost
in concentration, actually bumped into the back wall of
the stage, his guitar making a resonating clang. Looking
down, he appeared to consider what had happened, and
then playfully bashed the instrument into the wall a second time. I laughed, and despite the wealth of different
responses Bailey's music had already offered me, I never
thought it would provoke laughter. But something great
music shares with great comedy is the capacity to surprise,
to take us out of ourselves and engender a joyous, and not
necessarily mean-spirited or cynical, laughter. I've subsequently learned Bailey once played in the pit band for
Morecambe and Wise, when they toured theatres before
their 60's and 70's TV success. Banging your guitar into a
wall by accident, and then doing it again on purpose in a
spirit of clownish curiosity, seems to me like a classic Eric
Morecambe move.

There's a great documentary about stand-up comedy
currently winning awards all over the international film
festival circuit. *The Aristocrats*, directed by Paul Provenza
and Penn Jillette, shows sixty or so stand-ups telling a
shaggy dog story enjoyed privately by American comics,

but never inflicted on the public. I've never subscribed to the idea that stand-up is, along with jazz and comic books, one of America's great 20th century art forms. This seems a blinkered and isolationist observation. But *The Aristocrats* started to swing me. Halfway through, soon after one of the comics has gone off on a tangent involving the father repeatedly slamming his penis in a drawer for the audience's edification, somebody makes a case for stand-up's relationship with jazz. The distinct variations different performers can extrapolate from the Aristocrats tells us that stand-up is about 'the singer not the song'. Just as John Coltrane's 'My Favorite Things' is different to the Julie Andrews version, so George Carlin's Aristocrats, told with a world-weariness that suggests he has been compelled against his will to relate this horrible event, differs vastly from Billy Connolly's, which is delivered with typically infectious relish.

Carlin, a Fifties Catskills hack, turned Sixties radical, turned elder statesman of American stand-up, wisely draws the distinction between 'shock', a term that comes with pejorative overtones, and 'surprise', which has no obvious moral dimension. Though the endless variations in different versions of the Aristocrats mainly involve stacking up increasing levels of scatological or sexual symbols, what's really making us laugh is the pleasure of surprise, of things being simply unexpected and wrong, of reversing the usual order of things. Surprise is the reason a one-year-old child laughs if you put a shoe on your head. Shoes are for feet, not heads. Even a baby has a sense of inappropriate behaviour. Respectable looking families shouldn't smash their genitals into drawers onstage in the name of entertainment. And guitars shouldn't be banged into walls by elderly musicians, and then banged again. But how exciting is it to not know what's going to happen next? Sometimes Derek Bailey's music makes me feel like a kid on a roller-coaster. And Carlin, like some Native American shaman-clown, makes the need to subvert expectation, to continually surprise, sound like an artist's Holy Obligation.

It seems to me there are two broadly different approaches to stand-up, and by association to all art, each with their own strengths. At commercial British comedy chains like Jongleurs or The Comedy Store, performers tell you about your life, and things that always happen to you, and you may feel comforted by this. Go beyond the usual venues and you may see acts advance ideas that would not normally have occurred to you. In his book, *Improvisation*, Derek Bailey assumes a position in opposition to the very act of musical composition itself. But there's a kind of social need both for songs we can all sing, and for jokes about buses always being late, and men being different to women, and dogs being different to cats. Only the most extreme *Wire* subscriber would deny the potential of all-embracing, utilitarian art. It's just that all-embracing, utilitarian art tends to be a bit shit. When millions wept for their own mortality after the death of Princess Diana, all they were offered was an Elton John song with the words changed a bit.

Great art, whether it's laboriously crafted or spontaneously generated, tends towards the surprise factor that Carlin describes, and Bailey embodies. Derek Bailey is bold enough to refuse to gloss his work with emotional signifiers, just as George Carlin doesn't tell jokes as if they're supposed to be funny. Both make us do the work, and we get the reward of appearing to surprise ourselves. But the breakthrough moment, for me, of seeing Bailey bash his guitar into the back wall of the RFH, was realising that I could be made to laugh, against my will, in an atmosphere of high seriousness, in the temple of culture, by the simple childlike joy of surprise. Derek Bailey, it seemed, was giving me permission to laugh.

'Epiphanies', *Wire* magazine
comedy issue, June 2005

IV: Johnny Vegas – Instrument of God

Michael Pennington was born in St Helens, Lancashire, in 1971. He gave birth to Johnny Vegas sometime in the early 90's, after a difficult pregnancy involving pottery, the priesthood and at least one severe beating. Pennington is one of our most misunderstood and maligned talents, and Johnny is one of the greatest comedy characters ever created. Johnny's live performances, whether they succeed or fail, always do so spectacularly. Despite this, Johnny is best known to the public for his association with a woollen monkey in a series of TV commercials promoting a now bankrupt cable TV supplier. Almost hourly, people in the street shout at him, 'Where's your monkey?' Only once have I seen him crack and reply, 'It fucking died!'

I never knew Michael Pennington as Michael Pennington, only as Johnny Vegas, and he'll be the first to admit that the line between the two burly northern men is blurred. 'When I tell people about terrible things that have happened to me, they just seem sad,' he explains. 'But if I pretend they've happened to Johnny they become hilarious. But sometimes it's complicated. On *Shooting Stars* I had to sit there and join in. But Johnny Vegas would have just lost interest, wandered off, come back with a dead rabbit and said, "Look what I've found."' For the purposes of this piece, the Pennington–Vegas phenomenon will be referred to throughout as Johnny.

On location in the Peak District village of Castleton, where he is filming *Dead Man Weds*, a sit-com written by and staring *Phoenix Nights'* Dave Spikey, it is Johnny, not Michael Pennington, whom every passer-by feels entitled to engage in conversation. Moving through any public space with Johnny is a problematic exercise. Everyone wants to shake hands, buy him a drink, or get scraps signed. I have never spent time with a celebrity so genuinely loved, and yet also so unselfconsciously accessible. Nobody leaves Johnny's orbit without an anecdote or an authenticated fragment. Finally we wrangle him away, and Vegas drinks rum and coke in a Castleton pub, turning butts of smoking paraphernalia over in his hands, which are surprisingly small and gentle, like those of a spider monkey, or a young Victorian servant girl.

Johnny's ongoing presence in newspaper gossip columns, quiz shows and commercials means that although he himself is instantly recognisable, the talent that informs his incendiary live shows remains largely unrecognised. 'It's not my world but that doesn't stop me passing through,' he protests. 'I think anyone who is remotely normal would find it interesting to observe those kind of parties without considering yourself one of the people that ought to be there. The thing is though, you go along and you imagine you're just people-watching, but before you realise it, people are watching you.' But to see Johnny live at the Edinburgh fringe in the late 90's was an unforgettable experience. In some dark, dank room, this gargantuan figure would rage at the audience, often half naked, soaked with spilt pints, demanding their pity, or their respect, forcing them, often out of sheer terror, to enjoy themselves by joining in massed singalongs, whilst he displayed his genuine prowess on the potter's wheel, creating, as best he could, beautiful clay objects, moulded from muck and beer, within the midst of this maelstrom. Where did this character come from?

'When I was young I did get badly beaten up once and hospitalised. I went through a year of being really timid and I think doing Johnny allowed me to be as confrontational on stage as I'd like to be in real life. I might have been scared in reality, but I'd stand my ground on stage. And a lot of him is like local lads in St Helens where I grew up. You go in their club and they're dead happy to see you but you only want to have two pints with them, not six. You don't want to get drawn into it, otherwise it's, "Come on, sit with me, be my friend, and then watch me reach the point of exploding."' When Johnny embarks upon free-associating tirades, that often last literally hours, he conjures the same feeling of excitement, fear and hilarity experienced during the desperate revels of just such despairing drinkers. 'That's another drunk-style thing about Johnny,' he explains, 'nothing ever gets to a finished point. Drunks think there's always got to be somewhere else open. Otherwise it's the horror of going home and living with themselves. Johnny wouldn't care how much he bored other people. He'd satisfy his own need to be distracted first.'

Was using the potter's wheel onstage in the early days of the act an attempt to find something delicate in amongst all the violence, despair and anger? 'No,' says Johnny, 'the pottery was a kind of accident. When I was starting out doing stand-up I accepted a residency somewhere in Manchester and in my blissful ignorance I hadn't realised people spent years putting their first hour show together. I didn't have enough material so I just thought of anything I could do to fill the time. I remembered I'd done an arts foundation course and I'd really loved ceramics because I'd had a brilliant teacher. So I brought the Potter's Wheel on stage. The first time I did it I realised it had a mesmerising, magnetic effect on people. They were amazed I could do it. And the fact that I could actually make pots like I said I could, made them wonder how much else of the act was true. "God! He weren't lying? Maybe he was a Butlin's redcoat in the 60's like he says?" The problem with people that come and see me now is they're not a live comedy crowd. They're people who want to see someone off the telly. I do what I do and they say, "That's not what I paid to see. I was expecting stand-up. Not a frightening monster." I don't think you can defeat it. You just have to not water down what you do, and not start gearing it towards that kind of audience.'

The Johnny Vegas character has been thoughtfully and carefully drawn to embody blackly hilarious notions of desperation, loneliness and bewilderment. But it's so convincingly portrayed that, when it encounters an increasingly superficial media, Johnny's behaviour is portrayed as synonymous with Michael Pennington's. 'What you say on stage becomes a perception of your real life,' Vegas explains, 'they won't draw that line.' Last year some lads shouted out at Johnny on stage, 'Why did your wife leave you?' Confronted with such a personal question any stand-up who chose to answer it seriously, or else get angry, would have thrown the gig. Johnny replied, 'She didn't share my belief in sea monsters. I'd be swimming around in the sea looking for them, and she'd get bored,' brilliantly defusing the whole situation. The next day in the *Daily Mirror*, this comment was reported as evidence of Michael Pennington's deteriorating mental state, as had been a previous gig where he had invited men in the audience to lick his nipples, an old Johnny Vegas trick for breaking the ice that fans will have seen him use on stage many times. In the *Incredible Hulk* film, Eric Bana rampages through the Mojave desert destroying thousands of US army tanks, but he has so far escaped personal censure for this in the pages of the *Daily Mirror*. That said, I once criticised some friends for saying they had seen Johnny do a shit onstage. I said this was ridiculous and that whilst he may have pretended to do a shit onstage, he wouldn't actually do a shit on stage. He was a character comedian, an actor playing a role, not a psychopath. I subsequently related this story to Johnny as an example of people's failure to view Johnny Vegas as a character, but he made a kind of doubtful face, and I decided not to pursue the issue.

The irony is, such stories, whether true or not, add to the myth of Johnny Vegas. Johnny has never been honoured with his own TV vehicle. 'TV producers and commissioners come and see the show and love it but when you give them any more in that vein they don't seem to latch onto it and think you've gone too far,' he concedes. Ben Thompson's study of British TV comedy in the 90's, *Sunshine on Putty*, singles out Channel 4's failure to commission Johnny's 1998 pilot as a major downward turning point in British comedy. But, denied of its own TV format, the Johnny Vegas character seems instead to be creating its own narrative in the real world, funnier and more comically tragic than anything a team of writers could contrive.

Earlier this year, Vegas appeared in *Sex Lives Of The Potato Men*, a film subsequently described as 'the worst British film ever made', though presumably not by people who had seen *Love Actually*, *Shooting Fish* or that one with Lee Majors and Bradley Walsh riding around in golf carts. But though being in 'the worst British film ever made' might have been a blow for Michael Pennington, there's something perfect about it for Johnny Vegas. When I went to see *Sex Lives Of The Potato Men* in Leicester Square, the Warner West End ticket machine was broken, and the cashier had given me a handwritten note allowing me access to the film. The very act of going to see Vegas' film became inherently absurd and this is a typical by-product, somehow, of any of Johnny's interactions with popular culture. I couldn't resist ringing him from the largely empty cinema. 'It's the critics,' he said, 'they've taken to sabotaging the ticket machines now.' But whilst the film's other stars saw off the flack with various degrees of plausible denial, Vegas, honourably alone, embraced it. 'Even when one critic described me as "the ugliest man in British cinema" I still stood by what I've done,' he says. 'Everyone that read that script wanted to be in it. I don't moan about it. There are actors in it who've tried to distance themselves from it but it's like stand-up. When they go badly they blame the crowd, and when they go well it's because they themselves were amazing.'

Vegas may yet become a superstar by doing what he's actually good at. If not then there remains the consolation that his career will look like some kind of strange art project. Standing alongside soap opera celebs in TV listings magazines Johnny, like the skeleton at the feast, renders them all ridiculous, whilst he remains idiotically removed, so low in status that he cannot be harmed, a genius fool. 'You can't touch Johnny because he's never going to see the sense in taking the blame for anything anyway. That's another idea drawn from alcoholism too. Everything's always someone else's fault. If that butterfly had flapped its wing in Tokyo I'd have got the part in *Lord Of The Rings*. It's not my fault.'

The Johnny Vegas character seems entangled in notions of guilt and blame. It's no surprise that the young Johnny considered training for the Catholic priesthood. 'I thought of going into it until the age of ten,' he remembers, 'then at 11 I went to seminary, a private school funded and run by the church. The church work out what you can afford and your parents pay it out of shame. The idea was you'll be a priest, get a taste for the monastic lifestyle of the priesthood – it's indoctrination really. I don't want faith through fear. I think it's about the individual's acceptance. I thought it was quite good that at the age of 11 I wanted to read George Orwell in bed but they wouldn't even let me have a reading light because of rules and regulations and I found myself rallying against it. I was the great white hope of the parish and when I said I wasn't up for it everyone was very disappointed. I was made to feel very special when I wanted to be a priest and everyone was disappointed when I became ordinary again. But I craved the ordinary. I suppose Johnny Vegas is like that. He doesn't give people what they want. He's a revolutionary, like Martin Luther, but he doesn't have anything worked out that he can nail to the church door. Johnny Vegas believes he has something to share but he is constantly humiliated. God is trying to teach Johnny Vegas a lesson, but even the violence doesn't work on him. You could knock his head in and then he'd just put on baby's clothes. God is doing it to him. God is saying to Johnny Vegas "you are one of the men who deserve to be beaten". But he'd just tell God he was out of order.'

Does Johnny think God would like the Johnny Vegas act? 'God would see that by accident one man has got as much as he can out of misery,' is all he will say. And what if Johnny Vegas were to do a shit on stage, would God approve of that, would he see it as an expression of his love? 'Whatever happens,' Johnny Vegas concludes, 'I am God's instrument. Maybe I should have used me own name for some things, and kept Johnny as a character. But I didn't. And it's too late now.'

Esquire magazine,
December 2004

V: An Improvised Discussion about Russell Brand on *Big Brother's Little Brother*

This is an interrogation/interview that Johnny Vegas and I improvised from areas of conversation that I had suggested to him previously, included as an extra on the 41st Best Stand-Up Ever DVD, in order not to misrepresent Russell Brand, whom I had misquoted, knowingly, during the show itself. I maintained that I had no obligation to represent Brand's behaviour accurately as what I was doing was a 'meta-discussion'.

The actress Jackie Clune, who penned the poorly received Denise van Outen vehicle Blondes, had just written a news-paper piece about her opinion of a routine Vegas had recently performed in a live show I promoted, which the Guard-ian had described as being the literal equivalent of a sexual assault, implying that his audience volunteer should press charges. When I challenged Clune about the rights and wrongs of speculating at length about something that she hadn't seen, having not been present at the show, and that wasn't proven or even corroborated by the supposed victim, she said the truth of the events was immaterial, because her piece was a 'meta-discussion' about the issues it raised, rather than a piece of reportage.

VEGAS AND LEE SIT FACING ONE ANOTHER IN CHAIRS IN THE CELLAR OF THE KING'S HEAD, CROUCH END, LONDON.

336

JOHNNY VEGAS: But, er, is it right, I, I've got here ... Is it an actual quote that, um, that you have Russell Brand saying about racism on *Celebrity Big Brother*? 'Cause you claim ...

STEWART LEE: Yeah ... No, he ...

VEGAS: ... that he said, 'Ooh, there's some bad racism and stuff like that going down today and no mistake, my liege. It's made my winkle go right small, it has ...'

LEE: Yeah.

VEGAS: 'Oh yes it has, yeah, and my ball-bag, my ball-bag [*laughing*] has gone up my bum. Here's H from Steps.'

LEE: Yeah it was. When I saw it, it was literally about two days after that had broke. And I saw him say that. And I thought that he was, was trying to, like, smooth over the whole thing, and I thought, 'That is so brilliant, 'cause if you just say that onstage, if it will expose the kind of ridiculousness of the attempt of a light-entertainment celebrity in a light-entertainment programme to deal with something as serious as this kind of racial bullying ...' So, I mean, I just thought it was perfect, so I wrote it down and, um, and it, you know, people just laugh openly at it, 'cause it's so stupid.

VEGAS: Yeah, but ...

LEE: It was great.

VEGAS: Um, I've ... been back. I actually checked it.

LEE: Oh well, I'm glad.

VEGAS: Yeah, yeah ...

LEE: No, it's good, 'cause you should, you know ... I'm glad.

VEGAS: Yeah, yeah, but what he actually said was, 'Racism, it's such a wank thing, innit? It's such a pain in the arse that someone would go round being racist . . .'

LEE: [*quietly agreeing*] Mmm.

VEGAS: 'And individually, I think if people were made culpable for their actions and were made to look at themselves, they'd think, "Oh God, I shouldn't say that." And yet the way that they are behaving collectively is obviously abhorrent.' Now, do you think it's . . . you've got enough artistic licence to . . .

LEE: Well, I think . . .

VEGAS: To actually twist the words of another, of a fellow comedian?

LEE: I don't think they're really twisted, I think that the essence of what he said is, um . . . The essence of what he said is the same as what I said. The only, the only difference between what I said he said and what he actually said is that what he actually said, it starts to make quite a lot of sense towards the end, and obviously that wouldn't . . .

VEGAS: That didn't suit your . . .

LEE: Doesn't suit my . . .

VEGAS: Comedic . . .

LEE: . . . purposes. 'Cause what I'm looking at . . . This is like a meta-discussion about the event, it's not to do with what he actually said, it's to do with how celebrity culture cannot address a serious issue, and that is the important thing. It doesn't really matter, er . . .

VEGAS: I think it . . .

338

LEE: It doesn't really matter what he said. I mean the important thing is that he's . . . something . . . he said something like it. And it can just be changed to my own ends. And I think Russell himself would agree . . .

VEGAS: And where does that, where does that . . .

LEE: . . . that it's fine.

VEGAS: . . . where does that end, in terms of, you know . . . So you, so you see yourself as Stewart Lee, demigod, who can take anything out of context . . .

LEE: Well . . .

VEGAS: . . . as long as it suits the purpose of your comedy?

LEE: It's not taking it out of context, because it wasn't actually . . .

VEGAS: Well . . .

LEE: It wasn't said, it wasn't said.

VEGAS: Well, misquoting . . .

LEE: It's not even misquoted, it has almost no . . .

VEGAS: It's misquoting, 'cause he never said . . .

LEE: . . . relationship with it.

VEGAS: 'My winkle has gone right small . . .'

LEE: No, but he has said . . .

VEGAS: '. . . oh yes it has, and my ball-bag has gone right up my bum.'

LEE: He's said things like that on other, on other occasions.

VEGAS: Yeah, but maybe not in relationship to racism.

LEE: No, but he, you know . . .

VEGAS: [*something indistinct*] loves genocide . . .

LEE: But if he had, if he had, if he had tried to address racism, er, and he, and he had . . .

VEGAS: That's how you think he would have . . .

LEE: Yeah. And the fact that he didn't do that, and he actually said something quite good is not . . . that's not . . . it's not . . . that doesn't detract from what I'm trying to do. What I'm trying to do is look at the bigger picture about how . . . You know, racism's bad, we all agree with that. Yeah? But it's not something that can be easily dealt with by celebrity. And, and when you think of celebrity, the person you think of, I think, for most people is Russell Brand. And the way that they think he speaks is in the way that I've said. So to me, it doesn't really matter what he's said. The important thing is that, you know, it's . . . And I don't think he would mind either. I think he'd look at that piece and he'd go, 'Well, fair play, that's a good bit . . .'

VEGAS: Have you asked him?

LEE: I haven't asked him, no. But I think . . . I know that he likes my work, and I think if he saw that he'd feel flattered to be misquoted, rather than annoyed. I think he'd, d'you know what, I think he'd be delighted by it.

VEGAS: Doesn't that sound presumptuous?

LEE: It's not . . . It's . . . It is presumptuous, but I think that you . . . When you, when you're, when you're working with these kind of ideas, you're working in . . . You have to make

340

these kind of bold leaps, of connecting ideas. And if, in connecting them, you're not strictly . . . If, if in connecting them, you, er, betray someone and make them look worse than they are, then that, that's like a casualty of war. And the war is about trying to reach the greater truth. And the truth is that racism is a bad thing, and that's what . . . And I think that if . . . You know, oh what, 'He didn't say that, he said, "It's a wank,"' you know. It doesn't really matter, does it, what he said. The point is that, er, that the . . . there's a different . . . there's a thing we're driving at that's more important than what he actually said.

VEGAS: But, sorry, do you . . . Would you . . . Do you sort of see . . . I suppose it's a mad thing with comedy, isn't it, because you go . . . You'll . . . You'll make friends sort of within the industry . . .

LEE: Yeah.

VEGAS: . . . but then you have kind of got to intellectually remain completely impartial . . .

LEE: [*neutrally*] Mm.

VEGAS: Do you know what I mean? Do you ever, do you ever struggle with that, with going, 'This is perfect for having, like, the piss taken out of it, but . . . I'm going to see him in a bar, I'm going to come across this person' – do you know what I mean? – 'and I'll actually feel quite awkward about . . .'

LEE: Yeah, well, I mean . . .

VEGAS: '. . . what I've said about them'?

LEE: You know, I feel the same about Russell Brand as I would about Tom O'Connor. You know, the stuff's out

341

there now, and, er, you know, let's see, see what happens, you know. And I, er, it's not like throwing down a gauntlet to him. But, er, I'm just saying that I view him as a kind of resource now in the way that I would, you know, f– . . . a funny animal or something . . .

VEGAS: [*laughs.*]

LEE: Or, er . . . a bad . . . bad weather. It's just something to, to exaggerate. And like, he's become like a phenomena, you know . . .

VEGAS: Mmm.

LEE: Like a, a, a . . . a rain or something, and, and less like a . . . He's not like a person to me now, you know?

VEGAS: He's a product, or . . .

LEE: He's a product. And if I choose to attribute things to him that he didn't say, then that's my prerogative, I feel, now.

VEGAS: Right.

LEE: It's like if you, you know, when, if you're doing a routine about a funny dog, and you imagine what the dog's thinking, no one goes, 'Oh, you don't know that that dog thought, "Oh, I wish I could have a bone."' It's the same . . . That's how I feel about a celebrity, about a, about a Russell Brand character . . . I have to, I kind of have to impose my thoughts onto . . .

VEGAS: I know.

LEE: . . . canvas.

VEGAS: In theory, in theory, if he got in touch and said,

'Actually, I find that deeply offensive,' would you remove it?

LEE: Well, um, you know this is a discussion we had before filming the, er . . . the DVD. It was pointed out to me that he didn't actually say this. And I said, 'Well, the way we'll get round it is I'll get Johnny Vegas in the DVD extra to ask me a question about it, so we can put what he actually said out there and say, you know, we're covered,' but the, but most people won't watch this part . . .

VEGAS: Yeah [*laughs*].

LEE: And so, you know, it's sort of, it's covered legally, but not in such a way as it impacts on the, er, the actual piece itself.

VEGAS: Right.

LEE: So this in many ways is a, a coping mechanism.

VEGAS: So you've . . . I wondered why you'd bring in such a simpleton to interview you. I'm just a patsy.

LEE: Yeah. You're a patsy. And you've been given the . . . You've been primed with that quote so that it would come up and I can address the issue.

VEGAS: Am I allowed to . . .

LEE: It's like a footnote.

VEGAS: Am I allowed to feel stupid now?

LEE: Um, no, you need to feel that you've done . . .

VEGAS: Have I done great things here?

LEE: You've done great things here, yeah, yeah.

VI: Pestival Set, May 2007

Here is the set I actually performed at Pestival, not the insect observational comedy one I put into the show 41st Best Stand-Up Ever.

Hello. I am Stewart Lee. I've been asked to come here and do stand-up tonight. And I was reluctant because, as you can imagine, it's difficult to know how to pitch it. It's difficult to know how many of you are here because you are fans of insects, and how many of you are here because you are Resonance FM listeners, and thus fans of improvised and experimental music, and whether there is any cross-over between them.

So what I decided to do was to come out dressed as an insect and do about half an hour of stand-up from the point of view of an insect. So I investigated how much it would cost to have an insect costume made, and it was about four to five hundred pounds for quite a good insect costume, and I thought, 'There's no way I can justify that for this because it will make a huge loss.'

But I was supposed to be doing a pilot for the BBC of a stand-up show, so to try and offset the cost, at the last minute I put in that I wanted them to film me doing stand-up as an insect, and then they withdrew the offer of the programme. So thanks. Thanks for having me here. My TV series has been cancelled. Because of you. I hadn't set up any other work. I thought I was filming a TV series. This is all I have in my diary. Pestival.

Now, it is nice to be at this insect-themed event, but usually I start my act like this: 'Hello. I'm Stewart Lee. Later on I'll be talking to you about how my tragic and ultimately fatal addiction to various forms of hard drugs has helped me to overcome my previous dependence on Christianity,' and then I talk about religion, politics and despair. But I can't do that tonight . . .

So I am going to read you the letter I got through after I accepted the booking. This is dated 20th September last year and it's from Miss B. Nicholls.

Dear Mr Lee

I am delighted you have accepted our offer to perform a short stand-up comedy set at our Pestival event. Now the contracts are exchanged I was just checking that you appreciated that we require your humorous material on the night to deal exclusively with insects, and insects only.

Straying into any other areas of subject material will be considered a breach of contract, and if such a breach of contract occurs, we intend to prosecute you with the full force of the law.

I only mention this because at a recent entomological event in Beijing I am informed the comedian told an inappropriate joke about spiders which went thus:

Why do black widow spiders kill their males after mating?
To stop their snoring before it starts.

The joke is inappropriate for two reasons:
(1) it is crude, and there may be children present;

(2) the black widow spider (*Latrodectus mactans*) is not strictly an insect, an insect being defined as a creature with a body segmented into three parts, with three pairs of legs.

We would be grateful if you did not step outside your insect remit. If you are stuck, here are four insect jokes you might like to tell. One is about a wasp, two are about bees, and the other is about insects generally. Perhaps begin with the general insect joke, and then move on to the other three specific gags.

> *What car does an insect drive?*
> *A Volkswagen Beetle.*

> *Why do bees hum?*
> *Because they've forgotten the words.*

> *Why do bees have sticky hair?*
> *Because of the honey combs.*

> *Where do you take a sick wasp?*
> *To waspital.*

I hope you find these helpful.

Yours truly,
B. Nicholls, Pestival.

Now, I'm known as a maverick within the world of comedy, I play by my own rules, not the rules of entomologists. If I want to do a joke about a spider, no amount of entomologists are going to stop me. You can threaten me with court and I'm still not scared . . . except with that TV thing cancelled I need this to work out, I need this. I need this. I need Pestival.

So I wrote back to Miss Nicholls in a slightly facetious

manner, and asked her if there were any particular insects which she thought I should write a joke about.

And she replied:

Dear Mr Lee

For me the most suitable insect for your comedy would be the aphid. The aphid reproduces parthenogenetically, that is to say without mating, so you should at least be able to work clean. I think we at Pestival would be happy with a fifteen-minute routine about aphids, perhaps something about the initially mystifying discovery of Russian spruce aphids in Switzerland in 1947, which was ultimately explained as being the result of involuntary migration by wind. I am sure you could think of something amusing about that incident! Perhaps you might like to mention how some ants farm aphids for their juices, but you must be careful that this observation does not

(a) imply any sexual undercurrent;

(b) suggest that the aphid is harmed in any way, as an insect-friendly audience will not like to hear about injury to any insect.

Also, if you do go with my aphid suggestion, please do not draw attention to the potato peach aphid, which carries fifty different kinds of virus, as there may be people at the event who are unconvinced about insects, just casual attendees, and who are not great lovers of insects, and they are sure to take against the potato peach aphid, and by association all aphids, if you describe it in these terms. At Pestival this year we are hoping to brush the potato peach aphid under the carpet, metaphorically speaking. These restrictions apart, feel free to say pretty much anything you like about aphids. We in the entomological community pride ourselves on having a sense of humour. In fact, only the other day someone told me this joke:

> What do you call a top pop group made up of insects which infest the hair of children?
> You call them The Lice Girls.

Yours truly,
Miss B. Nicholls, Pestival

P.S. You can use the Lice Girls joke if you like, although it doesn't really make sense. It would be difficult to be sure that the group of singing lice were really The Lice Girls as the gender of the head louse (*Pediculus humanus capitis*) is only discernible in the later stages of its life.

So . . . a number of difficult restrictions placed on me. It was last week, while I was trying to write a funny story about aphids that I began to hate all insects. Try as I might, I couldn't see the humour in insects. And so I come here tonight, not to praise insects, but to bury them. Except for the ones that like living underground. Burying is too good for them. They will be dug up and exposed to the light.

Of all the creatures in the animal kingdom, insects are the most numerous. Likewise, of all the people in the world, the Chinese are the most numerous. Unlike insects, the Chinese have at least given us fireworks, fried rice and the bamboo flute. Insects live in swamps, jungles and deserts; they live in temperate zones and in severe mountain climates. Doubtless the insect fans here tonight choose to view this as evidence of their adaptability. I view it as evidence of the fact that insects are lazy and indiscriminate. Don't give them the oxygen of publicity.

So as you can see, I was sitting there, struggling to write

348

jokes about insects, and I was just about to give up. And then I remembered the story of Robert the Bruce. I don't know if you remember the story of Robert the Bruce. Robert the Bruce was fighting a battle against the English, and he wasn't getting on so well, so he ran away and he hid in a cave. And while he was there his eye fell on a little spider, which was trying to swing from one high rock ledge to another. And Robert the Bruce watched the spider once and it didn't quite make it and it fell down. And then Robert the Bruce watched the spider again and it didn't quite make it and it fell down again. And then Robert the Bruce watched the spider a third time, and the third time the spider attempted the swing, it made it from one ledge to the other. And Robert the Bruce thought about what he had seen, and he went back to the battle against the English, and remembering the example of the spider, he spun a huge web out of his own bodily fluids, in which the English soldiers became trapped, allowing Robert the Bruce to crawl stealthily from one soldier to the next, crushing them to death in his enormous mandibles. And so he won the battle and became the king of Scotland.

And that story of Robert the Bruce and the spider always reminds me of the story of Robert the Bruce and the head louse, I don't know if you know it. Robert the Bruce was fighting a battle against the English, and he wasn't getting on so well, so he ran away and he hid in a cave. And while he was there his eye fell on a little head louse, which was trying to jump from one Scottish soldier's head to another. And Robert the Bruce watched the head louse jump once and it didn't quite make it and it fell down. And then Robert the Bruce watched the head louse jump a second time and it didn't quite make it and it fell down again. And then Robert the Bruce watched the head louse a third time, and the third time the head louse attempted the jump, it made it from one Scottish soldier's head to the other. And Robert the Bruce thought about what he had seen, and he went back to the battle against the English, and remembering the example of the head louse (*Pediculus humanus capitis*), and when he got there he was able to infest the heads of the English soldiers, causing itching, leading to secondary infections and thus greatly demoralising the army of Edward II, and in that way he won the battle and became king of Scotland.

And that story of Robert the Bruce and the head louse always reminds me of the story of Robert the Bruce and the potato peach aphid, I don't know if you remember it. Robert the Bruce was fighting a battle against the English, and he wasn't getting on so well so he ran away and he hid in a cave. And while he was there his eye fell on a little potato peach aphid, which was trying to jump from a potato to a peach. And Robert the Bruce watched the potato peach aphid jump once and it didn't quite make it and it fell down between the potato and the peach. And then Robert the Bruce watched the potato peach aphid jump a second time and it didn't quite make it and it fell down again between the potato and the peach. And then Robert the Bruce watched the potato peach aphid a third time, and the third time the potato peach aphid attempted the jump, it made it from the potato to the peach. And Robert the Bruce thought about what he had seen, and he went back to the battle against the English, and remembering the example of the potato peach aphid (*Myzus periscae*), and when he got there he was able to live both upon the potato and peach reserves of the English army, robbing them initially of their staple food, the potato, and then subsequently of their peach, one of life's little luxuries which if denied to serving men can make them turn on their over-lords, and in that way, Robert the Bruce was able to win the battle and gain the Scottish crown.*

The story of Robert the Bruce and the potato peach aphid there, specially adapted for this evening's show, and being broadcast by Resonance FM all around the world, all around the world, and we can only hope that, statistically, there is someone, someone out there somewhere in the world who is now thinking, 'Yes, I always wanted to hear something like that.'

---

* Then I improvised the following end . . .

VII: 'I'll Only Go If You Throw Glass'

In 2002, I was invited to submit a 5,000-word piece for a book of writing by comedians called Sit Down Comedy. *I sent them the following poem, inspired by my time as Jerry Sadowitz's support act and as a teenage punter in the eighties observing the dying days of the first wave of post-punk stand-up in Britain. The characters of the two comedians in it, though, are fictional composites. The publishers said they liked it but felt they couldn't publish a poem as it would put potential buyers off. I knocked out all the commas, didn't change a word, and resubmitted it as prose, and they ran it. At the time of writing, it has been performed live twice, once at a Lewisham Library literary event, and once at Apples and Snakes Spoken Word Night at Battersea Arts Centre, where it was poorly received.*

'I'LL ONLY GO IF YOU THROW GLASS'

They say you play Bangor University
Student Union twice in your career.
I'll be there in an hour, for the second time.
I had run out of money.
There was nothing on the horizon,
At least nothing for me, nothing I could call mine.
Respective heads of TV comedy dept's had played musical
chairs again.

The ones that liked me missed their seats, and sighed,
And waited for sackings or suicides.
I grew pallid in Stoke Newington
And bled into the toilet bowl.
After six months lost in the NHS system,
I cashed my last cheque for a consultation
With a show-biz physician.
He prodded my liver and banned me from drinking.
So here was I, sober and dry,
Returning to the stand-up circuit to die,
Scrabbling for loose change, and at my age.
But I had a trade, see, something to fall back on,
Like a plumber or an electrician,
And I was going again, just a little ashamed,
To Bangor University Student Union.

Bangor was the worst stand-up gig
On the National Comedy Network.
It took pride in its hostility, and so,
Like the entire city of Glasgow,
Was regarded with suspicion.
'If you don't do the required time',
Explained the Entertainments Officer,
Complicit in the scheme,
'Your fee will be reduced according
To how short your set has been.'
Yes, last time I was in Bangor
Teenage drunks threw plastic glasses.
Experiences like this had crushed
My last faith in the masses.
'I'll only go if you throw glass,' I said,
Wittily, from the stage,
And security guards dodged the shards

To enter the melee.
It was a good line,
And it was funny,
But it wasn't one of mine,
And he still docked my money.

'I'll only go if you throw glass',
Was an old standard
From an old stand-up,
Malcolm Tracey.
And Malcolm Tracey was coming.
To Bangor.
With me.

Now he sits in the car un-speaking,
Reading pornography and smoking,
With Scott Walker quietly exploding
On his personal stereo.
He will not shut the window.
And it is starting to snow.
I don't think you can begin to understand
What Malcy's presence means to me,
At this strange stage in what I call
My so-called career.
I'll try and explain.

Five hours earlier, at the top
Of a council block in Finchley,
I rang the bell and waited
To be met by Malcolm's mother.
The door swung in and there she stood,
Pinch faced, small and shrewish,
An apron tied around her waist

And a rolling pin in hand,
As if assembled to express some absurd ideal
Of everything I'd feared.
'Who are you and what do you want?'
She hissed through lipstick lips.
'I'm Tim and I have come,' I said,
'To pick up Malcy, your only son.
I am going to Bangor to perform.
And he's coming too as my support.'
'You don't look old enough,' she said,
And took my hand and stroked my hair.
And studying my sick-thin face,
She laughed and led me in.
From the kitchen she called out,
'It's a young man called Tim.'
Malcy grunted from a box room,
A fifty-year-old teenage boy.
I looked over my shoulder
And glimpsed him through a door,
Going about his business,
Crouched upon the floor.
A black suit shape beside the bed,
Scratching at his balding head,
He stuffed debris into a bag
And searched for cigarettes.

Malcy's mother sat me down
And chattered as she worked.
Something about tranquillisers
And did I want some grub?
Not that Service Station muck,
But something she would rustle up.
We came to an agreement

And she made me a packed lunch.
She boxed it up in Tupperware
And sat it next to Malcy's fare,
Identical in all respects,
A cake, an apple and some crisps.
I drank my tea and looked around.
It had come to this.
Going back to the Bangor
For one hundred and fifty quid.
Thirty-five and finished,
And not allowed to drink.
But I would be accompanied
By my one consolation.
Malcolm Tracey, formerly known
As Mal Co-ordinated.

Malcy was the missing link
Between the perfume and the stink.
Between cheap Channel 5 stand-up filler,
Between a million sneering panel shows,
Between the alleged death of The Spirit of the Fringe,
Between the stage of the Hackney Empire
And the screen of the Empire Leicester Square,
Between squatted nineteen-seventies gigs in Stepney
And the comedy colonisation of the provinces,
Between the transfiguration of the mainstream,
Between a new generation of prancing nonces,
Between all that and more,
Back to the first time anybody chalked upon a board
The noble phrase,
That presaged change,
And turned the ripple to a wave,

The secret signal to the brave,
'Alternative Cabaret'.

No one knew how Malcy had begun,
Where he had sprung from and how he had grown.
Nor where he had gone to for most of the nineties,
When he appeared to disown his progeny,
And tied his talent in a sack and drowned it in the sea.
The history, such as it was, was contradictory.
Lisa Appignanesi's book on Cabaret
Included a photo of him in the final chapter.
He was wild-haired in a leotard and snarling like a
panther,
At a venue called the Earth Exchange that the comedy
circuit left to rot
Long before my first try-out spot.
A pamphlet I bought at Leicester Art Gallery
Tied Malcy in to 70s Arts Lab anarchy.
Victoria Wood once mentioned him
When asked who had inspired her to begin.
A journalist called John Connor
Wrote a book on the Fringe in Edinburgh.
But he had an ideological axe to grind,
And Malcy's work got left behind.

Someone told me it was Malcy who
First coined the term 'Alternative Cabaret'.
Working in South Devon in 1972,
He used it to advertise a Punch & Judy show.
From inside a stripy tent he increased the violence
content,
And threw in an act of anal sex between wooden puppets.

In the beer garden of a plush hotel
Malcy found he'd caused offence,
And was compelled to grab his effigies
And flee from the South-West.
Then there were the years of petty crime and drugs,
The years spent dancing naked in Soho in gay clubs,
And rumours of unsavoury acts and criminal convictions,
And of time spent in prison for unspecified actions.

On release Malcy played folk clubs and festivals
Until the Alternative Comedy scene coalesced.
He never had an act as such, it seemed,
But still he stormed the gigs
With only a harmonica, a pack of cards,
A dirty pair of Y-fronts, and a bag of different wigs.
Somehow he could usually hold a crowd.
You could almost hear them thinking aloud,
'Can this be it? It's fucking shit.'
They sat bewildered and entranced,
Waiting for Mal, as if by chance,
To achieve something recognisable,
Something tangible and definable.
But he never did.
A harmonica solo, a poem,
A song and then a joke.
A magic trick, a puppet show,
And then a puff of smoke.
A purple wig, an inflatable pig,
A visceral torrent of abuse,
A shambling dance in a tight red suit.
And then the climax, the *coup de grâce*.
Malcy turned round and dropped his pants.

I first saw him in '84,
At a club in Birmingham supporting The Fall.
The disgruntled fans showed their disdain
For Malcy's refusal to entertain.
Leaning drunk upon the mike stand
With a beer bottle in each hand,
He told the same joke again and again,
Until they tried to shift him with polystyrene
Cups and empty cans.
Acknowledging defeat he said,
'I'll only go if you throw glass,'
The immortal line, that would one day be mine.
But a shoe connected with his head,
And he died upon his arse.
The performance was recorded and released as a
seven-inch single.
I knew every shout and jeer and each embarrassed giggle.
But I did not know what I had seen.
Had Malcy failed, or did he succeed?
All I knew was that somewhere,
Beyond the suburbs where I went to school,
It seemed there were heroic deeds,
Irrational acts and holy fools.

I next saw Malcy in Edinburgh
In 1987,
Falling drunk down the Fringe club stairs
At a quarter past eleven,
Raising his glass and cursing heaven,
Dressed as Vladimir Lenin.
And two years later at the Glastonbury Festival,
Punching an inflatable woman in the face
At the other end of the cabaret tent.

My girlfriend called it a disgrace.
She had a point I must confess.

Three months later, I moved to London.
My fledgling career had begun.
I won five hundred pounds
In a new acts competition,
Got signed up to an agency
With a handshake and no conditions.
They took me to the top floor
Of a tiny West End office
And pointed out across the land,
Beyond the upstairs rooms of pubs,
At the uncharted territories
Of student union premises
That they promised would collapse
And fall into our waiting laps.
And soon I was out on the road,
Only twenty-one years old,
And support act to none other
Than Mal Co-ordinated.
Or, as he was currently billed,
Malcolm Tracey,
formerly Mal Co-ordinated.
Times had changed,
for the better in that respect at least.

Malcy didn't drive. So I chauffeured
Him hundreds of miles
Between bizarrely scheduled dates.
Aberdeen to Derby in a day.
Malcy was paid a thousand pounds a show,
Of which he gave me sixty.

Some days he was convivial,
Other days withdrawn.
Some days he was charming,
Other days a bore.
Once in Leeds, or Bradford,
He made me give him thirty pounds.
I had run into an ex-girlfriend
And slept at her house.
Malcy had booked me a hotel room
And felt I should pay.
I couldn't tell if he was joking.
But he kept my money anyway.
Each night, I did my fifteen minutes
Then watched him work,
Knocking back the drinks rider,
Smoking in the dark.

Nearly two decades since he first
Wrote 'Alternative Cabaret',
Malcy's act, such as it was,
Had reached its apogee.
After ten minutes' faff with harmonicas
And cards and wigs and coats,
Malcy held up a massive picture
Of four small brown stoats.
Then he began an hour's speculation
On their interconnected relationships,
Occasionally gesturing at individual stoats
With a pointed wooden stick.
Sometimes it worked,
And the students were spellbound.
But Malcy seemed to be seeing
How he could confound

Expectations, amusing himself
At the punters' expense,
As if holding them in contempt.
And in the closing ten minutes,
When the space had thinned
And the crowd was sparse,
Malcy could always win them back
By dropping his trousers
And showing his arse.
But even this traditional display,
With which he had all but made his name,
Seemed to be dispatched in a perfunctory way.
In short, Malcy's heart wasn't in it.

As we travelled the country, it became clear to me
Malcy wasn't that concerned about his comedy career.
It was of secondary importance to a social network
he maintained,
Which indulged his other interests up and down the land.
In Aberdeen a small fat man met Malcy after the show,
And they retired to practise card tricks in a hotel room,
Sharing junk food from the garage and a can of Irn Bru,
Lamenting Malcy's conflict with the Magic Circle crew.
In Nottingham he was ensnared
By the executive committee
Of the Robert Silverberg Appreciation Society,
For whose newsletter Malcy had appraised
The overrated science-fiction writer.
In Sheffield, Malcy was the sometime beau
Of a seventeen-stone widow,
Who had needs that only he could satisfy,
Apparently.
In Bristol, fluff-faced comic-book fans

362

Offered him a seventies copy of *Superman*
Which they knew Malcy, a famous collector,
Would not be able to resist.
It included the first appearance of
The Super Moby Dick of Space,
A sentient, speaking whale in a short red cape
Who patrolled the cosmos defending The American Way.
I assumed Malcy's interest was an ironic pose,
But he was hurt by the suggestion
And didn't speak till we reached Preston.
Malcy loved the Super Moby Dick of Space.
He felt that its creator was touched by divine intervention,
Chosen to communicate something beyond his
comprehension.

The route of our already strangely scheduled tour
Was further complicated
By the side-trips Malcy insisted on making,
And the peculiar rituals he was determined to observe.
After an average to bad show at Lancaster University,
Malcy made me drive him twelve miles to the coast
Where he stood on the seafront and took off his coat
And urinated in the face of a statue of Eric Morecambe,
Who hailed from the area, or at least had done.
He explained that he tried to do this at least once a year,
And considered Ernie Wise a genius unsung.

Malcy had sworn he would never play Glasgow,
But on the way to Stirling he insisted we drive through
The city centre while he, sporting a ginger wig and
clutching a haggis,
Leaned out of the car window shouting,
'Remember Culloden! That was tragic!'

At small children and old women.
Each day, Malcy would buy the dullest postcard of the
town we were in,
Inscribe it with the same description of an imaginary
Italian holiday and post it to an address in Ealing
That he had chosen at random from the telephone directory.
On an Irish leg, driving between Belfast, Dublin and Cork,
Malcy insisted on eating only at tiny tea-rooms,
Where he would order a baked potato, with no butter,
filling or salad,
And then seek out the chef to compliment him on
the meal.
Whenever we were in Devon he always tried to have
sex with men,
But even in Exeter's only gay nightclub,
The local queens could tell the difference
Between real lust and some situationist conceit.
Whenever we played a town with two 'b's in its name,
Malcy would order me two full English breakfasts in bed
And have them both delivered to my room at 5.45 a.m.
The cost of the two meals would then be deducted from
my fee.
But I grew to love these idiosyncrasies,
Just as I grew to love Malcy,
Over and above his act,
In spite of himself.

Malcy used to live in Peckham then,
Before he moved back to his mum's.
At the end of our two-month trip
I finally dropped him in his street.
He did not invite me in for tea,
Say goodbye or thank me.

Three months later in Edinburgh,
Malcy performed his 'farewell' show,
In a room above a shop.
The signs had been there I suppose,
But it still seemed hard to believe.
What would Malcy do instead?
He was dis-institutionalised.

After midnight Malcy stuck his face through a curtain
And addressed us for a quarter of an hour in the persona
of a head
Which had no body and was floating in the air.
Then he laid his props upon the floor,
The harmonica, the wigs, the pack of cards,
And invited us to speculate upon the perfect order
That these elements might integrate for the ultimate
comic effect.
Malcy lit an oil lamp, and sealed his mouth with
masking tape.
He arranged his props in every possible way,
Like some Mondrian ballet,
Until at last, at half past one,
With wigs scattered all around the room,
He admitted it could not be done,
And that the totems of his trade were powerless
To someone who no longer cared.
Even against his will Malcy was still funny,
But the friends that I took with me said it was a waste of
money.
Sold out for three weeks, then that was it,
Malcy packed up and disappeared.
The *Guardian* said the show was shit.
The *Observer* disagreed.

Five years later I saw Malcy on Oxford Street,
Hunched up, head down, staring at his feet.
I waved at him, but I don't think he noticed me.
When the money well ran dry and I went back to my old
promoters,
They laughed as if vindicated somehow and said they
could find me something.
Two weeks headlining on what remained of the student
circuit that I'd help create.
Of course I'd need a support.
Had I heard Malcolm Tracey was back on the boards?
No. He lives with his mum now in her council flat,
No one knows where he's been but he's blown all his cash.
It'll be just like the old days.
But if he really sucks promise you'll call
And we'll send someone up to replace him.

Malcy came in the kitchen where I sat with his mum.
He looked older but content in an indefinable way,
As if the black cloud that always used to surround him
had risen away.
'Malcy,' I said, 'it's Tim. Remember me?'
'Ah, Tim, yes. Did I see you on the TV?
Good luck to you, son, they'd never have me.
I dare say I could have made it if I'd given it a try
But sometimes these opportunities,
Well, they just pass one by.
Now. Bangor. In Wales. I assume that you'll drive.
Goodbye, Mother, I am sure that we will meet again.
But if I should die, think only this of me.
The stash of porn under the bed goes to kids with
cerebral palsy.
Everyone needs a wank, Mother, don't you agree . . .'

'Goodbye, Malcy,' she said, and passed him his packed
lunch.
Malcy kissed his mother on the cheek and handed me
his props.
'Sight gags, dear boy. You can't have too many.
You're still travelling light I assume?
You think that wig, no matter how funny,
Is beneath the likes of you.'

Malcy woke soon after Oswestry.
So far I'd restrained myself from asking him
Where he'd been the past ten years.
It seemed somehow impolite.
Instead I said how much I had enjoyed his farewell show,
In Edinburgh so long ago,
When he had spent an hour trying to align
His funny props for maximum effect.
'Yes. Well, I got there in the end you know, while I've
been away.
I was five years gone before I realised anyone might have
missed me.'
'What do you mean, Malcy?' I asked him.
'The problem was I'd taped up my mouth.
You remember, you were there,
So I couldn't play the harmonica
Or recite even the simplest joke or sing a silly song.
It was all very well moving wigs about
But even to a foreign ear there's something in
The rhythm of a perfect gag that can incite the
involuntary act
Of laughter, and I believe, there are absurd images that
transcend
Any cultural conditioning

And whack us on our funny bones at a primeval level.'
My head was spinning. I'd never heard Malcy wax theoretical
On comedy before. He'd always seen it as a chore.
What did he mean?
'A certain shape, a certain sound,
A certain colour and a certain move,
Combined at a special moment and timed
To perfection, will send a pulse of laughter out,
So powerful the earth will crack,
The lightning flash,
The sky turn black,
And everything will alter.'
I felt a little bit afraid
Hearing Malcolm Tracey talk this way,
But kept my eyes upon the road
And looked for signs to Bangor.
'Everything I need to implement
This comic day of judgement
Is in that bag on your back seat
Or here inside my skull.
And when I work my wonders
Everything I've fought against
Will wither, die and fall.
Can we stop for a piss soon?'

We checked into the Regency Hotel,
Opposite the station.
Outside the rain was chucking down
And waves were crashing on the shore.
I thought about the prophecy that Malcy had just made,
And wondered what exactly he'd been doing while away.
If he really had the power that he seemed to think he did,

Then having him as my opening act might not be ideal.
If Malcy had stumbled upon some comic formulae
That unleashed the energies he had described
Then if I had to follow him I would surely die,
And with it being Bangor I needed to do the time
Agreed, or with the petrol and the rooms I'd be in
negative equity.
I went into the hotel bar to get a drink and steady my
nerves,
And then I remembered I wasn't well enough.
But as I sat there smoking I realised there were two options.
Either Malcolm was a superbeing, or he'd just flipped
and lost it.
Tragically it seemed to me the second was most likely.
I resolved to get through the gig tonight,
Then have a think in the cold hard light
Of day as to whether my childhood hero really was going
to pay his way.
If he looked like a liability I could just put him on the train,
Phone the promoters and have them find me someone
new,
Who I could hook up with before the next show.
I knocked at Malcy's door.
'Show time,' I said.
'Come in,' he lay upon the bed,
Naked except for socks and an orange wig over his cock.
'Get dressed, Malcolm,' I said, 'Bangor Uni will dock
Our fee if we're not there by six thirty for an ineffectual
sound-check.
This is no time for messing around.'
'On the contrary, dear boy,' said Malcy,
'There's never been a better time for it.'

What can I say?
Malcy did OK.
His fifteen minutes came and went
Largely without incident.
At first he faltered, as well he might,
After ten years out of the light.
But he cut such an eccentric figure with his tight red suit
And revolving roster of wigs that the student pricks were
initially too confused
To go in for the kill, and before they knew it
He had their goodwill.
Twelve minutes in Malcy put down his puppet rubber
chicken
And reached inside his jacket pocket and pulled out a
piece of paper.
I wondered if it contained some spell, some charm, or
incantation,
With which he would make good his boast of earlier that
day,
To bring the mountains crashing down and make the
doubters pay.
But instead it was a poem he said he'd written that week,
About his relationship with his estranged daughter.
In all the time I'd spent with him,
Malcy had never mentioned her.
He read it sincerely in slow measured tones.
It was funny, but not cute, and clearly heartfelt.
The audience fell silent, with occasional laughs,
But they came in the right places,
And Malcy rode the pauses.
At the end they applauded but I noticed from my corner
That a girl by the toilets was crying.
Then as if to acknowledge the hiatus he'd caused,

Malcy bent over and pulled down his pants,
Showed his arse to the students and bowed.

I need not have worried.
Malcy still had it, and more.
After his set my own seemed a bore,
If not to the crowd then to me.
Once more I was learning from Malcolm Tracey.
But hey, what the hell, we both did our time.
The cunt from the union paid us both fine
And nobody had to go hungry.
As we walked back to the Regency Hotel
Malcy stopped for a piss by the chip shop.
'Though I say it myself,' he said, to himself,
'That went rather well. It might have been my best gig ever.
Yes. I was on fire, so I think I'll retire.
Things really can't get any better.'
Outside the hotel Malcy stood on the steps
And looked at the sea and the sky.
'A drink before bed,'
Malcy smiled. I said,
'I'm sorry I need to get some kip in.
I didn't tell you before but tomorrow
I'm afraid we are both due in Glasgow.'
To my surprise, Malcy took it in his stride.
'Good. Then we'd best be off early.
If you don't mind there's a stop I should like to make
Somewhere west of Greenock.'
It had been a long time since I'd had to drive
Malcy to his assignations.
But I felt kind of proud to have him around
And agreed, just this once, that I'd take him.

At Wemyss Bay Malcy pointed the way
Across the sea by ferry.
'We'll go to Bute, to a beach I know,
And there we will put on a show
To live in the halls of memory.'
Tired and confused I acquiesced
And drove the car onto the boat.
Malcy hurried to the bar,
Already on his second jar
By the time I'd bought the tickets.
I didn't think to question him,
I'd seen it all before.
He'd have a plan, to see a certain man
Or dally with a whore.
But when we drove onto the land
He took control and directed me
A little way, to Skelpsie Bay,
Some way south-west of Rothesay.
I parked the car above the beach,
In the distance I saw Arran,
And in the rain I helped Malcy
Get all the props that we could carry
And take them to the shore.
He handed me a pint glass that he'd
Brought with him from Bangor,
And told me to keep it safe
As he would need it later.
Across the sand he dragged his bags
And set them up upon some rocks,
That stretched some way into the sea,
A small performance promontory.
And as I watched him from the beach
He got down on his knees and reached

Into his pocket and pulled out
His old harmonica.
The wind carried the notes away,
But I assume he started to play
And as he did so little heads
Began to break above the waves.
Malcy was surrounded on three sides
By dolphins bobbing on the tide,
Clicking, waiting, watching him,
Wondering when he'd begin.
'I'll test my theory,' he cried,
'On these far superior minds.'
And in-between the wind and spray
I think I heard Malcy say
The first lines of his tried and tested set.

The story of a gherkin boy who lived inside a burger,
The suicide note of a mouse or something or other,
A funny kind of lullaby sung to a sleepless child,
I knew the pay-off, but before he spat it out
Malcy called, 'Throw the glass, throw it at me now.'
'What?' I answered him, appalled,
As Malcy stuck an orange wig upon his sodden hair,
And blew a last harmonica blast that cut the soggy air.
'I'll only go if you throw glass,' he shouted.
I threw it towards the waiting rocks. It shattered with a
crash.
The sea grew calm and duck pond still and then there was
a splash.
The dolphins dived beneath the waves.
Skulls cracked smiles in ancient graves.
A shadow fell across my face.
The Super Moby Dick of Space!

But not a cloud had crossed the sun.
I looked back.
Malcy?
He was gone.
And lying there upon the rocks,
His harmonica, alone, unloved.

I hung around the beach till dusk looking for Malcolm
Tracey.
If he had come back across the beach footprints would
have betrayed him.
If he'd swum underwater out to sea he'd have to have
swum a mile from me
Without breaking the surface.
I had to confront my fear.
Malcolm Tracey had disappeared.

I drove back to the ferry and phoned the promoters
To tell them my support act had spontaneously
combusted.
But back in London they pre-empted me.
There had been a complaint.
Malcy's poem had made a student cry.
This wasn't what comedy was for.
Admittedly in any other form of art,
Tugging the strings of someone's heart
Would be considered worthy.
But not in stand-up comedy.
Malcy was sacked and there would be
A new support waiting for me
When I arrived in Glasgow.

There's nowhere to hide in the University of Strathclyde.

The venue's on the top floor of a tower.
You're crushed into a backstage room that doubles as
an office.
And it was there that I met Malcolm Tracey's young
replacement.
A local lad, slotted in, new to the game, hungry, keen.
He was playing Jongleurs gigs up and down the country
And storming every one, he told me.
He wasn't interested in doing the Glastonbury,
How was that gonna help his career?
But would do a couple of Edinburghs to snag
A Perrier nomination and blag a TV deal.
I felt old and irrelevant, like someone cutting peat
While dreaming of electric fires and cursing their wet feet.
I offered him a cigarette, but he didn't smoke.
I said the rider was no use to me, and he packed it away
In his sports bag.
A pretty young girl flounced in and said it was time.
My support act stood and left the room and I went out
into the hall
And watched him walk onto the stage.

The crowd applauded his entrance but his opening line,
Something about how he resembled an Australian
soap star,
Hardly caught fire.
It shrivelled in the spotlight and then curled up and died.
He tried a condemnation of the students' refusal to laugh,
And then flipped onto his belly, begging for their love.
But the tricks of the trade were just tricks of the trade.
The emperor stood naked.
The crowd were betrayed.
The boy floundered, dry-mouthed, then looked around,

375

And bent his head, and bit his lip and bedded in for a
battle.
Something was different.
Something had changed.
I felt Malcy's harmonica in my pocket and put it to my
mouth.
It might have been seawater, or it might have been spittle,
But as I ran my tongue along the openings I could feel that
it was wet.
I pursed my lips and filled my cheeks and blew the liquid
out.

Acknowledgements

Everyone who encouraged me during the period described deserves great thanks. So thanks to The Managements – Avalon and Debi Allen Associates; The Promoters and venues – Brett Vincent for Underbelly, David Johnson and John Mackay, Tommy Sheppard and The Stand; The Bookers – Charlie Briggs and Dave Mauchline; The Opening Acts – Josie Long, Stephen Carlin, Henning Wehn and Greg Fleet; The Public Relations – Daniel Bee at Avalon, Mel Brown at Impressive, and especially Sally Homer; the DVD manufacturers – Avalon Productions, Chris Evans for Go Faster Stripe and Colin Dench for Real Talent; and at Faber, thanks to Stephen Page, Julian Loose, Ian Bahrami and everyone who worked on this book. Special thanks to my publisher Hannah Griffiths for her enthusiasm and support; to Richard Thomas and the hundreds of hands that shaped *Jerry Springer: The Opera*; to Adrienne Connors at the *Sunday Times* Culture, Christine Gettins and the Manchester International Festival, the Soho Theatre, the Bush Theatre, and Tom Morris and Battersea Arts Centre; and thanks for their patience and advice to the wife, Bridget Christie, and the editor, Andy Miller, who is a Mod.

Discography

Stewart Lee – Stand-Up Comedian (2005), 2entertain –
VCD7210 (DVD)

Jerry Springer: The Opera (2005), Pathe! – P-DGB
P917701000 (DVD)

Stewart Lee – '90s Comedian (2005), Go Faster Stripe –
GFS-01 (DVD)

Pea Green Boat (2006), Go Faster Stripe – GFS-04 –
(CD/10" vinyl)

What Would Judas Do? (2007), Go Faster Stripe – GFS-16
(3 × CD)

Stewart Lee – 41st Best Stand-Up Ever (2008), Real Talent –
RTDVD002 (DVD/CD)

Stewart Lee's Comedy Vehicle (2009), BBC/2entertain –
BBCDVD3010 (DVD)

RELEVANT WEBSITES
www.stewartlee.co.uk
www.myspace.com/stewlee
www.gofasterstripe.com